ISBN 978-1-330-15024-5
PIBN 10038231

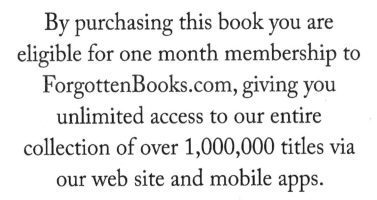

English
Français
Deutsche
Italiano
Español
Português

www.forgottenbooks.com

Mythology Photography **Fiction**
Fishing Christianity **Art** Cooking
Essays Buddhism Freemasonry
Medicine **Biology** Music **Ancient
Egypt** Evolution Carpentry Physics
Dance Geology **Mathematics** Fitness
Shakespeare **Folklore** Yoga Marketing
Confidence Immortality Biographies
Poetry **Psychology** Witchcraft
Electronics Chemistry History **Law**
Accounting **Philosophy** Anthropology
Alchemy Drama Quantum Mechanics
Atheism Sexual Health **Ancient History**
Entrepreneurship Languages Sport
Paleontology Needlework Islam
Metaphysics Investment Archaeology
Parenting Statistics Criminology
Motivational

SIR JOHN DICTATES HIS BOOK

49135

To

MY DEAR OLD FRIEND

H. B. BRABAZON

A. L.

LONDON, *October* 1895

[NOTE.—*I have to thank the Editor of the "Pall Mall Magazine" for the kind loan of such Drawings of mine as appeared in the February number 1894 of that publication, illustrating an article upon Sir John Maundevile by my cousin, Mr. George Somes Layard.*—A. L.]

English, French, Italian, Spanish, Dutch, Walloon, German, Bohemian, Danish, and even in Irish ; and as for the different MS. versions there are said to be over three hundred known. No book of any respectable age, except the Bible, and possibly Tyll Owlglass, has been so often copied or printed.

Sir John is withal intensely human, and therefore intensely interesting, and his dish has been, and must be, judged on its own merits and not analysed and dissected, and the various ingredients and their sources considered. I fear, were one to look into a good many literary larders, the owners would not fare better than has our Knight at the hands of some of his critics : moreover, at the period in which he wrote, literary plagiarism was as little thought of as highway robbery, or judicial torture, and in each instance drew protest from none but the individual sufferer.

It is evident that in the case of such a book as Maundevile's there must be an immense field for scholarship and research, and those who would go into the matter of text and textual criticism are referred to the preface of Halliwell and the magnificent bi-lingual edition published by the Roxburgh Society, where they will find all such matters fully treated of and in such a thorough way that it would hardly be interesting, even if possible, to give the veriest outlines of their labours in a preface to a popular edition such as is this last.

It may be mentioned, however, that the text generally followed throughout the present volume is that of the Cotton MS., with only such alterations as to make it easily readable by an Englishman of the Nineteenth Century, and, though in every instance it is not an actual verbal reproduction of the original, the spirit of the whole has been most faithfully reproduced without interpolation, and with scarcely an omission.

Where the Cotton MS. is obviously at fault on comparison with the French and Latin versions the better reading has been used ; for example, where the French version says " entre Montaignes," it has been expressed in the old English rendering as " between Mount Aygnes," an obvious absurdity and blunder on the part of the translator. Maundevile's work was first written in French. Or again where the first English translator has rendered "limons," limes or lemons, as "snails," obviously mistaking the word for " limaçons ; " or again where " Nuns of a hundred orders " is given as the translation of " Nonnes Cordres " viz., " Nuns Cordelers," where, for some

reason best known to himself, probably carelessness, the translator has separated the "c" from the "ordres" and treated the initial letter as the Roman numeral for a hundred.

Wherever any doubt could arise and wherever identification has been possible the real or modern names of places have been inserted in brackets, as for instance "Nyfland [Livonia]"; but though in this volume there have been some further identifications, it has been quite impossible to follow our author in all his peregrinations, mental or actual. For example, he tells us of an Island at which every traveller touches upon leaving Genoa. He calls it Greaf, but, with the delightful *insouciance* of the spelling of the period, also, indifferently, Gryffle, Gresse, Grif, &c. It has been surmised, though it seems on somewhat slender circumstantial evidence, that the place referred to is Corfu. The reader may judge the confusion likely to arise, and, in fact, often caused in the originals, from this airy way of treating proper names, a disorder which in this present edition has been reduced to the order of more modern exigencies. His Monkish Latin too is at times most distressing; and vague indeed his references to the Bible.

As it may interest some, I subject to the reader's

judgment a couple of passages which will show that the following of Sir John's quaint speech is not an altogether easy matter for the average Englishman of to-day, and the turning of it into English sufficiently modern to be easily read and yet preserving accurately the spirit, if not absolutely the actual words of the original, is not quite such a simple matter as some might be inclined to think.

"And than thei make Knyghtes to jousten in Armes fulle lustyly ; and thei rennen to gidre a gret randoum ; and thei frusschen to gidere fulle fiercely; and thei breken here speres so rudely, that the Tronchouns flen in sprotes and peces alle aboute the Halle. And than thei make to come in huntyng, for the Hert and fer the Boor, with Houndes rennynge with open Mouth."

Or again.

"This Bryd Men seen often tyme, fleen in tho Contrees : and he is not mecheles more than an Egle. And he hathe a Crest of Fedres upon his Hed more gret than the Poocok hathe ; and his Nekke is zalowe, aftre colour of an Orielle, that is a Ston well schynynge ; and his Bek is coloured blew, as Ynde; and his Wenges ben of Purpre Colour, and the

Taylle is zelow and red, castynge his Taylle azen in travers."

The above two passages are taken at random from the book and are fair samples of Maundevilese : I fear few ordinary readers would be able, straight off, to give the modern equivalent for " rennen to gidre a gret randoum," or " castynge his Taylle azen in travers."

For the first time, as far as I know, has a popular Edition of Maundevile been properly indexed : to my mind an immense gain to any volume—of course I do not refer to such splendid works as the Edition of the Roxburgh Society, and the like, which are quite of another order and practically inaccessible to the general public—and I think I am not in error when I say that in this Edition the text has for the first time been properly paragraphed.

Few have suffered so much as Sir John at the hands of some of his Editors. One widely circulated Edition contains—and this no solitary example—a laughable blunder. The text has it that Alexander the Great sent a message to the people of Bragman, whoever they were, that he would come and conquer them, and their reply was to beseech him not to think of doing so, as their only riches consisted of

love for one another "and accord and peace." Our
Classical Editor goes out of his way to state that
this people's only treasure was "*acorns and peas*,"
and the Editor of a sequent popular Edition had far
too much respect and appreciation for the care and
erudition of his Classical Colleague to dream of error,
and followed on cheerfully with the same rendering.
Poor Sir John! this is far from being the only or
even the most ridiculous mistake on the part of
some of your would-be correctors.

Happy are they whom privacy makes innocent,
who have no commentators, no laudators, no de-
tractors ; about whose relics play no cold winds of
after-criticism. It is better to be fast forgotten
than to suffer the correction of the careless. Much
that is true and truly written down is read out for
false, the eyes of the lector seeing not but the type
set prominent by his own perceptions. So comes
change, not alone from natural causes and the deter-
mining effects of nature, but also, in frequent case,
from the trenchant edge of accident.

> " The knight's bones are dust,
>   His good sword is rust,
>   His soul is with the Saints, we trust."

And with this last pious hope we will let all of him

CONTENTS

CHAPTER IX

CHAPTER X

CHAPTER XI

CHAPTER XII

CHAPTER XIII

CONTENTS

CONTENTS

CHAPTER XIX

CHAPTER XX

CHAPTER XXI

CHAPTER XXII

CHAPTER XXIII

CONTENTS

THE PROLOGUE

OR as much as the Land beyond the Sea, that is to say the Holy Land, that Men call the Land of Promise or of Behest, passing all other Lands, is the most worthy Land, most excellent, and Lady and Sovereign of all other Lands, and is blessed and hallowed by the precious Body and Blood of our Lord Jesu Christ; in the which Land it liked Him to take Flesh and Blood of the Virgin Mary, to honour that Holy Land with His blessed Feet; and there He would of His Blessedness enshadow Him in the said blessed and glorious Virgin Mary, and become Man, and work many Miracles, and preach and teach the Faith and the Law of Christian Men unto His Children; and there it liked Him to suffer many Reprovings and Scorns for us; and He that was King of Heaven, of Air, of Earth, of Sea and of all Things that be contained in them, would only for all be clept King of that Land, when He said, "*Rex sum Judeorum,*" that is to say, "*I am King of the Jews;*" and that Land He chose before all other Lands, as the best and most worthy Land, and the most virtuous Land of all the World : for it is the Heart and the Midst of all the World ; witness the Philosopher, that saith thus, "*Virtus Rerum in Medio consistit,*" that is to say, "*The Virtue of Things is in the Midst;*" and in that Land He would lead His Life, and suffer Passion and Death of the Jews, for us, to buy and deliver us from Pains of Hell, and from Death without End ; the which was ordained for us, for the Sin of our Forefather Adam, and for our own Sins also; for as for Himself, He had no Evil deserved : for He thought never Evil nor did Evil : and He that was King of Glory and of Joy, might best in that Place suffer Death ; because He chose in that Land rather than in any other, there to suffer His Passion and His Death. For he that will publish anything to make it openly known, he will make it to be cried and pronounced in the middle Place of a Town ; so that the Thing that is proclaimed and pronounced, may alike stretch to all Parts : right so, He that was Maker of all the World, would suffer for us at Jerusalem, that is the Midst of the World ; to that End and Intent, that His Passion and His Death, that was published there, might be known alike to all Parts of the World.

See now, how dear He bought Man, that He

made after His own Image, and how dear He again bought us, for the great Love that He had to us, and we never deserved it of Him. For more precious Chattel or greater Ransom might He not put for us, than His blessed Body, His precious Blood, and His holy Life, that He enthralled for us ; and all these He offered for us that never did Sin.

Dear God ! What Love had He to us His Subjects, when He that never trespassed, would for Trespassers suffer Death ! Right well ought we to love and worship, to dread and serve such a Lord ; and to worship and praise such an Holy Land, that brought forth such Fruit, through the which every Man is saved, but it be by his own Default. Well may that Land be called delectable and a fruitful Land, that was be-bled and moisted with the precious Blood of our Lord Jesu Christ ; the which is the same Land that our Lord plighted us in Heritage. And in that Land He would die as seised, to leave it to us, His Children.

Wherefore every good Christian Man, that is of Power, and hath whereof, should strengthen him to conquer our right Heritage, and chase out all the misbelieving Men. For we be clept Christian Men, after Christ our Father. And if we be right Children of Christ, we ought to challenge the Heritage, that our Father left us, and take it out of heathen Men's Hands. But now Pride, Covetousness, and Envy have so inflamed the Hearts of Lords of the World, that they are more busy to dis-herit their Neighbours, than to challenge or to conquer their right Heritage.

before-said. And the common People, that would put their Bodies and their Chattels, to conquer our Heritage, they may not do it without the Lords. For an Assembly of People without a Chieftain, or a chief Lord, is as a Flock of Sheep without a Shepherd; the which departeth and disperseth and wist never whither to go. But would God, that the temporal Lords and all worldly Lords were at good Accord, and with the common People would take this holy Voyage over the Sea! Then I trow well, that within a little time, our right Heritage before-said should be recovered and put in the Hands of the right Heirs of Jesu Christ.

And, for as much as it is long time passed, that there was no general Passage nor Voyage over the Sea; and many Men desire to hear speak of the Holy Land, and have thereof great Solace and Comfort;—I, John Maundevile, Knight, all be it I be not worthy, that was born in England, in the Town of St. Albans, passed the Sea in the Year of our Lord Jesu Christ, 1322, in the Day of St. Michael; and hitherto have been long time over the Sea, and have seen and gone through many diverse Lands, and many Provinces and Kingdoms and Isles, and have passed through Tartary, Persia, Ermony (Armenia) the Little and the Great; through Lybia, Chaldea, and a great Part of Ethiopia; through Amazonia, Ind the Less and the More, a great Part; and throughout many other Isles, that be about Ind; where dwell many diverse Folks, and of diverse Manners and Laws, and of diverse Shapes of Men.

Of which Lands and Isles I shall speak more plainly hereafter.

And I shall advise you of some Part of Things that there be, when Time shall be hereafter, as it may best come to my Mind ; and specially for them, that will and are in Purpose to visit the Holy City of Jerusalem and the holy Places that are thereabout. And I shall tell the Way that they shall hold thither. For I have often times passed and ridden the Way, with good Company of many Lords. God be thanked !

And ye shall understand, that I have put this Book out of Latin into French, and translated it again out of French into English, that every Man of my Nation may understand it ; and that Lords and Knights and other noble and worthy Men that know Latin but little, and have been

FRENCH NOBLEMAN, 14TH CENTURY

beyond the Sea, may know and understand, that if I err in devising, from forgetting or other Thing, they may redress or amend it. For Things passed out of long time from a Man's Mind or from his Sight, turn soon into forgetting ; because that the Mind of Man may not be comprehended or withheld, by reason of the Frailty of Mankind.

CHAPTER I

To teach you the Way out of England to Constantinople

PILGRIM WITH DOUBLE CROSS

N the Name of God, Glorious and Almighty! He that will pass over the Sea, to go to the City of Jerusalem, he may go by many Ways, both on Sea and Land, after the Country that he cometh from; for many of them come to the one End.

But trow not that I will tell you all the Towns, and Cities and Castles that Men shall go by; for then should I make too long a Tale; but only some Countries and most principal Stages that Men shall go through to go the right Way.

First, if a Man come from the West Side of the World, as England, Ireland, Wales, Scotland, or

Norway, he may, if that he will, go through Almayne (Germany), and through the Kingdom of Hungary, that marcheth with the Land of Polayne (Poland), and with the Land of Pannonia, and so to Silesia.

And the King of Hungary is a great Lord and a mighty, and holdeth great Lordships and much Land in his Hand. For he holdeth the Kingdom of Hungary, Sclavonia, and of Comania a great Part, and of Bulgaria that Men call the Land of Bougiers, and of the Realm of Russia a great Part, whereof he hath made a Duchy, that stretcheth unto the Land of Nyfland (Livonia), and marcheth with Prussia. And Men go through the Land of this Lord, through a City that is clept Cypron (Ödenburg), and by the Castle of Neasburghe (Meseburch), and by the evil Town, that sitteth toward the End of Hungary. And there Men pass the River of Danube. This River of Danube is a full great River, and it goeth into Almayne, under the Hills of Lombardy, and it receiveth into him 40 other Rivers, and it runneth through Hungary and through Greece and through Thrace, and it entereth into the Sea, toward the East so rudely and so sharply, that the Water of the Sea is fresh and holdeth his Sweetness 20 Mile within the Sea. ·

And after, go Men to Belgrade, and enter into the Land of Bougiers; and there Men pass a Bridge of Stone that is upon the River of Marrok (Morava). And Men pass through the Land of Pyncemartz (Petschenegs), and come to Greece to the City of Nye (Sofia), and to the City of Fynepape (Philip-

THE BRIDGE OVER THE RIVER OF MARROK

oppolis), and after to the City of Dandrenoble (Adrianople), and after to Constantinople, that was wont to be clept Bezanzon (Byzantium). And there dwelleth commonly the Emperor of Greece. And there is the most fair Church and the most noble of all the World; and it is that of Saint Sophia.

And before that Church is the Image of Justinian the Emperor, covered with Gold, and he sits upon an Horse a-crowned. And he was wont to hold a round Apple of Gold in his Hand : but it is fallen out thereof. And Men say there, that it is a Token that the Emperor hath lost a great Part of his Lands and of his Lordships; for he was wont to be Emperor of Roumania and of Greece, of all Asia the Less, and of the Land of Syria,

PILGRIM

of the Land of Judea in the which is Jerusalem, and of the Land of Egypt, of Persia, and of Arabia. But he hath lost all but Greece ; and that Land he holds only. And Men would many times put the Apple into the Image's Hand again, but it will not hold it. This Apple betokeneth the Lordship that he had over all the World, that is round. And the tother Hand he lifteth up against the East, in token to menace the Misdoers. This Image stands upon a Pillar of Marble at Constantinople.

CHAPTER II

Of the Cross and the Crown of our Lord Jesu Christ

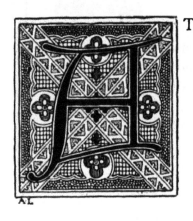

A T Constantinople is the Cross of our Lord Jesu Christ, and His Coat without Seams, that is clept *Tunica inconsutilis*, and the Sponge, and the Reed, with which the Jews gave our Lord Vinegar and Gall, on the Cross. And there is one of the Nails, that Christ was nailed with on the Cross.

And some Men trow that half the Cross, that Christ was put on, is in Cyprus, in an Abbey of Monks, that Men call the Hill of the Holy Cross; but it is not so. For that Cross that is in Cyprus, is the Cross, on the which Dismas the good Thief was hanged. But all Men know not that; and that is evilly done, that for Profit of the Offerings, they say that it is the Cross of our Lord Jesu Christ.

And ye shall understand that the Cross of our Lord was made of four Manner of Trees, as it is contained in this Verse,—

"*In Cruce fit Palma, Cedrus, Cypressus, Oliva.*" For that Piece that went upright from the Earth to the Head was of Cypress ; and the Piece that went overthwart, to the which His Hands were nailed, was of Palm ; and the Stock, that stood within the Earth, in the which was made the Mortise, was of Cedar ; and the Tablet above His Head, that was a Foot and a half long, on the which the Title was written in Hebrew, Greek and Latin, that was of Olive.

And the Jews made the Cross of these four Manner of Trees ; for they thought that our Lord Jesu Christ should have hanged on the Cross, as long as the Cross might last. And therefore made they the Foot of the Cross of Cedar ; for Cedar may not rot in Earth nor Water, and therefore they would that it should have lasted long. For they trowed that the Body of Christ should have stunken ; therefore they made that Piece, that went from the Earth upwards of Cypress, for it is well-smelling, so that the Smell of His Body should not grieve Men that went thereby. And the overthwart Piece was of Palm, for in the Old Testament it was ordained, that when one overcame he should be crowned with Palm ; for they trowed that they had the Victory of Christ Jesus, therefore made they the overthwart Piece of Palm. And the Tablet of the Title they made of Olive; for Olive betokeneth Peace. And the Story

of Noah witnesseth that when the Culver brought
the Branch of Olive, that betokened Peace made
between God and Man.   And so trowed the Jews
to have Peace, when Christ was dead; for they
said that He made Discord and Strife amongst
them.   And ye shall understand that our Lord was
a-nailed on the Cross lying, and therefore He
suffered the more Pain.

And the Christian Men, that dwell beyond the
Sea, in Greece, say that the Tree of the Cross, that
we call Cypress, was of that Tree that Adam ate the
Apple off; and that find they written.   And they
say also, that their Scripture saith, that Adam was
sick, and said to his Son Seth, that he should go to
the Angel that kept Paradise, that he would send
him Oil of Mercy, to anoint his Members, that he
might have Health.   And Seth went.   But the
Angel would not let him come in; but said to him,
that he might not have of the Oil of Mercy.   But
he took him 3 Grains of the same Tree, that his
Father ate the Apple off; and bade him, as soon as
his Father was dead, that he should put these 3
Grains under his Tongue, and bury him so : and he
did.   And of these 3 Grains sprang a Tree, as
the Angel said that it should, and bare a Fruit,
through the which Fruit Adam should be saved.
And when Seth came again, he found his Father
near dead.   And when he was dead, he did with
the Grains as the Angel bade him; of the which
sprung 3 Trees, of the which the Cross was made,
that bare good Fruit and blessed, our Lord Jesu

Constantinople is a full fair City, and a good, and well walled; and it is 3-cornered. And there is an Arm of the Sea of Hellespont : and some Men call it the Mouth of Constantinople ; and some Men call it the Brace (or Arm) of Saint George : and that Arm closeth the 2 Parts of the City. And upward to the Sea, upon the Water, was wont to be the great City of Troy, in a full fair Plain : but that City was destroyed by them of Greece, and little appears now thereof, because it is so long since it was destroyed.

About Greece there be many Isles, as Calliste, Calcas (Carki), Critige (Ortygia), Tesbria, Mynia, Flaxon, Melo, Carpate (Scarpanto) and Lemnos. And in this latter Isle is the Mount Athos, that passeth the Clouds. And there be many diverse Languages and many Countries, that be obedient to the Emperor ; that is to say, Turcople, Pyneynard, Cornange, and many other, as Thrace and Macedonia, of the which Alexander was King. In this Country was Aristotle born, in a City that Men call Stagyra, a little Way from the City of Thrace. And at Stagyra lieth Aristotle ; and there is an Altar upon his Tomb. And there make Men great Feasts for him every Year, as though he were a Saint. And at his Altar they hold their great Councils and their Assemblies, and they hope, that through Inspiration of God and of him, they shall have the better Council.

In this Country be right high Hills, toward the End of Macedonia. And there is a great Hill, that Men call Olympus, that parteth Macedonia and Thrace. And it is so high, that it passeth the Clouds. And there is another Hill, that is clept Athos, that

PHILOSOPHERS ON MOUNT ATHOS

is so high, that the Shadow of him reacheth to Lemne, that is an Isle; and it is 76 Mile between. And above at the Top of the Hill is the Air so clear, that Men may find no Wind there, and therefore may no Beast live there; and so is the Air dry.

AND THEY POUND THE SAME LETTERS

the Diversity that is between our Faith and theirs. For many Men have great Liking, to hear speak of strange Things of divers Countries.

KNIGHT, 14TH CENTURY

CHAPTER IV

*Of the Way from Constantinople to Jerusalem. Of Saint
John the Evangelist. And of the Daughter
of Ypocras, transformed from a
Woman to a Dragon*

VENETIAN PAGE, 14TH CENTURY

OW return I again, to teach you the way from Constantinople to Jerusalem. He that will, goeth through Turkey toward the city of Nyke (Nicea,) and passeth through the Gate of Chienetout (Gemlik,) and always Men see before them the Hill of Chienetout, that is right high; and it is a Mile and a half from Nyke.

And whoso will go by Water, by the Brace of St. George, and by the Sea where St. Nicholas lieth, and toward many other Places—first Men go to an Isle that is clept Sylo (Scio). In that Isle groweth Mastick on small Trees, and out of them cometh Gum, as it were of Plum-trees or of Cherry-trees.

And after Men go through the Isle of Patmos;

and there wrote St. John the Evangelist the Apocalypse. And ye shall understand, that St. John was of Age 32 Year, when our Lord suffered His Passion; and after His Passion, he lived 67 Year, and in the 100th Year of his Age he died.

From Patmos Men go unto Ephesus, a fair City and nigh to the Sea. And there died St. John, and was buried behind the high Altar in a Tomb. And there is a fair Church; for Christian Men were wont to hold that Place always. And in the Tomb of St. John is nought but Manna, that is clept Angels' Meat; for his Body was translated into Paradise. And the Turks now hold all that Place, and the City and the Church (and all Asia the Less is a-clept Turkey). And ye shall understand, that St. John let make his Grave there in his Life, and laid himself therein all alive; and therefore some Men say, that he died not, but that he resteth there till the Day of Doom. And, forsooth, there is a great Marvel; for Men may see there the Earth of the Tomb openly many times stir and move, as though there were alive Things underneath.

And from Ephesus Men go through many Isles in the Sea, unto the City of Patera, where St. Nicholas was born, and so to Martha (Myra), where he was chosen to be Bishop; and there groweth right good Wine and strong, and that Men call Wine of Martha. And from thence go Men to the Isle of Crete, that the Emperor gave sometime to the Genoese.

And then pass Men through the Isles of Colos and

of Lango (Cos,) of the which Isles Ypocras* was
Lord.   And some Men say, that in the Isle of Lango
is yet the Daughter of Ypocras, in Form and Likeness of a great Dragon, that is a 100 Fathom of

THE KNIGHT SAW HER IN THAT
FORM SO HIDEOUS

Length, as Men say,
for I have not seen her.
And they of the Isles
call her Lady of the
Land.   And she lieth in an old Castle, in a Cave,
and sheweth twice or thrice in the Year, and she
doth no Harm to no Man, but if Men do her Harm.
And she was thus changed and transformed, from a

* Hippocrates, the celebrated Physician, who was born at Lango
(another name for Cos).

SHE CAST HIM INTO THE SEA

fair Damosel, into Likeness of a Dragon, by a God-
dess that was clept Diana.   And Men say, that she
shall so endure in that Form of a Dragon, unto the
Time that a Knight come, that is so hardy, that
dare come to her and kiss her on the Mouth ; and
then shall she turn again to her own Kind, and
be a Woman again, but after that she shall not
live long.

And it is not long since, that a Knight of Rhodes,
that was hardy and doughty in Arms, said that he
would kiss her.   And when he was upon his Courser,
and went to the Castle, and entered into the Cave,
the Dragon lift up her Head against him.   And when
the Knight saw her in that Form so hideous and so
horrible he fled away.   And the Dragon bare the
Knight upon a Rock, maugre his Head ; and from
that Rock, she cast him into the Sea.   And so was
lost both Horse and Man.

And also a young Man, that wist not of the
Dragon, went out of a Ship, and went through the
Isle till that he came to the Castle, and came into
the Cave, and went so long, till that he found a
Chamber ; and there he saw a Damosel that combed
her Head and looked in a Mirror ; and she had much
Treasure about her.   And he trowed that she had
been a common Woman, that dwelled there to receive
Men to Folly.   And he abode, till the Damosel saw
the Shadow of him in the Mirror.   And she turned
her toward him, and asked him what he would ?
And he said, he would be her Leman or Paramour.
And she asked him, if that he were a Knight ?   And

he said, Nay.   And then she said, that he might not be her Leman ; but she bade him go again unto his Fellows, and make him Knight, and come again upon the Morrow, and she should come out of the Cave before him, and then he should come and kiss her on the Mouth and have no Dread,—"for I shall do thee no manner of Harm, albeit that thou see me in Likeness of a Dragon ; for though thou see me hideous and horrible to look on, I charge thee to know that it is made by Enchantment ; for without Doubt, I am none other than thou seest now, a Woman, and therefore dread thou nought. And if thou kiss me, thou shalt have all this Treasure, and be my Lord, and Lord also of all the Isle."

And he departed from her and went to his Fellows to the Ship, and let make him a Knight and came again upon the Morrow to kiss this Damosel.   And when he saw her come out of the Cave in Form of a Dragon, so hideous and horrible, he had so great Dread, that he fled again to the Ship, and she followed him.   And when she saw that he turned not again, she began to cry, as a Thing that had much Sorrow ; and then she turned again into her Cave.   And anon the Knight died.   And since then might no Knight see her, but that he died anon. But when a Knight cometh, that is so hardy to kiss her, he shall not die ; but he shall turn the Damosel into her right Form and natural Shape, and he shall be Lord of all the Countries and Isles above-said.

And from thence Men come to the Isle of Rhodes,

the which Isle the Hospitallers hold and govern;
and that took they some-time from the Emperor.
And it was wont to be clept Collos;* and so the
Turks call it yet.   And Saint Paul in his Epistle
writes to them of that Isle *ad Colossenses*.† This Isle
is nigh 800 Mile from Constantinople.

And from this Isle of Rhodes Men go to Cyprus,
where be many Vines, that first be red and after one
Year they become white; and those Wines that be
most white, be most clear and best of Smell.

And Men pass by that Way, by a Place that was
wont to be a great City, and a great Land; and the
City was clept Cathailye (Satalia), the which City and
Land was lost through Folly of a young Man. For he
had a fair Damosel, that he loved well for his Paramour; and she died suddenly, and was put in a Tomb
of Marble.   And for the great Lust that he had to
her, he went in the Night unto her Tomb and opened
it, and went in and lay by her, and went his Way.
And when it came to the End of 9 Months, there
came a Voice to him and said, "Go to the Tomb of
that Woman, and open it and behold what thou hast
begotten on her; and if thou fail to go, thou shalt
have a great Harm."   And he went and opened the
Tomb, and there fled out an Head right hideous to
see; the which all swiftly flew about the City and
the Country, and soon after the City sank down.
And there be many perilous Passages.‡

---

* From the Colossus of Rhodes.
† As a matter of fact, St. Paul's Epistle is to the people of Colossæ
in Phrygia Major.   ‡ For ships, that is.

From Rhodes to Cyprus be 500 Mile and more.
But Men may go to Cyprus, and not touch at
Rhodes. Cyprus is a right good Isle, and a fair and
a great, and it hath 4 principal Cities within him.
And there is an Archbishop at
Nicosea, and 4 other Bishops in
that Land.   And at
Famagusta is one

THERE FLED OUT
AN HEAD RIGHT
HIDEOUS

of the principal Havens of the Sea that is in the
World ; and there arrive Christian Men and Saracens
. and Men of all Nations.   In Cyprus is the Hill of
the Holy Cross ; and there is an Abbey of black
Monks, and there is the Cross of Dismas the good
Thief, as I have said before.   And some Men

trow, that there is half the Cross of our Lord ; but it is not so, and they do Evil that make Men to believe so.

In Cyprus lieth Saint Zenonimus, of whom Men of that Country make great Solemnity.   And in the Castle of Amours lieth the Body of Saint Hilarion, and Men keep it right worshipfully.   And beside Famagusta was Saint Barnabas the Apostle born.

In Cyprus Men hunt with Papyonns, that be like Leopards, and they take wild Beasts right well, and they be somewhat more big than Lions ; and they take more sharply the Beasts, and more nimbly than do Hounds.

In Cyprus it is the Manner of Lords and all other Men to eat on the Earth.   For they make Ditches in the Earth all about in the Hall, deep to the Knee, and they do pave them ; and when they will eat, they go therein and sit there.   And the Reason is that they may be the more cool ; for that Land is much more hotter than it is here.   And at great Feasts, and for Strangers, they set Forms and Tables, as Men do in this Country, but they had rather sit in the Earth.

From Cyprus, Men go to the Land of Jerusalem by the Sea : and in a Day and in a Night, he that hath good Wind may come to the Haven of Tyre, that is now clept Sur.   There was some-time a great City and a good of Christian Men, but Saracens have destroyed it a great Part ; and they keep that Haven right well, for Dread of Christian Men.   Men might go more straight to that Haven, and touch not at Cyprus, but they go gladly to Cyprus to rest them on the Land, or else to buy Things, that they have need for their Living. On the Sea-side Men may find many Rubies. And there is the Well, the which Holy Writ speaketh of, and saith, " *Fons Orto-rum, et Puteus Aquarum viventium:* " that is to say, " *The Well of Gardens, and the Ditch of Living Waters.* "

In this City of Tyre, said the Woman to our Lord, " *Beatus Venter qui Te portavit, et Ubera que suc-cisti :* " that is to say, " *Blessed be the Body that bare Thee, and the Paps that Thou suckedst.* " And there our Lord forgave the Woman of Canaan her Sins. And before Tyre was wont to be the Stone, on the which our Lord sat and preached, and on that Stone was founded the Church of Saint Saviour.

And 8 mile from Tyre, toward the East, upon the Sea, is the City of Sarphen (Sûrafend) in Sarepta of the Sidonians. There was wont to dwell Elijah the Prophet; and there raised he Jonas, the Widow's Son, from Death to Life. And 5 Mile from Sarphen is the City of Sidon ; of the which City, Dido was Lady, that was Eneas' Wife, after the Destruction of Troy, and that founded the City of Carthage in Africa, now clept Didonsarte. And in the City of Tyre, reigned Agenor, the Father of Dido. And 16 Mile from Sidon is Beirout. And from Beirout to Sardenare is 3 Days' Journey. And from Sard-enare it is 5 Mile to Damascus.

And whoso will go long time on the Sea, and come nearer to Jerusalem, he shall go by Sea to the Port Jaffa. For that is the next Haven to Jeru-

salem; for from that Haven is not but one Day's
Journey and an half to Jerusalem. And the Town
is called Jaffa; for one of the Sons of Noah named
Japhet founded it, and now it is clept Joppa. And
ye shall understand, that it is one of the oldest Towns
of the World, for it was founded before Noah's
Flood. And even yet the Rock showeth there, how
the Iron Chains were fastened, that Andromeda, a
great Giant, was bounden with,* and put in Prison
before Noah's Flood. And there be Bones of the
Giant's Side 40 Foot long.

And whoso will arrive at the Port of Tyre or of
Sur, that I have first spoken of before, may go by
Land, if he will, to Jerusalem. And Men go from Sur
unto the City of Acre in a Day. And it was clept
some-time Ptolemaïs. And it was some-time a City
of Christian Men, and full fair, but it is now destroyed;
and it stands upon the Sea. And from Venice to
Acre, by Sea, is 2080 Lombardy Miles; and from
Calabria, or from Sicily to Acre, by Sea, is 1300
Lombardy Miles; and the Isle of Crete is right
in the Midway.

And beside the City of Acre, toward the Sea,
120 Furlongs on the right Side, toward the South, is
the Hill of Carmel, where Elijah the Prophet dwelled,
and there was the Order of Friars Carmelites first
founded. This Hill is not right great, nor full high.
And at the Foot of this Hill was some-time a good
City of Christian Men, that Men clept Caiffa, for Caiaphas first founded it; but it is now all waste. And

* A queer subversion of the old legend.

on the left Side of the Hill of Carmel is a Town, that Men call Saffre (Sephoris,) and that is set on another Hill. There Saint James and Saint John were born; and, in Worship of them there is a fair Church. And from Ptolemaïs, that Men now call Acre, unto a great Hill, that is clept the Scale (or Ladder) of Tyre, is 100 Furlongs. And beside the City of Acre runneth a little River, that is clept Belon (Belus).

And there nigh is the Foss of Mennon that is all round; and it is 100 Cubits of Largeness, and it is all full of Gravel, shining bright, of the which Men make fair and clear Verres (or Crystal Glasses). And Men come from far, by Water in Ships, and by Land with Carts, to fetch of that Gravel. And though there be never so much taken away thereof in the Day, at the Morrow it is as full again as ever it was; and that is a great Marvel. And there is evermore great Wind in that Foss, that stirreth evermore the Gravel, and maketh it troubled. And if any Man put therein any sort of Metal, it turneth anon to Glass. And the Glass, that is made of that Gravel, if it be put again into the Gravel, it turneth anon into Gravel as it was first. And therefore some Men say, that it is a Whirlpool of the gravelly Sea.

And from Acre, above-said, Men go forth 4 Days' Journey to the City of Palestine, that was of the Philistines, that now is clept Gaza, that is a gay City and a rich; and it is right fair and full of Folk, and it is a little from the Sea. And from this City brought Samson the Strong the Gates upon an high

Land, when he was taken in that City, and there he slew in a Palace the King and himself, and great Number of the best of the Philistines, the which had put out his Eyes and shaved his Head, and imprisoned him by Treason of Delilah his Paramour. And therefore he made fall upon them a great Hall, when they were at Meat.

And from thence go Men to the city of Cesarea, and so to the Castle of Pilgrims (Athlêt), and so to Ascalon ; and then to Jaffa, and so to Jerusalem.

ARQUEBUSE AND BANDEROLE, 14TH CENTURY

SIR JOHN COMES TO THE CASTLE OF DARON

CHAPTER V

*Of many Names of Sultans, and of
the Tower of Babylon*

AND whoso will go by Land through
the Land of Babylon, where the
Sultan dwelleth commonly, he
must get Grace of him and Leave
to go more securely through those
Lands and Countries.

And to go to the Mount of Sinai, before that Men
go to Jerusalem, they shall go from Gaza to the
Castle of Daire (Daron). And after that, Men come
out of Syria, and enter into a Wilderness, and there
the Way is sandy ; and that Wilderness and Desert
lasteth an 8 Days' Journey, but always Men find
good Inns, and all that they need of Victuals.

And Men call that Wilderness Achelleke.   And
when a Man cometh out of that Desert, he entereth
into Egypt, that Men call Egypt-Canopac, and after
other Languages, Men call it Morsyn.   And there
first Men find a good Town, that is clept Belethe
(Belbais) ; and it is at the End of the Kingdom of
Aleppo.   And from thence Men go to Babylon and
to Cairo.

At Babylon there is a fair Church of our Lady,
where she dwelled 7 Year, when she fled out of
the Land of Judea for Dread of King Herod.   And
there lieth the Body of Saint Barbara the Virgin and
Martyr.   And there dwelled Joseph, when he was
sold by his Brethren.   And there made Nebuchadnezzar the King to be put 3 Children into the
Furnace of Fire, because they were in the right Truth
of Belief, the which Children Men call Anania, Aza-
riah, Mishael, as the Psalm of *Benedicite* saith : but
Nebuchadnezzar clept them otherwise, Shadrach,
Meshach, and Abednego, that is to say, God glorious,
God victorious, and God over all Things and Realms :
And that was for the Miracle, that he saw God's Son
go with the Children through the Fire, as he said.

There dwelleth the Sultan in his Calahelyke (for
there is commonly his Seat) in a fair Castle, strong
and great, and well set upon a Rock.   In that Castle
dwell always, to keep it and to serve the Sultan,
more than 6000 Persons, that take all their
Necessaries from the Sultan's Court.   I ought right
well to know it ; for I dwelled with him as Soldier a
great while, in his Wars against the Bedouins.   And

he would have married me full highly to a great Prince's Daughter, if I would have forsaken my Law and my Belief; but I thank God, I had no Will to do it, for anything that he promised me.

And ye shall understand, that the Sultan is Lord of 5 Kingdoms, that he hath conquered and appropriated to himself by Strength. And these be the Names: the Kingdom of Canapac, that is Egypt; and the Kingdom of Jerusalem, where that David and Solomon were Kings; and the Kingdom of Syria, of the which the City of Damascus was chief; and the Kingdom of Aleppo in the Land of Mathe; and the Kingdom of Arabia, that belonged to one of the 3 Kings, that made Offering to our Lord, when He was born. And many other Lands he holdeth in his Hand. And therewithal he holdeth Caliphs, that is a full great Thing in their Language, and it is as much as to say King.

" A GREAT PRINCE'S
DAUGHTER "

And there were wont to be 5 Sultans; but now there is no more but he of Egypt. And the first Sultan was Zarocon, that was of Media, as was Father to Saladin that took the Caliph of Egypt and slew him, and was made Sultan by Strength. After him was Sultan Saladin, in whose Time the King of England, Richard the First, with many others, kept the Passage, that Saladin might not pass. After

Saladin reigned his Son Boradin, and after him his
Nephew. After that, the Comanians that were in
Servage in Egypt, feeling themselves that they were
of great Power, chose them a Sultan amongst them,
the which made himself to be clept Melechsalan :
and in his Time entered into the Country of the
Kings of France, Saint Louis, and fought with him;
and the Sultan took him and imprisoned him ; and
this Sultan was slain by his own Servants. And
after, they chose another to be Sultan, that they
called Tympieman ; and he let deliver Saint Louis
out of Prison for a certain Ransom. And after, one
of these Comanians reigned, that was called Cachas,
and slew Tympieman, to be Sultan ; and made himself be clept Melechmenes. And after was another
that had to Name Bendochdare, that slew Melechmenes to be Sultan, and called himself Melechdare.
In his Time entered the good King Edward of England into Syria, and did great Harm to the Saracens.
And after, was this Sultan empoisoned at Damascus,
and his Son thought to reign after him by Heritage,
and made himself to be clept Melechsache ; but
another that had to Name Elphy, chased him out of
the Country and made himself Sultan. This Man
took the City of Tripoli and destroyed many of the
Christian Men, the Year of Grace 1289, but he was
anon slain. After that was the Son of Elphy chosen
to be Sultan, and called himself Melechasseraff, and
he took the City of Acre and chased out the Christian
Men ; and this Sultan was also empoisoned, and then
was his Brother made Sultan, and was clept Melech-

nasser.   And after, one that was clept Guytoga took
him and put him in Prison in the Castle of Mountroyal, and made himself Sultan by Strength, and
called himself Melechadel; and he was of Tartary.
But the Comanians chased him out of the Country,
and did him much Sorrow, and made one of themselves Sultan, that had to Name Lachin.   And he
made himself to be clept Melechmanser, the which
on a Day played at Chess, and his Sword lay beside
him ; and so it befell, that one angered him, and
with his own proper Sword he was slain.   And
after that, they were at great Discord, to make a
Sultan ; and finally were accorded for Melechnasser,
that Guytoga had put in Prison at Mountroyal.
And this Sultan reigned long and governed wisely,
so that his eldest Son was chosen after him, Melech-
mader, the which his Brother caused to be slain
privily to have the Lordship, and made himself to be
clept Melechmadabron, and he was Sultan when I
departed from these Countries.*

And wit ye well that the Sultan may lead out of
Egypt more than 20,000 Men of Arms, and out of
Syria, and out of Turkey and out of other Countries
that he holds, he may raise more than 50,000.   And
all those be at his Wages, and they be always with
him, besides the Folk of his Country, that are without
Number.   And every one of them hath by the Year
the Amount of 6 Score Florins ; but it behoveth,

* By this we are able to settle the date of Sir John's leaving
Egypt ; this must have been at the end of 1341, as Melechmadabron
only reigned six months, and was deposed on the 11th January, 1342.

that every one of them hold 3 Horses and a
Camel. And in the Cities and in the Towns be
Admirals, that have the Governance of the People ;
one hath to govern 4, and another hath to govern
5, another more, and another not a few more.
And as much Pay taketh the Admiral to himself
alone, as have all the other Soldiers under him ;
and therefore, when the Sultan will advance any
worthy Knight, he maketh him an Admiral. And
when there is any Dearth, the Knights be right poor,
and then they sell both their Horses and their
Harness.

And the Sultan hath 4 Wives, one Christian
and 3 Saracens, of the which one dwelleth at
Jerusalem, and another at Damascus, and another
at Ascalon ; and when they list, they remove to
other Cities, and when the Sultan will he may go
visit them. And he hath as many Paramours as he
liketh. For he maketh to come before him the
fairest and the noblest of Birth, and the gentlest
Damosels of his Country, and he maketh them to be
kept and served full honourably. And when he will
have one to lie with him, he maketh them all to
come before him, and he beholdeth them all, which
of them is most to his Pleasure, and to her anon he
sendeth or casteth a Ring from his Finger. And then
anon she shall be bathed and richly attired, and
anointed with delicate Things of sweet Smell, and
then led to the Sultan's Chamber ; and thus he doth
as often as he list, when he will have any of them.

And before the Sultan cometh no Stranger, but if

he be clothed in Cloth of Gold, or of Tartary or of Camaka, in the Saracens' Guise, and as the Saracens use. And it behoveth, that anon at the first Sight that Men see the Sultan, be it in a Window or in what Place else, that Men kneel to him and kiss the Earth, for that is the Manner to do Reverence to the Sultan of them that speak with him. And when that Messengers of strange Countries come before him, the People of the Sultan, when the Strangers speak to him, be about the Sultan with Swords drawn and Gisarmes * and Axes, their Arms lift up on high with the Weapons to smite upon them, if they say any Word that is Displeasure to the Sultan. And also, no Stranger cometh before him, but that he maketh him some Promise and Grant if that the Stranger asketh reasonably ; if it be so it be not against his Law. And so do other Princes beyond, for they say that no Man shall come before no Prince, but that he be the better, and shall be more gladder in departing from his Presence than he was at the coming before him.

And understand ye, that that Babylon that I have spoken of, where that the Sultan dwelleth, is not that great Babylon where the Diversity of Language was first made for Vengeance by the Miracle of God, when the great Tower of Babel was begun to be made ; of the which the Walls were 64 Furlongs of Height ; that is in the great Desert of Arabia, upon the Way as Men go toward the Kingdom of Chaldea. But it is full long since that any

* Bills or battle-axes.

Man durst nigh to the Tower; for it is all deserted
and full of Dragons and great Serpents, and full of
diverse venomous Beasts all about.   That Tower,
with the City, was of 25 Mile in Circuit of the
Walls, as they of the Country say, and as Men
may deem by Estimation, from what Men tell of
the Country.

And though it be clept the Tower of Babylon, yet
nevertheless there were ordained within many Man-
sions and many great Dwelling-places, in Length and
Breadth.   And that Tower contained great Country
in its Circuit, for the Tower alone contained 10 Mile
square.   That Tower founded King Nimrod that
was King of that Country; and he was first King
of the World.   And he had made an Image in the
Likeness of his Father, and constrained all his
Subjects to worship it; and anon began other Lords
to do the same, and so began first the Idols and
Simulacres.

The Town and the City were full well set in a fair
Country and a Plain that Men call the Country of
Samar, of the which the Walls of the City were
200 Cubits in Height, and 50 Cubits in Breadth;
and the River of Euphrates ran throughout the City
and about the Tower also.   But Cyrus the King of
Persia took from them the River, and destroyed all
the City and the Tower also; for he parted that
River into 60 small Rivers, because that he had
sworn, that he should put the River in such point,
that a Woman might well pass there, without
casting off of her Clothes, forasmuch as he had

lost many worthy Men that trowed to pass that River by swimming.

And from Babylon where the Sultan dwelleth, to go right between the Orient (East) and the Septentrion (North) toward the great Babylon, is a 40 Days' Journey to pass by Desert. But the great Babylon is not in the Land and in the Power of the said Sultan, but is in the Power and the Lordship of Persia, and is held of the great Chan, that is the greatest Emperor and the most Sovereign Lord of the Parts beyond, and is Lord of the Isles of Cathay and of many other Isles and of a great Part of Ind, and his Land marcheth with Prester John's Land, and he holdeth so much Land, that he knoweth not the End : and he is more mighty and a greater Lord without Comparison than is the Sultan : of his royal Estate and of his Might I shall speak more fully, when I shall speak of the Land and of the Country of Ind.

Also the City of Mecca where Mohammet lieth is in the great Deserts of Arabia ; and there lieth his Body full honourably in their Temple, that the Saracens call Mosque. And it is from Babylon the Less, where the Sultan dwelleth, unto Mecca above-said, near a 32 Days' Journey.

And wit well, that the Realm of Arabia is a full great Country, but therein is over-much Desert. And no Man may dwell there in that Desert for Default of Water, for that Land is all gravelly and full of Sand. And it is dry and in no way fruitful, because it hath no Moisture ; and therefore is there

so much Desert. And if it had Rivers and Wells, and the Land also were as it is in other Parts, it should be as full of People and as full inhabited with Folk as in other Places; for there is full great Multitude of People, where the Land is inhabited. Arabia endureth from the Ends of the Realm of Chaldea unto the last End of Africa, and marcheth with the land of Idumea toward the End of Botron (Bozra). And in Chaldea the chief City is Bagdad. And of Africa the chief City is Carthage, that Dido, that was Eneas's Wife, founded; the which Eneas was of the City of Troy, and after was King of Italy.

Mesopotamia stretcheth also unto the Deserts of Arabia, and it is a great Country. In this Country is the city of Haran, where Abraham's Father dwelled, and from whence Abraham departed by Commandment of the Angel. And of that City was Ephraim, that was a great Clerk and a great Doctor. And Theophilus was of that City also, that our Lady saved from our Enemy.* And Mesopotamia endureth from the River of Euphrates, unto the River of Tigris, for it is between those two Rivers.

And beyond the River of Tigris is Chaldea, that is a full great Kingdom. In that Realm, at Bagdad above-said, was wont to dwell the Caliph, that was wont to be both Emperor and Pope of the Arabians, so that he was Lord Spiritual and Temporal; and he was Successor to Mahommet, and of his Lineage.

* Theophilus sold himself to the Devil, and, repenting, was saved by the Virgin Mary: a legend of the Middle Ages.

That City of Bagdad was wont to be clept Susa,
and Nebuchadnezzar founded it ; and there dwelled
the holy Prophet Daniel, and there he saw Visions
of Heaven, and there he made the Exposition of
Dreams.*

And in old Time there were wont to be 3
Caliphs, and they dwelled in the City of Bagdad
above-said.

And at Cairo beside Babylon dwelled the Caliph
of Egypt ; and at Morocco, upon the West Sea,
dwelled the Caliph of the People of Barbary and of
the Africans.   And now are there none of the
Caliphs, nor nought have been since the Time of the
Sultan Saladin; for from that Time hither the Sultan
calleth himself Caliph, and so have the Caliphs lost
their Name.

And wit well, that Babylon the Less, where the
Sultan dwelleth, and at the City of Cairo that is nigh
beside it, be great huge Cities many and fair ; and
the one sits nigh the other.   Babylon sits upon the
River of Gyson, sometimes clept Nile, that cometh
out of Terrestrial Paradise.

That River of Nile, all the Year, when the Sun
entereth into the Sign of Cancer, beginneth to wax,
and it waxeth always, as long as the Sun is in Cancer
and in the Sign of the Lion ; and it waxeth in such
Manner, that it is sometimes so great, that it is
20 Cubits or more of Deepness, and then it doth
great Harm to the Goods that be upon the Land.
For then may no Man travail to plough the Lands

* A spurious book, popular in those times.

for the great Moisture, and therefore is there dear Time in that Country. And also, when it waxeth but little, it is dear Time in that Country, for Default of Moisture. And when the Sun is in the Sign of Virgo, then beginneth the River to wane and to decrease little by little, so that when the Sun is entered into the Sign of Libra, then Men enter between these Rivers that are made. This River cometh, running from Terrestrial Paradise, between the Deserts of Ind, and after it smiteth into the Land, and runneth long time through many great Countries under Earth. And after it goeth out under an high Hill, that Men call Alothe, that is between Ind and Ethiopia the distance of 5 Months' Journeys from the Entry of Ethiopia; and after it environeth all Ethiopia and Mauritania, and goeth all along from the Land of Egypt unto the City of Alexandria to the End of Egypt, and there it falleth into the Sea. About this River be many Birds and Fowls, as Sikonies, that they call Ibes.

Egypt is a long Country, but it is strait, that is to say narrow, for they may not enlarge it toward the Desert for Default of Water. And the Country is set along upon the River Nile, so that that River may serve by Floods or otherwise, that when it floweth it may spread abroad through the Country; so is the Country large of Length. For it raineth not but little in that Country, and for that Cause they have no Water, but if it be of the Flood of that River. And forasmuch as it raineth not in that Country, but the Air is always pure and clear, therefore in that

Country be the good Astronomers, for they find there no Clouds to hinder them. Also the City of Cairo is right great and more huge than that of Babylon the Less, and it sits above toward the Desert of Syria, a little above the River above-said.

A GOOD ASTRONOMER

In Egypt there be 2 Parts : the Upper, that is toward Ethiopia, and the Lower, that is toward Arabia. In Egypt is the Land of Rameses and the Land of Goshen. Egypt is a strong Country, for it hath many bad Havens because of the great Rocks that be strong and dangerous to pass by. And in Egypt, toward the East, is the Red Sea, that endureth unto the City of Coston ; and toward the West is the Country of Lybia, that is a full dry Land and little of Fruit, for there is overmuch plenty of Heat, and that Land is called Fusthe. And toward the Meridional (South) Part is Ethiopia. And toward the North is the Desert, that endureth unto Syria, and so is the Country strong on all Sides. And it is well a 15 Days' Journey of Length, and more than twice

THE HOLY HERMIT AND THE MONSTER

so much of Desert, and it is but a 2 Days' Journey
in Width.   And between Egypt and Nubia it hath
well 12 Days' Journeys of Desert.   And the Men of
Nubia be Christians, but they be black as the Moors
for the great Heat of the Sun.

In Egypt there be 5 Provinces: that one is
called Sahythe; that other Demeseer; another
Resith, that is an Isle in the Nile; another Alexandria; and another the Land of Damietta.   That
City of Damietta was wont to be right strong, but
it was twice won of the Christian Men, and therefore
after that the Saracens beat down the Walls; and
with the Walls and the Tower thereof, the Saracens
made another City more far from the Sea, and called
it the new Damietta; so that now no Man dwelleth
at the former Town of Damietta.   And that City of
Damietta is one of the Havens of Egypt; and at
Alexandria is the other.   That is a full strong City,
but there is no Water to drink, but if it come by
Conduit from the Nile, that entereth into their
Cisterns; and if any one stopped that Water from
them, they might not endure there.   In Egypt there
be but few Forts or Castles, because that the Country
is so strong of himself.

At the Deserts of Egypt was a worthy Man, that
was an holy Hermit, and there met with him a
Monster, (that is to say, a Monster is a Thing de-
formed against Kind both of Man or of Beast or of
anything else, and that is clept a Monster).   And
this Monster, that met with this holy Hermit, was as
it had been a Man, that had 2 trenchant Horns on

his Forehead; and he had a Body like a Man unto the Navel, and beneath he had a Body like a Goat. And the Hermit asked him what he was. And the Monster answered him, and said he was a deadly Creature, such as God had formed, and dwelled in those Deserts in purchasing his Sustenance. And he besought the Hermit, that he would pray God for him, the Which came from Heaven to save all Mankind, and was born of a Maiden and suffered Passion and Death (as we well know) and by Whom we live and be. And the Head with the 2 Horns of that Monster is yet at Alexandria for a Marvel.

In Egypt is the City of Heliopolis, that is to say, the City of the Sun. In that City there is a Temple, made round after the Shape of the Temple of Jerusalem. The Priests of that Temple have all their Writings, under the Date of the Fowl that is clept Phœnix; and there is but one in all the World. And he cometh to burn himself upon the Altar of the Temple at the end of 500 Year; for so long he liveth. And at the 500 Years' End, the Priests array their Altar nobly, and put thereupon Spices and live Sulphur and other Things that will burn lightly; and then the Bird Phœnix cometh and burneth himself to Ashes. And the first Day next after, Men find in the Ashes a Worm; and the second Day next after, Men find a Bird alive and perfect; and the third Day next after, he flieth his Way. And so there is no more Bird of that Kind in all the World, but it alone, and truly that is a great Miracle of God. And Men may well liken that Bird unto

God, because that there is no God but one; and also, that our Lord arose from Death to Life the third Day. This Bird Men see often-time flying in those Countries; and he is not much more big than an Eagle. And he hath a Crest of Feathers upon his Head more great than the Peacock hath; and his Neck is yellow after the Colour of an Oriel that is a fine shining Stone; and his Beak is coloured blue as Azure; and his Wings be of purple Colour, and the Tail is yellow and red, cast in Streaks across his Tail. And he is a full fair Bird to look upon, against the Sun, for he shineth full gloriously and nobly.

Also in Egypt be Gardens, that have Trees and Herbs, the which bear Fruits 7 Times in the Year. And in that Land Men find many fair Emeralds and enough; and therefore be they more cheap. Also when it raineth once in the Summer in the Land of Egypt, then is all the Country full of great Mires. Also at Cairo, that I spake of before, sell Men commonly both Men and Women of other Laws as we do here Beasts in the Market. And there is a common House in that City that is all full of small Furnaces, and thither bring Women of the Town their Eggs of Hens, of Geese, and of Ducks to be put into those Furnaces. And they that keep that House cover them with Heat of Horse Dung, without Hen, Goose or Duck or any other Fowl. And at the End of 3 Weeks or of a Month they come again and take their Chickens and nourish them and bring them forth, so that all the Country is full of them. And so Men do there both Winter and Summer.

Also in that Country and in others also, Men find long Apples to sell, in their Season, and Men call them Apples of Paradise; and they be right sweet and of good Savour. And though ye cut them in never so many Gobbets or Parts, overthwart or end-long, evermore ye shall find in the Midst the Figure of the Holy Cross of our Lord Jesu. But they will rot within 8 Days, and for that Cause Men may not carry off the Apples to far Countries; and they have great Leaves of a Foot and a half of Length, and they be conformably large. And Men find there also the Tree of Adam's Apples, that have a Bite at one of the Sides; and there be also Fig Trees that bear no Leaves, but Figs upon the small Branches; and men call them Figs of Pharaoh.

Also beside Cairo, without that City, is the Field where Balm groweth; and it cometh out on small Trees, that be none higher than a Man's Breeks' Girdle, and they seem as of Wood that is of the Wild Vine. And in that Field be 7 Wells, that our Lord Jesu Christ made with one of His Feet, when He went to play with other Children. That Field is not so well closed, but that Men may enter at their own List; but in that Season that the Balm is growing, Men put the Place into good Keeping, that no Man dare be hardy enough to enter.

This Balm groweth in no Place, but only there. And though that Men bring of the Plants, to plant in other Countries, they grow well and fair; but they bring forth no fruitful Thing, and the Leaves of Balm fall not at all. And Men cut the Branches with a sharp Flintstone, or with a sharp Bone, when Men will go to cut them ; for whoso would cut them with Iron, it would destroy its Virtue and its Nature.

And the Saracens call the Word "*Enonch-balse*," and the Fruit, the which is as Cubebs, they call "*Abebissam*," and the Liquor that droppeth from the Branches they call "*Guybalse*." And Men make always that Balm to be tilled by the Christian Men, or else it would not fructify ; as the Saracens say themselves, for it hath been often-time proved. Men say also, that the Balm groweth in Ind the Greater, in that Desert where the Trees of the Sun and of the Moon spake to Alexander, but I have not seen it ; for I have not been so far above upward, because that there be too many perilous Passages.

And wit ye well, that a Man ought to take good Care in buying Balm, but an if he know it right well, for he may right lightly be deceived. For Men sell a Gum, that Men call Turpentine, instead of Balm, and they put thereto a little Balm to give good Odour. And some put Wax in Oil of the Wood of the Fruit of Balm, and say that it is Balm. And some distil Cloves of Gilofre* and Spikenard of Spain and other Spices, that be well smelling ; and the Liquor that goeth out thereof they call it Balm, and they think that they have Balm, and they have none. For the Saracens counterfeit it by Subtlety of Craft to deceive the Christian Men, as I have

* A kind of clove.

seen full many a time; and after them the Merchants and the Apothecaries counterfeit it soon after, and then it is less worth, and a great deal worse.

But if it like you, I shall show how ye shall know and prove it, to the End that ye shall not be deceived. First ye shall well know, that the natural Balm is full clear, and of citron Colour and strong smelling; and if it be thick, or red or black, it is sophisticated, that is to say, counterfeited and made like it for Deceit.   And understand, that if ye will put a little Balm in the Palm of your Hand against the Sun, if it be fine and good, ye shall not be able to suffer the Heat of the Sun against your Hand.   Also take a little Balm with the Point of a Knife, and touch it to the Fire, and if it burn it is a good Sign.   After take also a Drop of Balm, and put it into a Dish, or in a Cup with Milk of a Goat, and if it be natural Balm anon it will take and curdle the Milk.   Or put a Drop of Balm in clear Water in a Cup of Silver or in a clear Basin, and stir it well with the clear Water; and if the Balm be fine and of his own Kind, the Water shall never trouble; and if the Balm be sophisticated that is to say counterfeited, the Water shall become anon troubled; and also if the Balm be fine it shall fall to the Bottom of the Vessel, as though it were Quicksilver, for the fine Balm is more heavy twice than is the Balm that is sophisticated and counterfeited.   Now I have spoken of Balm.

And now I shall speak of another Thing that is beyond Babylon, above the Flood of the Nile, toward the Desert between Africa and Egypt; that is to

say, of the Granaries of Joseph, that he had made, to keep the Grains for the Peril of the dear Years. And they be made of Stone, full well made of Masons' Craft ; of the which 2 be marvellously great and high, and the tothers be not so great.   And every Granary hath a Gate to enter within, a little high from the Earth ; for the Land is wasted and fallen since the Granaries were made.   And within they be all full of Serpents.   And above the Granaries without be many Scriptures of diverse Languages.   And some Men say, that they be Sepultures of great Lords, that were sometime, but that is not true, for all the common Rumour and Speech of all the People there, both far and near, is that they be the Granaries of Joseph ; and so find they in their Scriptures, and in their Chronicles.   On the other Hand, if they were Sepultures, they would not be void within ; for ye may well know, that Tombs and Sepultures be neither made of such Greatness, nor of such Highness ; wherefore it is not to be believed, that they be Tombs or Sepultures.

In Egypt also there be diverse Languages and diverse Letters, and of other Manner and Condition than there be in other Parts.   As I shall advise you, such as they be, and the Names how they call them, to such Intent, that ye may know the Difference of them and of others,—Athoimis, Bunchi, Chinok, Durain, Eni, Fin, Gomor, Hecket, Janny, Karacta, Luzanim, Miche, Naryn, Oldache, Pilon, Quyn, Yron, Sichen, Thola, Urmron, Yph and Zarm, Thoit (θ).

E

Now I will return again, ere I proceed any further, to declare to you the other Ways, that draw toward Babylon, where the Sultan himself dwelleth, that is at the Entry of Egypt; for as much as many Folk go thither first and after that to Jerusalem, as I have said to you here before. For they fulfil first the more long Pilgrimage, and after return again by the nearest Ways, because that the more nigh Way is the more worthy, and that is Jerusalem; for no other Pilgrimage is like in Comparison to it. But to fulfil their Pilgrimages more easily and more securely, Men go first by the longer Way.

But whoso will go to Babylon by another Way, more short from the Countries of the West that I have rehearsed before, or from other Countries next to them—then Men go by France, by Burgundy and by Lombardy. It needeth not to tell you the Names of the Cities, nor of the Towns that be in that Way, for the Way is common, and it is known of many Nations. And there be many Havens where Men take the Sea. Some Men take the Sea at Genoa, some at Venice, and pass by the Sea Adriatic, that is clept the Gulf of Venice, that parteth Italy and Greece on that side; and some go to Naples, some to Rome, and from Rome to Brindisi and there they take the Sea, and in many other Places where that Havens be. And Men go by Tuscany, by Campania, by Calabria, by Apulia, and by the Hills of Italy, by Corsica, by Sardinia, and by Sicily, that is a great Isle and a good.

In that Isle of Sicily there is a manner of a Garden,

in the which be many diverse Fruits ; and the Garden is always green and flourishing, all the Seasons of the Year as well in Winter as in Summer. That Isle holds in Compass about 350 French Miles. And between Sicily and Italy there is but a little Arm of the Sea, that Men call the Faro of Messina. And Sicily is between the Sea Adriatic and the Sea of Lombardy. And from Sicily into Calabria is but 8 Mile of Lombardy.

And in Sicily there is a kind of Serpent, by the which Men assay and prove, whether their Children be Bastards or not, or of lawful Marriage : for if they be born in right Marriage, the Serpents go about them, and do them no Harm, and if they be born in Adultery, the Serpents bite them and envenom them. And thus many wedded Men prove if their Children be their own.

Also in that Isle is the Mount Etna, that Men call Mount Gybelle, and the Volcanoes that be evermore burning. And there be 7 Places that burn and cast out diverse Flames of diverse Colour: and by the changing of those Flames, Men of that Country know when it shall be Dearth or good Time, or cold or hot or moist or dry, or in all other Manners how the Time shall be governed. And from Italy unto the Volcanoes is but 25 Mile. And Men say, that the Volcanoes be Ways to Hell.

And whoso goeth by Pisa, if that Men list to go that Way, there is an Arm of the Sea, where that Men go to other Havens in those Coasts, and then Men pass by the Isle of Greaf (Corfu ?) that is at

Genoa. And after Men arrive in Greece at the Haven of the City of Myrok, or at the Haven of Valone, or at the City of Duras ; and there is a Duke at Duras, or at other Havens in those Coasts; and so Men go to Constantinople. And after Men go by Water to the Isle of Crete and to the Isle of Rhodes, and so to Cyprus, and so to Athens, and from thence to Constantinople.

To hold the more straight Way by Sea, it is well 1880 Mile of Lombardy. And after from Cyprus Men go by Sea, and leave Jerusalem and all the Country on the left Hand, unto Egypt, and arrive at the City of Damietta, that was wont to be full strong, and it sits at the Entry of Egypt. And from Damietta go Men to the City of Alexandria, that sits also upon the Sea. In that City was Saint Catherine beheaded : and there was Saint Mark the Evangelist martyred and buried, but the Emperor Leo made his Bones to be brought to Venice.

And there is yet at Alexandria a fair Church, all white without Paintings ; and so be all the other Churches that were of the Christian Men, all white within, for the Paynims and the Saracens made them white to do away with the Images of Saints that were painted on the Walls. That City of Alexandria is well 30 Furlongs in Length, but it is but 10 in Breadth; and it is a full noble City and a fair. At that City entereth the River Nile into the Sea, as I to you have said before. In that River Men find many precious Stones, and much also of Lignum Aloes ; and it is a manner of Wood, that cometh

out of Terrestrial Paradise, the which is good for many diverse Medicines, and it is right costly. And from Alexandria men go to Babylon, where the Sultan dwelleth ; that sits also upon the River Nile : and this Way is the most short, to go straight unto Babylon.

Now shall I say to you also the Way, that goeth from Babylon to the Mount of Sinai, where Saint Catherine lieth. Ye must pass by the Deserts of Arabia, by the which Deserts Moses led the People of Israel. And then pass Men by the Well that Moses made with his Hand in the Deserts, when the People grumbled ; for they found nothing to drink. And then pass Men by the Well of Marah, of the which the Water was at first bitter ; but the Children of Israel put therein a Tree, and anon the Water was sweet and good to drink. And then go Men by Desert unto the Vale of Elim, in the which Vale be 12 Wells ; and there be 72 Trees of Palm, that bear the Dates the which Moses found with the Children of Israel. And from that Valley is but a good Day's Journey to the Mount of Sinai.

And who so will go by another Way from Babylon, then go by the Red Sea, that is an Arm of the Sea-Ocean. And there passed Moses with the Children of Israel, overthwart the Sea all dry, when Pharaoh the King of Egypt chased them. And that Sea is well a 6 Mile of Largeness in Breadth ; and in that Sea was Pharaoh drowned and all his Host that he led. That Sea is not more red than another Sea ; but in some Place thereof is the Gravel red, and therefore Men call it the Red Sea. That Sea runneth to the Ends of Arabia and of Palestine.

That Sea lasteth more than a 4 Days' Journey, and then go Men by Desert unto the Vale of Elim, and from thence to the Mount of Sinai. And ye may well understand, that by this Desert no Man may go on Horseback, because that there is neither Meat for Horse nor Water to drink; and for that Cause Men pass that Desert with Camels. For the Camel finds always Meat in Trees and on Bushes, that he feedeth him with: and he may well fast from Drink 2 days or 3. And that may no Horse do.

And wit well, that from Babylon to the Mount Sinai is well a good 12 Days' Journey, and some Men make them more. And some Men hasten and pain themselves, and so they make them less. And always Men find Latiners or Dragomen to go with them in these Countries, and further beyond, until the Time they know the Language : and it behoveth Men to bear Victuals with them, that shall last them in those Deserts, and other Necessaries to live by.

And the Mount of Sinai is clept the Desert of Sin, that is to say, the Bush burning ; because there Moses saw our Lord God many times in Form of Fire burning upon that Hill, and also in a Bush burning, and spake to Him. And that was at the Foot of the Hill. There is an Abbey of Monks, well builded and well closed with Gates of Iron for Dread of the Wild Beasts ; and the Monks be Arabians or Men of

Greece. And there is a great Convent, and they all be as Hermits, and they drink no Wine, but if it be on principal Feasts; and they be full devout Men, and live poorly and simply with Joutes* and with Dates, and they do great Abstinence and Penance.

There is the Church of Saint Catherine, in the which be many Lamps burning; for they have of Oil of Olives enough, both to burn in their Lamps and to eat also. And that Plenty have they by the Miracle of God; for the Ravens and the Crows and the Choughs and other Fowls of the Country assemble them there every Year once, and fly thither as in Pilgrimage; and every one of them bringeth a Branch of Bays or of Olive in their Beaks instead of Offering, and leave them there; of the which the Monks make great Plenty of Oil. And this is a great Marvel. And since that Fowls that have no natural Wit or Reason go thither to seek that glorious Virgin, well more ought Men then to seek her, and to worship her.

Also behind the Altar of that Church is the Place where Moses saw our Lord God in a burning Bush. And when the Monks enter into that Place, they doff both Hose and Shoes or Boots always, because that our Lord said to Moses, "*Do off thy Hose and thy Shoes, for the Place that thou standest on is Land holy and blessed.*" And the Monks call that Place Bezaleel, that is to say, the Shadow of God. And beside the high Altar, on 3 Steps of Height is the

* An ancient dish in cookery, made probably of gourds.

Feretrum or Shrine of Alabaster, where the Bones
of Saint Catherine lie. And the Prelate of the
Monks sheweth the Relics to the Pilgrims, and
with an Instrument of Silver he fretteth the Bones;
and then there goeth out a little Oil, as though they

ST. CATHERINE'S SHRINE

were in a manner sweating, that is neither like
to Oil nor to Balm, but it is full sweet of Smell;
and of that they give a little to the Pilgrims, for
there goeth out but little Quantity of the Liquor.
And after that they shew the Head of Saint Catherine,
and the Cloth that she was wrapped in, that is yet
all bloody; and in that same Cloth so wrapped, the
Angels bare her Body to the Mount Sinai, and there
they buried her with it. And then they shew the
Bush, that burned and wasted nought, in the which
our Lord spake to Moses, and other Relics enough.

Also, when the Prelate of the Abbey is dead, I

that they make of Skins of Beasts, as of Camels and
of other Beasts that they eat ; and beneath these they
couch them and dwell in any Place where they may
find Water, as on the Red Sea or elsewhere : for in
that Desert is full great Default of Water, and often-
time it befalleth that where Men find Water at one
time in a Place it faileth another time ; and for that
reason, they make no Habitations there. These
Folk that I speak of, they till not the Land, and they
labour nought ; for they eat no Bread, but and if they
be any that dwell nigh a good Town, that go thither
and eat Bread sometimes. And they roast their
Flesh and their Fish upon hot Stones against the
Sun. And they be strong Men and well-fighting; and
there so is much Multitude of that Folk, that they be
without Number. And they neither reck of anything, nor do anything but chase after Beasts to eat
them. And they reck nothing of their Lives, and
therefore they fear not the Sultan, nor any other
Prince ; but they dare well war with them, if they
do anything that is a Grievance to them. And
they have often-times War with the Sultan, and,
to wit, at that Time that I was with him. And
they bear but one Shield and one Spear, without
other Arms ; and they wrap their Heads and their
Necks with a great Quantity of white linen Cloth ;
and they be right felonous and foul, and of cursed
Kind.

And when Men pass this Desert, in coming toward
Jerusalem, they come to Beersheba, that was wont
to be a full fair Town and a delectable of Christian

Men; and there be some of their Churches there
yet.   In that Town dwelled Abraham the Patriarch, a long time.   And that Town of Beersheba
founded Bathsheba, the Wife of Sir Uriah the
Knight, on the which King David begat Solomon
the Wise, that was King after David over the
12 Kindreds or Tribes of Jerusalem and reigned
40 Year.

And from thence go Men to the City of Hebron,
that is the Amount distant of 12 good Mile.
And it was clept sometime the Vale of Mamre, and
some-time it was clept the Vale of Tears, because
that Adam wept there an 100 Year for the
death of Abel his Son, that Cain slew.   Hebron was
wont to be the principal City of the Philistines, and
there dwelled some time the Giants.   And that
City was also Sacerdotal, that is to say, Sanctuary
of the Tribe of Judah; and it was so free, that
Men received there all Manner of Fugitives of
other Places for their evil Deeds.   In Hebron
Joshua, Caleb and their Company came first to
a-spy, how they might win the Land of Behest.
In Hebron reigned first King David 7 Year and
a half; and in Jerusalem he reigned 33 Year and
a half.

And in Hebron be all the Sepultures of the
Patriarchs, Adam, Abraham, Isaac, and of Jacob;
and of their Wives, Eve, Sarah and Rebecca and of
Leah; the which Sepultures the Saracens keep full
carefully, and have the Place in great Reverence for
the holy Fathers, the Patriarchs that lie there.   And

HEBRON WAS WONT
TO BE THE PRIN-
CIPAL CITY OF THE
PHILISTINES, AND
THERE DWELLED
SOME - TIME THE
GIANTS

ARTHUR LAYARD

they suffer no Christian Man to enter into the Place,
but if it be of special Grace of the Sultan ; for they
hold Christian Men and Jews as Dogs, and they say,
that they should not enter into so holy a Place.
And Men call that Place, where they lie, Double
Spelunk (*Spelunca Duplex*), or Double Cave, or
Double Ditch, forasmuch as one lieth above another.
And the Saracens call that Place in their Language,
"*Karicarba,*" that is to say, "*The Place of Patriarchs.*"   And the Jews call that Place "*Arboth.*"
And in that same Place was Abraham's House, and
there he sat and saw 3 Persons, and worshipped
but one ; as Holy Writ saith, "*Tres vidit et unum
adoravit,*" that is to say, "*He saw 3 and wor-
shipped one :*" and those same were the Angels that
Abraham received into his House.

And right fast by that Place is a Cave in the Rock,
where Adam and Eve dwelled when they were put
out of Paradise ; and there got they their Children.
And in that same Place was Adam formed and
made, after that, that some Men say : (for Men were
wont to call that Place the Field of Damascus, because that it was in the Lordship of Damascus), and
from thence was he translated into the Paradise of
Delights, as they say ; and after he was driven out of
Paradise he was left there.   And the same Day that
he was put in Paradise, the same Day he was put •
out, for anon he sinned.   There beginneth the
Vale of Hebron, that endureth nigh to Jerusalem.
There the Angel commanded Adam that he should
dwell with his Wife Eve, of the which he begat

Seth ; of the which Tribe, that is to say Kindred, Jesu Christ was born.

In that Valley is a Field, where Men draw out of the Earth a Thing that Men call Cambile, and they eat it instead of Spice, and they bear it away to sell. And Men may not make the Hole or the Cave, where it is taken out of the Earth, so deep or so wide, but that it is, at the Year's End, full again up to the Sides, through the Grace of God.

And 2 Mile from Hebron is the Grave of Lot, that was Abraham's Brother.

And a little from Hebron is the Mount of Mamre, from the which the Valley taketh his Name. And there is a Tree of Oak, that the Saracens call "*Dirpe*," that is of Abraham's Time : the which Men call the Dry Tree. And they say that it hath been there since the Beginning of the World, and was some-time green and bare Leaves, unto the Time that our Lord died on the Cross, and then it dried : and so did all the Trees that were then in the World. And some say, by their Prophecies, that a Lord, a Prince of the West Side of the World, shall win the Land of Promise that is the Holy Land with Help of Christian Men, and he shall have sung a Mass under that dry Tree ; and then the Tree shall wax green and bear both Fruit and Leaves, and through that Miracle many Saracens and Jews shall be turned to Christian Faith : and, therefore, they do great Worship thereto, and guard it full busily. And, albeit so, that it be dry, nevertheless yet it beareth great Virtue, for certainly he that hath a little thereof upon him, it

THE MIRACLE OF THE ROSES

healeth him of the Falling Evil, and his Horse shall
not be a-foundered : and many other Virtues it hath,
wherefore Men hold it full precious.

From Hebron Men go to Bethlehem in half a Day,
for it is but 5 Mile ; and it is a full fair Way, by
Plains and Woods full delectable.   Bethlehem is a
little City, long and narrow and well walled, and on
each Side enclosed with good Ditches : and it was
wont to be clept Ephrata, as Holy Writ saith, "*Ecce,
audimus eum in Ephrata*," that is to say, "*Lo, we
heard it in Ephrata.*"   And toward the East End
of the City is a full fair Church and a gracious, and
it hath many Towers, Pinacles and Corners, full
strong and curiously made ; and within that Church
be 44 Pillars of Marble, great and fair.

And between the City and the Church is the Field
"*Floridus,*" that is to say, the "*Field Beflowered.*"
For a fair Maiden was blamed with Wrong, and
slandered that she had done Fornication ; for which
Cause she was condemned to Death, and to be burnt
in that Place, to the which she was led.   And, as
the Fire began to burn about her, she made her
Prayers to our Lord, that as certainly as she was
not guilty of that Sin, that He would help her and
make it to be known to all Men, of His merciful
Grace.   And when she had thus said, she entered
into the Fire, and anon was the Fire quenched and
out ; and the Brands that were burning became red
Rose-trees, and the Brands that were not kindled
became white Rose-trees, full of Roses.   And these
were the first Rose-trees and Roses, both white and

red, that ever any Man saw; and thus was the
Maiden saved by the Grace of God. And therefore
is that Field clept the Field of God Beflowered, for it
was full of Roses.

Also beside the Choir of the Church, at the right
Side, as Men come downward 16 Steps, is the
Place where our Lord was born, that is full well
adorned with Marble, and full richly painted with
Gold, Silver, Azure and other Colours. And 3
Paces beyond is the Crib of the Ox and the Ass.
And beside that is the Place where the Star fell, that
led the 3 Kings, Jaspar, Melchior and Balthazar:
(but Men of Greece call them thus, " *Galgalathe,
Malgalathe, and Seraphie*," and the Jews call them,
in this manner, in Hebrew, "*Appelius, Amerrius,
and Damasus*.") These 3 Kings offered to our
Lord, Gold, Incense and Myrrh, and they met together through Miracle of God; for they met together in a City in Ind, that Men call Cassak, that
is a 53 Days' Journey from Bethlehem; and they
were at Bethlehem the 13th Day; and that was
the 4th Day after that they had seen the Star,
when they met in that City, and thus they were in
9 Days from that City at Bethlehem, and that was
a great Miracle.

Also, under the Cloister of the Church, by 18
Steps at the right Side, is the Charnel-house of
the Innocents, where their Bodies lie. And before
the Place where our Lord was born is the Tomb
of Saint Jerome, that was a Priest and a Cardinal,
that translated the Bible and the Psalter from

Hebrew into Latin : and without the Minster is the Chair that he sat in when he translated it. And fast beside that Church, at 60 Fathom, is a Church of Saint Nicholas, where our Lady rested her after she was delivered of our Lord ; and forasmuch as she had too much Milk in her Paps, that grieved her, she milked them on the red Stones of Marble, so that the Traces may yet be seen, in the Stones, all white.

And ye shall understand, that all that dwell in Bethlehem be Christian Men.

And there be fair Vines about the City, and great plenty of Wine, that the Christian Men have made. But the Saracens till not the Vines, neither drink they any Wine : for their Books of their Law, that Mohammet gave them, which they call their "*Al Koran*," (and some call it "*Mesaph*," and in another language it is clept "*Harme*,")—the same Book forbiddeth them to drink Wine. For in that Book, Mohammet cursed all those that drink Wine and all them that sell it : for some Men say, that he slew once an Hermit in his Drunkenness, that he loved full well ; and therefore he cursed Wine and them that drink it. But his Curse be turned on to his own Head, as Holy Writ saith, "*Et in verticem ipsius iniquitas ejus descendet*," that is to say, "*His Wickedness shall turn and fall on to his own Head.*"

And also the Saracens breed no Pigs, nor eat they any Swine's Flesh, for they say it is Brother to Man, and it was forbidden by the old Law ; and they hold him accursed that eateth thereof. Also in the Land of Palestine and in the Land of

Egypt, they eat but little or none of Flesh of Veal or
of Beef, but if the Beast be so old, that he may no
more work for old Age ; for it is forbidden, because
they have but few of them ; therefore they nourish
them to till their Lands.

SOLDIER IN BY-COCKET WITH GLAIVE,
14TH CENTURY

In this City of Beth-
lehem was David the
King born ; and he had
60 Wives, and the first
Wife was called Michal ;
and also he had 300
Lemans.

And from Bethlehem
unto Jerusalem is but
2 Mile ; and in the Way
to Jerusalem half a Mile
from Bethlehem is a
Church, where the Angel
said to the Shepherds of the Birth of Christ.   And
in that Way is the Tomb of Rachel, that was the
Mother of Joseph, the Patriarch ; and she died
anon after that she was delivered of her Son Benjamin.   And there she was buried by Jacob her
Husband, and he made set 12 great Stones on her,
in Token that she had born 12 Children.*   In the
same Way, half a Mile from Jerusalem, appeared
the Star to the 3 Kings.   In that Way also be many
Churches of Christian Men, by the which Men go
towards the City of Jerusalem.

* Rachel had twelve grandchildren.

CHAPTER VII

Of the Pilgrimages in Jerusalem, and of the Holy Places thereabout

AFTER, to speak of Jerusalem the Holy City. Ye shall understand, that it stands full fair between 2 Hills, and there be no Rivers or Wells, but Water cometh by Conduit from Hebron. And ye shall understand, that Jerusalem of old Time, unto the Time of Melchisadech, was clept Jebus; and after it was clept Salem, unto the Time of King David, that put these 2 Names together, and clept it Jebusalem; and after that, King Solomon clept it Jerosoloma; and after that, Men clept it Jerusalem, and so it is clept yet.

And about Jerusalem is the Kingdom of Syria. And there beside is the Land of Palestine, and beside it is Ascalon, and beside that is the Land of Maritaine. But Jerusalem is in the Land of Judea, and

it is clept Judea, for that Judas Maccabeus was King
of that Country ; and it marcheth Eastward with the
Kingdom of Arabia ; on the South Side with the
Land of Egypt ; and on the West Side with the
Great Sea ; on the North Side, toward the Kingdom
of Syria and to the Sea of Cyprus.   In Jerusalem
was wont to be a Patriarch ; and Archbishops and
Bishops about in the Country.   About Jerusalem be
these Cities : Hebron, at 7 Mile ; Jericho, at 6 Mile ;
Beersheba, at 8 Mile ; Ascalon, at 17 Mile ; Jaffa,
at 16 Mile ; Ramath, at 3 Mile ; and Bethlehem, at
2 Mile.   And a 2 Mile from Bethlehem, toward the
South, is the Church of St. Karitot, that was Abbot
there, for whom they made much Dole amongst the
Monks when he died ; and they be yet mourning in
the Wise that they made their Lamentation for him
the first Time ; and it is full great Pity to behold.

This Country and Land of Jerusalem hath been in
many divers Nations' Hands, and often, therefore,
hath the Country suffered much Tribulation for the Sin
of the People that dwell there.   For that Country
hath been in the Hands of all Nations ; that is to say,
of Jews, of Canaanites, Assyrians, Persians, Medes,
Macedonians, of Greeks, Romans, of Christian Men,
of Saracens, Barbarians, Turks, Tartars, and of
many other divers Nations ; for God will not that it
be long in the Hands of Traitors nor of Sinners, be
they Christian or other.   And now have the Heathen
Men held that Land in their Hands 40 Year and
more ; but they shall not hold it long, if God will.

And you shall understand, that when Men come

PILGRIMS·IN·THE·TABERNACLE

to Jerusalem, their first Pilgrimage is to the Church
of the Holy Sepulchre, where our Lord was buried,
that is without the City on the North Side; but it
is now enclosed in by the Town Wall.   And there
is a full fair Church, all round, and open above,
and covered with Lead; and on the West Side is a
fair Tower and an high for Bells, strongly made.

And in the midst of the Church is a Tabernacle, as
it were a little House, made with a low little Door,
and that Tabernacle is made in manner of half a
Compass, right curiously and richly made of Gold
and Azure and other rich Colours fully nobly made.
And in the right Side of that Tabernacle is the
Sepulchre of our Lord; and the Tabernacle is
8 Foot long, and 5 Foot wide, and 11 Foot in
height.   And it is not long since the Sepulchre was
all open, that Men might kiss it and touch it; but
as Pilgrims that came thither laboured to break the
Stone in Pieces or in Powder, therefore the Sultan
hath had made a Wall about the Sepulchre that no
man may touch it : but in the left Side of the Wall of
the Tabernacle is, well the Height of a Man, a great
Stone of the Quantity of a Man's Head, that was
of the Holy Sepulchre; and that Stone kiss the Pilgrims that come thither.   In that Tabernacle be no
Windows, but it is all made light with Lamps that
hang before the Sepulchre.   And there is a Lamp
that hangeth before the Sepulchre, that burneth
alight; and on the Good Friday it goeth out by
himself, and lighteth again by himself at that Hour
that our Lord rose from Death to Life.

And there beside be 4 Pillars of Stone, that always drop Water; and some Men say that they weep for our Lord's Death. And nigh that Altar is a place under Earth, 42 Steps of Deepness, where the Holy Cross was found, by the Wit of Saint Helen, under a Rock where the Jews had hid it. And that was tested as the true Cross; for they found 3 Crosses, one of our Lord, and 2 of the two Thieves; and Saint Helen proved them by a dead Body that arose from Death to Life, when that it was laid on it, that our Lord died on. And thereby in the Walls is the Place where the 4 Nails of our Lord were hid: for He had 2 in His Hands and 2 in His Feet. And, of one of these, the Emperor of Constantinople made a Bridle to his Horse to bear him in Battle; and, through Virtue thereof, he overcame his Enemies, and won all the Land of Asia the Less, that is to say, Turkey, Armenia the Less and the More, and from Syria to Jerusalem, from Arabia to Persia, from Mesopotamia to the Kingdom of Aleppo, from Egypt the High and the Low and all the other Kingdoms unto the Depth of Ethiopia, and into Ind the Less that then was Christian.

And there were in that Time many good Holy Men and Holy Hermits, of whom the Book of the Fathers' Lives speaketh, and they be now in Paynims' and Saracens' Hands: but when God Almighty will, right so as the Lands were lost through Sin of Christian Men, so shall they be won again by Christian Men through Help of God.

And in Midst of that Church is a Compass, in the which Joseph of Arimathea laid the Body of our Lord when he had taken Him down off the Cross ; and there he washed the Wounds of our Lord. And that Compass, say Men, is the Midst of the World.

And in the Church of the Sepulchre, on the North Side, is the Place where our Lord was put in Prison ; (for He was in Prison in many Places) and there is a Part of the Chain that He was bounden with ; and there He appeared first to Mary Magdalene when He was risen, and she thought that He had been a Gardener.

In the Church of Saint Sepulchre were wont to be Canons of the Order of Saint Augustine, and they had a Prior, but the Patriarch was their Sovereign.

And without the Doors of the Church, on the Right Side as Men go upward 18 Steps, said our Lord to His Mother, "*Mulier, ecce Filius tuus ;*" that is to say, "*Woman, Lo! thy Son!*" And after that He said to John, His Disciple, "*Ecce Mater tua ;*" that is to say, "*Lo! Behold thy Mother!*" And these Words He said on the Cross. And on these Steps went our Lord when He bare the Cross on His Shoulder. And under these steps is a Chapel, and in that Chapel sing Priests (Indians, that is to say, Priests of Ind), not after our Law, but after theirs ; and always they make their Sacrament of the Altar, saying, "*Pater Noster*" and other Prayers therewith ; with the which Prayers they say the Words that the Sacrament is made of, for they know not the Additions that many Popes have made ; but they sing with good Devotion. And there near, is the Place where that our Lord rested Him when He was weary for the bearing of the Cross.

And ye shall understand that before the Church of

"SING PRIESTS, INDIANS"

the Sepulchre is the City more feeble than in any other Part, for the great Plain that is between the Church and the City. And toward the East Side, without the Walls of the City, is the Vale of Jehosaphat that toucheth to the Walls as though it were a large Ditch. And anent that Vale of Jehosaphat, out of the City, is the Church of Saint Stephen where he was stoned to Death. And there beside, is the Golden Gate, that may not be opened, by the which Gate our Lord entered on Palm-Sunday upon an Ass : and the Gate opened to Him when He would go unto the Temple ; and the Steps of the Ass's Feet appear yet in 3 Places on the Stairs that be of full hard Stone.

And before the Church of Saint Sepulchre, toward

the South, at 200 Paces, is the great Hospital of Saint John, of which the Hospitallers had their Foundation. And within the Palace of the Sick Men of that Hospital be 124 Pillars of Stone. And in the Walls of the House, beside the Number above-said, there be 54 Pillars that bear up the House. And from that Hospital to go toward the East is a full fair Church, that is clept "*Nôtre Dame la Grande.*" And then is there another Church right nigh, that is clept "*Nôtre Dame de Latine.*" And there were Mary Cleophas and Mary Magdalene, and tore their Hair when our Lord was in Pain on the Cross.

MONK, AND VALE OF JEHOSAPHAT

CHAPTER VIII

*Of the Temple of our Lord. Of the Cruelty of King
Herod. Of the Mount Sion. Of
Probatica Piscina ; and
of Natatorium Siloe*

 ND from the Church
of the Sepulchre,
toward the East, at
160 Paces, is *Temp-
lum Domini*. It is
a right fair House,
and it is all round
a n d hig h, a n d
covered with Lead.
And it is well paved
with white Marble.
But the Saracens will
suffer no Christian Man nor Jews to come therein,
for they say that none such foul sinful Men should
come in so holy a Place : but I came in there
and in other Places where I would, for I had
Letters of the Sultan with his great Seal, and

commonly other Men have but his Signet. In the which Letters he commanded, of his special Grace, to all his Subjects, to let me see all the Places, and to inform me fully of all the Mysteries of every Place, and to conduct me from City to City, if it were needed, and buxomly to receive me and my Company, and to obey all my reasonable Requests if they were not greatly against the Royal Power and Dignity of the Sultan or of his Law. And to others, that ask him Grace, such as have served him, he giveth not but his Signet, the which they make to be borne before them hanging on a Spear. And the Folk of the Country do great Worship and Reverence to his Signet or Seal, and kneel thereto as lowly as we do to *Corpus Domini*. And Men do yet full greater Reverence to his Letters; for the Admiral and all other Lords that they be shewed to, before ere they receive them, they kneel down; and then they take them and put them on their Heads; and after, they kiss them and then they read them, kneeling with great Reverence; and then they offer themselves to do all that the Bearer asketh.

And in this *Templum Domini* were some-time Canons Regular, to whom they were obedient; and in this Temple was Charlemagne when that the Angel brought him the Prepuce of our Lord Jesus Christ of his Circumcision; and after, King Charles had it brought to Paris into his Chapel, and after that he had it brought to Peyteres (Poitiers), and after that he had it brought to Chartres.

And ye shall understand, that this is not the

Temple that Solomon made, for that Temple
endured but 1102 Year. For Titus, Vespasian's
Son, Emperor of Rome, had laid Siege about Jerusalem to discomfit the Jews; for they put our Lord
to Death, without Leave of the Emperor. And, when
he had won the City, he burnt the Temple and beat
it down, and all the City, and took the Jews and did
them to Death,—1,100,000; and the others he put
in Prison and sold them to Servage,—30 for one
Penny; for they said they bought Jesu for 30
Pennies, and he made them more cheap when he
gave 30 for one Penny.

And after that time, Julian the Apostate, that was
Emperor, gave leave to the Jews to make the Temple
of Jerusalem, for he hated Christian Men. And yet
he was christened, but he forsook his Law, and
became a Renegade. And when the Jews had
made the Temple, came an Earthquaking, and cast
it down (as God would) and destroyed all that they
had made.

And after that, Hadrian, that was Emperor of
Rome, and of the Lineage of Troy, made Jerusalem
again and the Temple as Solomon made it. And he
would suffer no Jews to dwell there, but only
Christian Men. For although it were so that he
was not christened, yet he loved Christian Men
more than any other Nation save his own. This
Emperor made enclose the Church of Saint Sepulchre, and walled it within the City; that, before,
was without the City, long time before. And he
would have changed the Name of Jerusalem, and

have clept it Ælia, but that Name lasted not long.

Also, ye shall understand, that the Saracens do much Reverence to that Temple, and they say, that that Place is right holy. And when they go in they go bare-foot, and kneel many Times. And when my Fellows and I saw that, when we came in we did off our Shoes and came in bare-foot, and thought that we should do as much Worship and Reverence thereto, as any of the misbelieving Men should, and have as great Compunction of Heart.

This Temple is 64 Cubits of Wideness, and as many in Length ; and of Height it is 120 Cubits. And it is within, all about, made with Pillars of Marble. And in the middle Place of the Temple be many high Stages, of 14 Steps of Height, made with good Pillars all about : and this Place the Jews call "*Sancta Sanctorum* ;" that is to say, "*Holy of Holies.*" And, in that Place, cometh no Man save only the Prelate, that maketh here Sacrifice. And the Folk stand all about, in diverse Stages, according as they be of Dignity or of Worship, so that they all may see the Sacrifice. And in that Temple be 4 Entries, and the Gates be of Cypress, well made and curiously bedight : and within the East Gate our Lord said, "*Here is Jerusalem.*" And in the North Side of that Temple, within the Gate, there is a Well, but it runneth nought, of the which Holy Writ speaketh and saith, "*Vidi Aquam egredientem de Templo ;*" that is to say, "*I saw Water come out of the Temple.*"

And on that other Side of the Temple there is a Rock that Men call Moriach (but after it was called Bethel), where the Ark of God with Relics of the Jews were wont to be put. That Ark or Hutch with the Relics Titus led with him to Rome, when he had discomfited all the Jews. In that Ark were the 10 Commandments, and Aaron's Yard (or Rod), and Moses' Yard with the which he made the Red Sea part, as it had been a Wall, on the right Side and on the left Side, whiles that the People of Israel passed the Sea dry-foot : and with that Yard he smote the Rock, and the Water came out of it : and with that Yard he did many Wonders. And therein was a Vessel of Gold full of Manna, and Clothing and Ornaments and the Tabernacle of Aaron, and a square Tabernacle of Gold with 12 Precious Stones, and a Box of green Jasper with 4 Figures and 8 Names of our Lord, and 7 Candlesticks of Gold, and 12 Pots of Gold, and 4 Censers of Gold, and an Altar of Gold, and 4 Lions of Gold upon the which they bare Cherubim of Gold 12 Spans long, and the Circle of Swans of Heaven with a Tabernacle of Gold and a Table of Silver, and 2 Trumpets of Silver, and 7 Barley Loaves and all the other Relics that were before the Birth of our Lord Jesu Christ.

And upon that Rock was Jacob sleeping when he saw the Angels go up and down by a Ladder, and he said, " *Vere Locus iste sanctus est, et ego ignorabam;*" that is to say, "*Forsooth this Place is holy, and I wist it nought.*" And there an Angel held Jacob still, and changed his Name, and called him Israel. And in

that same Place David saw the Angel that smote the
Folk with a Sword, and put it up bloody in the
Sheath.   And on that same Rock was Saint Simeon
when he received our Lord into the Temple.   And
on that Rock he set Him when the Jews would have
stoned Him ; and a Star came down and gave Him
Light.   And upon that Rock preached our Lord often-
time to the People.   And out of that said Temple our
Lord drove the Buyers and the Sellers.   And upon
that Rock our Lord set Him when the Jews would
have stoned Him ; and the Rock clave in 2, and in
that Cleaving was our Lord hid, and there came down
a Star and gave Light and served Him with Clear-
ness.   And upon that Rock sat our Lady, and learned
her Psalter.   And there our Lord forgave the Woman
her Sins, that was found in Adultery.   And there was
our Lord circumcised.   And there the Angels shewed
Tidings to Zacharias of the Birth of Saint Baptist his
Son.   And there offered first Melchisadech Bread
and Wine to our Lord, in Token of the Sacrament
that was to come.   And there fell David praying to
our Lord and to the Angel that smote the People,
that he would have Mercy on him and on the People:
and our Lord heard his Prayer, and therefore would
he make the Temple in that Place, but our Lord
forbade him by an Angel ; for he had done Treason
when he made slay Uriah the worthy Knight, to have
Bathsheba his Wife.   And therefore, all the Provision
that he had ordained to make the Temple with took
Solomon his Son, and he made it, and he prayed our
Lord, that all those that prayed to Him in that Place

with good Heart—that He would hear their Prayer and grant it them if they asked it rightfully : and our Lord granted it him, and therefore Solomon clept that Temple the Temple of Counsel and of Help of God.

And without the Gate of the Temple is an Altar where Jews were wont to offer Doves and Turtles.

KNIGHT TEMPLAR

And between the Temple and that Altar was Zacharias slain. And upon the Pinnacle of that Temple was our Lord brought to be tempted of the Enemy, the Fiend. And on the Height of that Pinnacle the Jews set Saint James, and cast him down to the Earth, that first was Bishop of Jerusalem. And at the Entry of that Temple, toward the West, is the Gate that is clept "*Porta Speciosa*" (the Gate Beautiful). And nigh beside that Temple, upon the right Side, is a Church covered with Lead that is clept Solomon's School.

And from that Temple towards the South, right nigh, is the Temple of Solomon, that is right fair and well polished. And in that Temple dwell the Knights of the Temple that were wont to be clept Templars ; and that was the Foundation of their Order, so that there dwelled Knights and Canons Regular in *Templo Domini.*

From that Temple toward the East, a 120 Paces, in the Corner of the City, is the Bath of our Lord; and in that Bath was wont to come Water from Paradise, and it droppeth yet. And there beside is our Lady's Bed. And fast by is the Temple of Saint Simeon, and without the Cloister of the Temple, toward the North, is a full fair Church of Saint Anne, our Lady's Mother; and there was our Lady conceived; and before that Church is a great Tree that began to grow the same Night. And under that Church, in going down by 22 Steps, lieth Joachim, our Lady's Father, in a fair Tomb of Stone; and there beside lay some-time Saint Anne, his Wife; but Saint Helen had her translated to Constantinople. And in that Church is a Well, in manner of a Cistern, that is clept *Probatica Piscina*, that hath 5 Entries. Into that Well Angels were wont to come from Heaven and bathe within. And that Man, that first bathed him after the moving of the Water, was made whole of what manner of Sickness that he had. And there our Lord healed a Man of the Palsy that lay sick 38 Year, and our Lord said to him, "*Tolle Grabatum tuum et ambula;*" that is to say, "Take thy Bed and go." And there beside was Pilate's House.

And fast by is King Herod's House, that made slay the Innocents. This Herod was over-much cursed and cruel. For first he made slay his Wife that he loved right well; and for the passing Love that he had to her when he saw her dead, he fell in a Rage and out of his Wit a great while ; and then he came again to his Wit. And after he made slay his 2 Sons that he had of that Wife. And after that he made slay another of his Wives, and a Son that he had by her. And after that he made slay his own Mother ; and he would have slain his Brother also, but he died suddenly. And after he fell into Sickness. And when he felt that he should die, he sent after his Sister and after all the Lords of his Land. And when they were come he had them commanded to Prison. And then he said to his Sister, he wist well that Men of the Country would make no Sorrow for his Death. And therefore he made his Sister swear that she should make smite off all the Heads of the Lords when he were dead ; and then should all the Land make Sorrow for his Death, and else, nought. And thus he made his Testament. But his Sister fulfilled not his Will. For, as soon as he was dead, she delivered all the Lords out of Prison and let them go, each Lord to his own, and told them all the Purpose of her Brother's Ordinance. And so was this cursed King never made Sorrow for, as he had supposed. And ye shall understand, that in that Time there were 3 Herods, of great Name and Fame for their Cruelty. This Herod, of which I have spoken, was Herod the Ascalonite ; and he that made behead Saint John the Baptist was Herod Antipas ; and he that made smite off Saint James's head was Herod Agrippa, and he put Saint Peter in Prison.

And, furthermore, in the City is the Church of Saint Saviour; and there is the left Arm of John Chrisostome, and the greater Part of the Head of Saint Stephen. And on that other Side of the Street, toward the South as Men go to Mount Sion, is a Church of Saint James, where he was beheaded.

And from that Church, a 120 Paces, is the Mount Sion. And there is a fair Church of our Lady, where she dwelled; and there she died. And there was wont to be an Abbot of Canons Regular. And from thence was she borne of the Apostles unto the Vale of Jehosaphat. And there is the Stone that the Angel brought to our Lord from the Mount of Sinai, and it is of that same Colour that is the Rock of St. Catherine. And there beside is the Gate where through our Lady went, when she was with Child, when she went to Bethlehem. Also at the Entry of the Mount Sion is a Chapel. And in that Chapel is a Stone great and large, with the which the Sepulchre was covered, when Joseph of Arimathea had put our Lord therein; the which Stone the 3 Marys saw turn upward when they came to the Sepulchre the Day of His Resurrection, and there found an Angel that told them of our Lord's uprising from Death to Life. And there also in the Wall, beside the Gate, is a Stone of the Pillar that our Lord was scourged at. And there was Annas's House, that was Bishop of the Jews in that Time. And there was our Lord examined in the Night, and scourged and smitten and violently entreated. And in that same Place Saint Peter forsook our Lord thrice ere the Cock crew. And there is a Part of the Table that He made His Supper on, when He made His Maundy with His Disciples, when He gave them His Flesh and His Blood in Form of Bread and Wine.

And under that Chapel, 32 Steps down, is the Place where our Lord washed His Disciples' Feet,

"THE COCK CREW"

and the Vessel for the Water is there yet. And there beside that same Vessel was Saint Stephen buried. And there is the Altar where our Lady heard the Angels sing Mass. And there appeared first our Lord to His Disciples after His Resurrection, the Gates closed, and said to them, "*Pax vobis!*" that is to say, "*Peace to you!*" And on that Mount appeared Christ to Saint Thomas the Apostle and bade him assay His Wounds; and there believed he first, and said, "*Dominus meus et Deus meus!*" that is to say, "*My Lord and my God!*" In the same Church, beside the Altar, were all the Apostles on Whit-Sunday, when the Holy Ghost descended on them in Likeness of Fire. And there made our Lord His Passover with His Disciples.

And there slept Saint John the Evangelist upon the Breast of our Lord Jesu Christ, and saw sleeping many heavenly Privities.

Mount Sion is within the City, and it is a little higher than the other Side of the City ; and the City is stronger on that Side than on that other Side. For at the Foot of the Mount Sion is a fair Castle and a strong that the Sultan had made. In the Mount Sion were buried King David and King Solomon, and many other Kings, Jews of Jerusalem. And there is the Place where the Jews would have cast up the Body of our Lady when the Apostles bare the Body to be buried in the Vale of Jehosaphat. And there is the Place where Saint Peter wept full tenderly after that he had forsaken our Lord. And a Stone's Cast from that Chapel is another Chapel, where our Lord was judged, for there, at that Time, was Caiaphas's House. From that Chapel, to go toward the East, at 140 Paces, is a deep Cave under the Rock, that is clept the Galilee of our Lord, where Saint Peter hid him when he had forsaken our Lord. *Item*, between the Mount Sion and the Temple of Solomon is the Place where our Lord raised the Maiden in her Father's House.

Under the Mount Sion, toward the Vale of Jehosaphat, is a Well that is clept "*Natatorium Siloe*," the Pool of Siloam. And there was our Lord washed after His Baptism ; and there made our Lord the blind Man to see. And there was a-buried Isaiah the Prophet. Also, straight from *Natatorium*

Siloe, is an Image of Stone of old ancient Work that Absalom had made, and because thereof Men call it the Hand of Absalom. And fast by is yet the **Tree** of Elder that Judas hanged himself upon, for Despair that he had, when he sold and betrayed our Lord. And there beside was the Synagogue, where the Bishops of the Jews and the Pharisees came together and held their Council; and there cast Judas the 30 Pence before them, and said that he had sinned betraying our Lord. And there nigh was the House of the Apostles Philip and James the Son of Alpheus. And on that other Side of Mount Sion, toward the South, beyond the Vale a Stone's Cast, is Aceldama; that is to say, the Field of Blood, that was bought for 30 Pence, that our Lord was sold for. And in that Field be many Tombs of Christian Men, for there be many Pilgrims buried. And there be many Oratories, Chapels and Hermitages, where Hermits

were wont to dwell.   And toward the East, an 100
Paces, is the Charnel of the Hospital of Saint John,
where Men were wont to put the Bodies of dead
Men.

And from Jerusalem, toward the West, is a fair
Church, where the Tree of the Cross grew.   And 2
Mile from thence is a fair Church, where our Lady
met with Elizabeth, when they were both with
Child ; and Saint John stirred in his Mother's Womb,
and made Reverence to his Creator that he saw not.
And under the Altar of that Church is the Place
where Saint John was born.   And from that Church
is a Mile to the Castle of Emmaus : and there also
our Lord shewed Him to 2 of His Disciples after
His Resurrection.   Also on that other Side, 200
Paces from Jerusalem, is a Church, where was wont
to be the Cave of the Lion.   And under that
Church, at 30 Steps of Deepness, were interred
12,000 Martyrs, in the time of King Cosrhoes that
the Lion met with, all in a Night, by the Will of
God.

Also from Jerusalem, 2 Mile, is the Mount Joy,
a full fair Place and a delicious ; and there lieth
Samuel the Prophet in a fair Tomb.   And Men call
it Mount Joy, for it giveth Joy to Pilgrims' Hearts,
because that there Men see first Jerusalem.

Also between Jerusalem and the Mount of Olivet
is the Vale of Jehosaphat, under the Walls of the
City, as I have said before.   And in the Midst of
the Vale is a little River that Men call Brook
Cedron, and above it, overthwart, lay a Tree that

the Cross was made of, that Men went over on. And fast by it is a little Pit in the Earth, where the Foot of the Pillar is yet interred; and there was our Lord first scourged, for He was scourged and villainously entreated in many Places. Also in the middle Place of the Vale of Jehosaphat is the Church of our Lady: and it is of 43 Steps under the Earth unto the Sepulchre of our Lady. And our Lady was of Age, when she died, 72 Year. And beside the Sepulchre of our Lady is an Altar, where our Lord forgave Saint Peter all his Sins. And from thence, toward the West, under an Altar, is a Well that cometh out of the River of Paradise. And wit well, that that Church is full low in the Earth, and some is altogether within the Earth. But I suppose well, that it was not so founded. But because that Jerusalem hath often-time been destroyed and the Walls broken down and tumbled into the Vale, and that they have been so filled up again and the Ground raised — for that Reason is the Church so low within the Earth. And, nevertheless, Men say there commonly, that the Earth hath so been cloven since the Time that our Lady was there buried; and Men yet say there, that it waxeth and groweth every Day, without Doubt.

A BLACK MONK

In that Church were wont to be black Monks, that had their Abbot.

And beside that Church is a Chapel, beside the Rock that is called Gethsemane. And there was our Lord kissed by Judas ; and there was He taken by the Jews. And there left our Lord His Disciples, when He went to pray before His Passion, when He prayed and said, " *Pater, si fieri potest, transeat a me Calix iste ;*" that is to say, " *Father, if it may be, do let this Chalice go from me :*" and, when He came again to His Disciples, He found them sleeping. And in the Rock within the Chapel yet appear the Print of the Fingers of our Lord's Hand, when He put them in the Rock, when the Jews would have taken Him.

And from thence, a Stone's Cast toward the South, is another Chapel, where our Lord sweat Drops of Blood. And there, right nigh, is the Tomb of King Jehosaphat, of whom the Vale beareth the Name. This Jehosaphat was King of that Country, and was converted by an Hermit, that was a worthy Man and did much Good. And from thence, a Bow's Draw toward the South, is a Church, where Saint James and Zachariah the Prophet were buried.

And above that Vale is the Mount of Olivet ; and it is clept so for the Plenty of Olives that grow there. That Mount is more high than the City of Jerusalem is ; and, therefore, may Men upon that Mount see many of the Streets of the City. And between that Mount and the City is but the Vale of Jehosaphat that is not full large. And from that Mount rose our Lord Jesu Christ to Heaven upon Ascension Day ; and there sheweth yet the Shape of

His left Foot in the Stone. And there is a Church where was wont to be an Abbot and Canons Regular. And a little thence, 28 Paces, is a Chapel; and therein is the Stone on the which our Lord sat, when He preached the 8 Blessings and said thus: "*Beati Pauperes Spiritu :*" and there He taught His Disciples the *Pater Noster;* and wrote with His Finger on a Stone. And there nigh is a Church, Saint Mary the Egyptian, and there she lieth in a Tomb. And from thence toward the East, a 3 Bow Shot, is Bethphage, to the which our Lord sent Saint Peter and Saint James to fetch the Ass upon the Palm-Sunday, and rode upon that Ass to Jerusalem.

And in coming down from the Mount of Olivet, toward the East, is a Castle that is clept Bethany. And there dwelt Simon the Leper, and there lodged our Lord: and after he was baptised by the Apostles and was clept Julian, and was made Bishop; and this is the same Julian that Men call to for good Lodging, for our Lord lodged with him in his House. And in that House our Lord forgave Mary Magdalene her Sins: there she washed His Feet with her Tears, and wiped them with her Hair. And there served Saint Martha our Lord. There our Lord raised Lazarus from Death to Life, that was dead 4 Days and stank, that was Brother to Mary Magdalene and to Martha. And there dwelt also Mary Cleophas. That Castle is well a Mile long from Jerusalem. Also in coming down from the Mount of Olivet is the Place where our Lord wept upon Jerusalem.

And there beside is the Place where our Lady appeared to Saint Thomas the Apostle after her Assumption, and gave him her Girdle. And right nigh is the Stone where our Lord often-time sat when He preached; and upon that same shall He sit at the Day of Doom, right as He Himself said.

Also after the Mount of Olivet is the Mount of Galilee. There assembled the Apostles when Mary Magdalene came and told them of Christ's Uprising. And there, between the Mount Olivet and the Mount Galilee, is a Church, where the Angel spoke to our Lady of her Death.

Also going from Bethany to Jericho was sometime a little City, but it is now all destroyed, and now is there but a little Village. That City took Joshua by Miracle of God and Commandment of the Angel, and destroyed it, and cursed it and all them that built it again. Of that city was Zaccheus the Dwarf that clomb up into the Sycamore Tree to see our Lord, because he was so little he might not see Him for the People. And of that City was Rahab the common Woman that escaped alone with them of her Lineage: and she often-time refreshed and fed the Messengers of Israel, and kept them from many great Perils of Death; and, therefore, she had good Reward, as Holy Writ saith: "*Qui accipit Prophetam in Nomine Meo, Mercedem Prophetæ accipiet;*" that is to say, "*He that taketh a Prophet in My Name, he shall take the Meed of a Prophet.*" And so had she. For she prophesied to the Messengers, saying,

"*Novi quod Dominus tradet vobis Terram hanc.*" that is to say, "*I wot well, that our Lord shall give you this Land:*" and so He did. And after, Salmon.* Naasson's Son, wedded her, and from that Time was she a worthy Woman, and served God well.

Also from Bethany go Men to the River Jordan by a Mountain and through Desert. And it is nigh a Day's Journey from Bethany, toward the East, to a great Hill, where our Lord fasted 40 Days. Upon that Hill the Enemy of Hell bare our Lord and tempted Him, and said, "*Dic ut Lapides isti Panes fiant;*" that is to say, "*Say, that these Stones be made Loaves.*" In that Place, upon the Hill, was wont to be a fair Church ; but it is all destroyed, so that there is now but an Hermitage, that a manner of Christian Men hold, that be clept Georgians, for Saint George converted them. Upon that Hill dwelt Abraham a great while, and therefore Men call it Abraham's Garden. And between the Hill and this Garden runneth a little Brook of Water that was wont to be bitter ; but, by the Blessing of Elisha the Prophet, it became sweet and good to drink. And at the Foot of this Hill, toward the Plain, is a great Well, that entereth into River Jordan.

From that Hill to Jericho, that I spake of before, is but a Mile in going toward River Jordan. Also as Men go to Jericho sat the blind Man crying, "*Jesu, Fili David, miserere mei ;*" that is to say, "*Jesu, David's Son, have Mercy on me.*" And anon he had his Sight. Also, 2 Mile from Jericho, is

* Matt. i. 5.

River Jordan.   And, an half Mile more nigh, is a
fair Church of Saint John the Baptist, where he baptised our Lord.   And there beside is the House of
Jeremiah the Prophet.

CHAPTER IX

*Of the Dead Sea ; and of the River Jordan. Of the
Head of Saint John the Baptist ; and of
the Usages of the Samaritans*

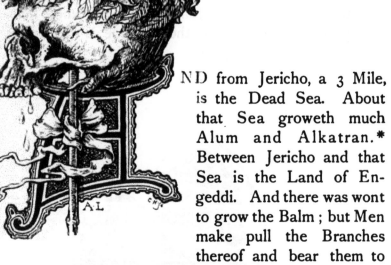

AND from Jericho, a 3 Mile,
is the Dead Sea. About
that Sea groweth much
Alum and Alkatran.*
Between Jericho and that
Sea is the Land of En-
geddi. And there was wont
to grow the Balm ; but Men
make pull the Branches
thereof and bear them to
be grafted at Babylon ; and Men call them yet
Vines of Geddi. At a Coast of that Sea, as Men
go from Arabia, is the Mount of the Moabites,

* Arabic, Katrân, Bitumen.

where there is a Cave, that Men call Karua.   Upon that Hill Balak, the Son of Boaz, led Balaam the Priest to curse the People of Israel.

That Dead Sea parteth the Land of Ind and of Arabia, and that Sea lasteth from Soara (Segor) unto Arabia.   The Water of that Sea is full bitter and salt, and if the Earth were made moist and wet with that Water, it would never bear Fruit.   And the Earth and the Land changeth often its Colour.   And it casteth out of the Water a Thing that Men call Asphalt, also great Pieces, as the Greatness of an Horse, every Day and on all Sides.   And from Jerusalem to that Sea is 200 Furlongs.   That Sea is in Length 580 Furlongs, and in Breadth 150 Furlongs; and it is clept the Dead Sea, for it runneth nought, but is ever un-movable.   And neither Man, Beast, nor anything that beareth Life in him may die in that Sea.   And that hath been proved many times, by Men that have deserved to be dead that have been cast therein and left there 3 Days or 4, and they might never die therein ; for it receiveth no Thing within him that beareth Life.   And no Man may drink of the Water for Bitterness.   And if a Man cast Iron therein, it will float above.   And if Men cast a Feather therein, it will sink to the Bottom, and these be Things against Nature.

And also, the Cities there were lost because of Sin. And there beside grow Trees that bear full fair Apples, and fair of Colour to behold ; but whoso breaketh them or cutteth them in 2, he shall find within them Coals and Cinders, in Token that by the

Wrath of God the Cities and the Land were burnt and
sunk into Hell.   Some Men call that Sea the Lake of
Asafœtida; some, the River of Devils; and some
the River that is ever stinking.   And into that Sea
sunk the 5 Cities by the Wrath of God; that is to
say, Sodom, Gomorrah, Admah, Zeboim, and Zoar,
for the abominable Sin that reigned in them.   But
Zoar, by the Prayer of Lot, was saved and kept a
great while, for it was set upon a Hill; and some
Part yet sheweth thereof above the Water, and Men
may see the Walls when it is fair Weather and clear.
In that City Lot dwelt a little while; and there he
was made drunk by his Daughters, and lay with them,
and engendered of them Moab and Ammon.   And
the Cause for which his Daughters made him drunk
to lie with him was this: because they saw no Man
about them, but only their Father, and therefore they
trowed that God had destroyed all the World as He
had done the Cities, as He had done before by Noah's
Flood.   And therefore they would lie with their
Father to have Issue, and to replenish the World
again with People to restore the World again by
them; for they trowed that there had been no more
Men in all the World; and if their Father had not
been drunk, he had not lain with them.

And the Hill above Zoar Men called it then Edom
and after Men called it Seir, and after Idumea.   Also
at the right Side of that Dead Sea, dwelleth yet the
Wife of Lot in Likeness of a salt Stone; for that she
looked behind her when the Cities sunk into Hell.

This Lot was Haran's Son, that was Brother to

ARTHUR LAYARD

LOT'S WIFE

Abraham; and Sarah, Abraham's Wife, and Milcah,
Nahor's Wife, were Sisters to the said Lot.   And
the same Sarah was of Age 90 Year when Isaac her
Son was gotten on her.   And Abraham had another
Son Ishmael that he gat upon Hagar his Handmaid.
And when Isaac his Son was 8 Days old, Abra-
ham his Father made him be circumcised, and
Ishmael with him that was 14 Year old: wherefore
the Jews that come of Isaac's Line be circumcised
the 8th Day, and the Saracens that come of
Ishmael's Line be circumcised when they be 14
Year of Age.

And ye shall understand, that the River Jordan
runneth within the Dead Sea, where it dieth, for it
runneth no further more, at a Place that is a Mile
from the Church of Saint John the Baptist toward
the West, a little beneath the Place where that
Christian Men bathe them commonly.   And a Mile
from River Jordan is the River of Jabbok, the which
Jacob passed over when he came from Mesopotamia.
This River Jordan is no great River, but it is plenteous of good Fish; and it cometh out of the Hill of
Lebanon by 2 Wells that be clept Jor and Dan, and
of the 2 Wells hath it the Name.   And it passeth
by a Lake that is clept Maron (Merom).   And after
it passeth by the Sea of Tiberias, and passeth under
the Hills of Gilboa; and there is a full fair Vale, both
on that one Side and on that other of the same River.
And Men go on the Hills of Lebanon, all their Length
unto the Desert of Pharan; and those Hills part the
Kingdom of Syria and the Country of Phœnicia;

and upon those Hills grow Trees of Cedar that be full high, and they bear long Apples, and as great as a Man's Head.

And also this River Jordan parteth the Land of Galilee and the Land of Idumea and the Land of Betron (? Arabia Petrea), and runneth under Earth a great Way unto a fair Plain and great that is clept "*Meldan*" in Sarmois; that is to say, Fair or Market in their Language, because that there are often Fairs in that Plain. And there becometh the Water great and large; and in that Plain is the Tomb of Job.

And in that River Jordan above-said was our Lord baptised of Saint John, and the voice of God the Father was heard saying; "*Hic est Filius Meus dilectus, &c;*" that is to say, "*This is My beloved Son, in the which I am well pleased; hear Him!*" and the Holy Ghost alighted upon him in Likeness of a Culver; and so at His baptising was all the Holy Trinity.

And through that River passed the Children of Israel, all dry Feet; and they put Stones there in the middle Place, in Token of the Miracle that the Water withdrew him so. Also in that River Jordan Naaman of Syria bathed him, that was full rich, but he was leprous; and there anon he took his Heal.

About the River Jordan be many Churches where that many Christian Men dwelled. And nigh thereto is the City of Hay (Hazor) that Joshua assailed and took. Also beyond the River Jordan is the

Vale of Mamre, and that is a full fair Vale. Also upon the Hill that I spake of before, where our Lord fasted 40 Days, a 2 Mile long from Galilee, is a fair Hill and an high, where the Enemy the Fiend bare our Lord the 3rd Time to tempt Him, and shewed Him all the Regions of the World and said, "*Hec omnia Tibi dabo, si cadens adoraveris me ;*" that is to say, "*All this shall I give Thee, if Thou fall and worship me.*"

Also from the Dead Sea going Eastward, out of the Borders of the Holy Land that is clept the Land of Promise, is a strong Castle and a fair, on an Hill, that is called "*Carak*" in Sarmois ; that is to say, Royal. That Castle made King Baldwin, that was King of France, when he had conquered that Land, and put it in Christian Men's Hands to keep that Country ; and for that Cause was it clept the Mount Royal. And under it there is a Town that is called Sobach, and there, all about, dwell Christian Men, under Tribute.

From thence go Men to Nazareth, of the which our Lord beareth the Surname. And from thence Men go by the Province of Galilee by Ramath, by Sothim and by the high Hill of Ephraim, where Elkanah and Hannah the Mother of Samuel the Prophet dwelled. There was born this Prophet ; and, after his Death, he was buried at Mount Joy, as I have said to you before.

And then Men go to Shiloh, where the Ark of God with the Relics were kept long time under Eli the Prophet. There made the People of Hebron

Sacrifice to our Lord, and there they yielded up their Vows. And there spake God first to Samuel, and shewed him the Mutation of the Order of Priesthood, and the Mystery of the Sacrament. And right nigh, on the left Side, is Gibeon and Ramah and Benjamin, of the which Holy Writ speaketh.

And after Men go to Sichem, some-time clept Sichar; and that is in the Province of Samaritans. And there is a full fair Vale and a fructuous; and there is a fair City and a good that Men call Neople (Neapolis). And from thence is a Day's Journey to Jerusalem. And there is the Well, where our Lord spake to the Woman of Samaria. And there was wont to be a Church, but it is beaten down. Beside that Well King Rehoboam had made 2 Calves of Gold and made them to be worshipped, and put the one at Dan and the other at Bethel. And a Mile from Sichar is the City of Luz; and in that City dwelt Abraham a certain Time. Sichem is a 10 Mile from Jerusalem, and it is clept Neople; that is to say, the New City. And nigh beside is the Tomb of Joseph the Son of Jacob that governed Egypt: for the Jews bare his Bones from Egypt and buried them there, and thither go the Jews often-time in Pilgrimage with great Devotion. In that City was Dinah, Jacob's Daughter, ravished, for whom her Brethren slew many Persons and did many Harms to the City. And there beside is the Hill of Gerizim, where the Saracens make their Sacrifice: in that Hill would Abraham have sacrificed his Son Isaac. And there beside is the Vale of Dotaim. And there is the Cistern, where Joseph, which they sold, was cast in of his Brethren; and that is a 2 Mile from Sichar.

From thence go Men to Samaria that Men call now Sebast; and that is the chief City of that Country, and it sits between Hills as Jerusalem doth. In that City were the Sittings of the 12 Tribes of Israel; but the City is not now so great as it was wont to be. There was buried Saint John the Baptist between 2 Prophets, Elisha and Abdon; but he was beheaded in the Castle of Macharim (Machærus) beside the Dead Sea, and after he was translated by his Disciples, and buried at Samaria. And there Julian the Apostate had him digged up and his Bones burnt, (for he was at that time Emperor) and the Ashes winnowed in the Wind. But the Finger that shewed our Lord, saying, " *Ecce Agnus Dei;*" that is to say, " *Lo! the Lamb of God,*" would never burn, but is all whole;—that Finger Saint Thecla, the holy Virgin, had born unto the Hill of Sebast; and there make Men great Feast.

There was wont to be the Head of Saint John Baptist, enclosed in the Wall. But the Emperor Theodosius had it drawn out, and found it wrapped in a little Cloth, all bloody; and so he had it born to Constantinople. And the hinder Part of the Head is yet at Constantinople; and the fore Part of the Head, to under the Chin, is at Rome under the Church of Saint Silvester, where be Nuns Cordelers: and it is yet all broiled, as though it were half-burnt, for the Emperor Julian above-said, of his Cursedness and Malice, had that Part burnt with the other Bones, and it sheweth yet; and this Thing hath been proved both by Popes and by Emperors. And the Jaws beneath, that hold to the Chin, and a Part of the Ashes and the Platter that the Head was laid in, when it was smitten off, are at Genoa; and the Genoese make for it great Feast, and so do the Saracens also.

"AND IT IS ALL BROILED"

And some Men say that the Head of Saint John is at Amiens in Picardy; and other Men say that it is the Head of Saint John the Bishop. I wot never, but God knoweth; but in whateverwise wise Men worship it, the blessed Saint John holds himself a-paid.

From this City of Sebast unto Jersualem is 12 Mile. And between the Hills of that Country there is a Well that 4 Times in the Year changeth his Colour, sometime green, sometime red, sometime clear and sometime troubled; and Men call that Well, Job. And the Folk of that Country, that Men call Samaritans, were converted and baptized by the Apostles; but they hold not well their Doctrine, and always they hold Laws by themselves, varying from Christian Men, from Saracens, Jews and Paynims. And the Samaritans believe in one God, and they say well that there is but one God that formed all, and All shall doom; and they hold the Bible according to the Letter, and they use the Psalter as the Jews do. And they say that they be the right

Sons of God.   And, among all other Folk, they say that they be best beloved of God, and that to them belongeth the Heritage that God plighted to His beloved Children.   And they have also different Clothing and Shape to look on than' other Folk have; for they wrap their Heads in red Linen Cloth, in Difference from others.   And the Saracens wrap their Heads in white Linen Cloth; and the Christian Men, that dwell in the Country, wrap them in blue of Ind; and the Jews in yellow Cloth.   In that Country dwell many of the Jews, paying Tribute as Christian Men do.

And if ye will know the Letters that the Jews use they be such, and the Names be as they call them here written above, in manner of A. B. C.

Aleph	Beth	Gymel	Deleth	He	Vau	Zay
א	ב	ג	ד	ה	ו	ז
Cy	Thet	Joht	Kapho	Lampd	Mem	Nun
ח	ט	י	כ	ל	מ	נ
Sameth	Ey	Fhee	Sade	Coph	Resch	Son	Tau
ס	ע	פ	צ	ק	ר	שׁ	ת

CHAPTER X

*Of the Province of Galilee, and where Anti-Christ shall
be born. Of Nazareth. Of the age of Our Lady.
Of the Day of Doom. And of the Customs of
the Jacobites and the Syrians ; and of
the Usages of the Georgians*

ROM this Country of the Samaritans that I have spoken of before go Men to the Plains of
Galilee, and Men leave the Hills
on the one Side.

And Galilee is one of the
Provinces of the Holy Land, and in that
Province is the City of Nain—and Ca-
pernaum, and Chorazin and Bethsaida.
In this Bethsaida were Saint Peter and
Saint Andrew born. And thence, a
4 Mile, is Chorazin. And 5 Mile from
Chorazin is the City of Kedar whereof
the Psalter speaketh : " *Et habitavi cum
Habitantibus Kedar ;* " that is to say,
" *And I have dwelled with the Men dwelling in
Kedar.* " In Chorazin shall Antichrist be born, as

some Men say. And other Men say he shall be born in Babylon; for the Prophet saith: "*De Babilonia Coluber exiet, qui totum Mundum devorabit*;" that is to say, "*Out of Babylon shall come a Worm that shall devour all the World.*" This Antichrist shall be nourished in Bethsaida, and he shall reign in Capernaum: and therefore saith Holy Writ; "*Væ tibi, Chorazin! Væ tibi Bethsaida! Væ tibi Capernaum!*" that is to say, "*Woe be to thee, Chorazin! Woe to thee, Bethsaida! Woe to thee, Capernaum.*" And all these Towns be in the Land of Galilee. And also Cana of Galilee is 4 Mile from Nazareth: of that City was Simon the Canaanite and his Wife Canee, of the which the Holy Evangelist speaketh: there did our Lord the first Miracle at the Wedding, when He turned Water into Wine.

And in the End of Galilee, at the Hills, was the Ark of God taken; and on the other Side is the Mount Hendor or Hermon. And, thereabout, goeth the Brook of Kishon; and there beside Barak that was Abimelech's * Son with Deborah the Prophetess overcame the Host of Idumea, when Sisera the King was slain of Jael the Wife of Heber. And Gideon† chased beyond the River Jordan, by Strength of Sword, Zeeb and Zebah and Zalmunna, and there he slew them. Also a 5 Mile from Nain is the City of Jezreel that sometime was clept Zarim, of the which City Jezabel, the cursed Queen,

* Should be Abinoam.
† The name of Gideon is omitted in the originals.

was Lady and Queen, that took away the Vine of
Naboth by her Strength. Fast by that City is the
Field Megiddo, in the which the King Joram was
slain of the King of Samaria and after was translated and buried in the Mount Sion.

And a Mile from Jezreel be the Hills of Gilboa,
where Saul and Jonathan, that were so fair, died ;
wherefore David cursed them, as Holy Writ saith :
"*Montes Gilboæ, nec Ros nec Pluvia, &c ;*" that is to
say, " *Ye Hills of Gilboa, neither Dew nor Rain come
upon you.*" And a Mile from the Hills of Gilboa
toward the East is the City of Cyropolis, that was
clept before Bethshan ; and upon the Walls of that
City was the Head of Saul hanged.

After go Men by the Hill beside the Plains of
Galilee unto Nazareth, where was wont to be a
great City and a fair ; but now there is but a
little Village, and Houses abroad here and there.
And it is not walled. And it sits in a little Valley,
and there be Hills all about. There was our Lady
born, but she was begotten at Jerusalem. And
because that our Lady was born at Nazareth, therefore bare our Lord this Surname of that Town.
There took Joseph our Lady to Wife, when she was
14 Year of Age. And there Gabriel greet our
Lady, saying, "*Ave Gratia plena, Dominus tecum !*"
that is to say, "*Hail, full of Grace, our Lord is with
thee !*" And this Salutation was done on the Place
of a great Altar of a fair Church that was wont to be
sometime, but it is now all down, and Men have
made a little Receptacle, beside a Pillar of that

Church, to receive the Offerings of Pilgrims.   And
the Saracens keep that Place full dearly, for the
Profit that they have thereof.   And they be full
wicked Saracens and cruel, and more despiteful
than in any other Place, and have destroyed all the
Churches.   There nigh is Gabriel's Well, where our
Lord was wont to bathe Him, when He was young,
and from that Well bare
the Water often-time to
His Mother.   And in that
Well she washed often-
time the Clothes of her
Son Jesu Christ.   And
from Jerusalem unto
thither is 3 Days' Journey.
At Nazareth was our Lord
nourished.   Nazareth is
as much as to say, "*Flower
of the Garden;*" and by
good Reason may it be

" THEY BE FULL WICKED SARACENS "

clept Flower, for there was nourished the Flower
of Life that was Christ Jesu.

    And 2 Mile from Nazareth is the City of
Sephor, by the Way that goeth from Nazareth to
Acre.   And an half Mile from Nazareth is the Leap
of our Lord.   For the Jews led Him upon an high
Rock to make Him leap down, and to have slain
Him ; but Jesu passed amongst them, and leapt upon
another Rock, and the Steps of His Feet be yet in the
Rock, where He alighted.   And therefore say some
Men, when they dread them of Thieves on any Way,

or of Enemies; "*Jesus autem transiens per Medium illorum ibat;*" that is to say, "*Jesus, forsooth, passing by the Midst of them, went:*" in Token and Mind, that as our Lord passed through, out of the Jews' Cruelty, and escaped safely from them, so surely Men pass the Peril of Thieves. And then say Men 2 Verses of the Psalter 3 Times: "*Irruat super eos Formido et Pavor, in magnitudine Brachii Tui, Domine. Fiant immobiles, quasi Lapis, donec pertranseat Populus Tuus, Domine; donec pertranseat Populus Tuus iste, quem possedisti;*" ("*May Fear and Dread fall upon them; by the Greatness of Thine Arm, O Lord let them be still as a Stone; till Thy People pass over, O Lord, till Thy People pass over, which Thou hast purchased,*") and then may Men pass without Peril.

And ye shall understand, that our Lady had Child when she was 15 Year old. And she was conversant with her Son 33 Year and 3 Months. And after the Passion of our Lord she lived 24 Year.

Also from Nazareth Men go to the Mount Tabor; and that is a 4 Mile. And it is a full fair Hill and well high, where was wont to be a Town and many Churches; but they be all destroyed. But there is yet a Place that Men call the School of God, where He was wont to teach His Disciples, and told them the Privities of Heaven. And, at the Foot of that Hill, Melchisadech that was King of Salem, in the Turning of that Hill met Abraham in coming again from the Battle, when he had slain

Abimalech.   And this Melchisadech was both King and Priest of Salem that now is clept Jerusalem. In that Hill Tabor our Lord transfigured Him before Saint Peter, Saint John and Saint James; and there they saw, ghostly, Moses and Elias the Prophets beside them.   And therefore said Saint Peter; "*Domine, bonum est nos hic esse; faciamus*

"4 ANGELS WITH 4 TRUMPETS SHALL BLOW."

tria Tabernacula"; that is to say, "*Lord, it is good for us to be here; make we here 3 Dwelling-places.*" And there heard they a Voice of the Father that said; "*Hic est Filius Meus dilectus, in Quo Mihi bene complacui.* ("*This is My beloved Son, in whom I am well pleased.*") And our Lord forbid them that they should tell that Vision till that He were risen from Death to Life.

On that Hill and in that same Place, at the Day of Doom, 4 Angels with 4 Trumpets shall blow and raise all Men that have suffered Death, since that the World was formed, from Death to Life; and they shall come in Body and Soul in Judgment, before the Face of our Lord in the Vale of Jehosaphat. And the Doom shall be on Easter Day, such Time as our Lord arose. And the Doom shall begin, such Hour as our Lord descended to Hell and despoiled it. For at such Hour shall He despoil the World and lead His chosen to Bliss; and the others shall He condemn to perpetual Pains. And then shall every Man have after his Desert, either Good or Evil, but and if the Mercy of God passeth His Righteousness.

Also a Mile from Mount Tabor is the Mount Hermon; and there was the City of Nain. Before the Gate of that City raised our Lord the Son of Widow, that had no more Children. Also 3 Mile from Nazareth is the Castle Safra, of the which the Sons of Zebedee and the sons of Alpheus were. Also a 3 Mile from Nazareth is the Mount Cain, and under that is a Well; and beside that Well Lamech, Noah's Father, slew Cain with an Arrow. For this Cain went through Briars and Bushes as a wild Beast; and he had lived from the Time of Adam his Father unto the Time of Noah, and so he lived nigh to 2000 Year. And this Lamech was all blind for Eld.

From Safra Men go to the Sea of Galilee and to the City of Tiberias, that sits upon the same Sea. And albeit that Men call it a Sea, yet is it neither Sea nor Arm of the Sea. For it is but a Tank of fresh

Water that is in Length 100 Furlongs, and of Breadth 40 Furlongs, and hath within him great Plenty of good Fish, and runneth into River Jordan. The City is not full great, but it hath good Baths within him.

And there, as the River Jordan passeth from the Sea of Galilee, is a great Bridge, where men pass from the Land of Promise to the Land of Bashan and the Land of Gennesaret, that be about the River Jordan and the Beginning of the Sea of Tiberias. And from thence Men may go to Damascus, in 3 Days, by the Kingdom of Traconitis, the which Kingdom lasteth from Mount Hermon to the Sea of Galilee, or to the Sea of Tiberias, or to the Sea of Gennesaret; and all is one Sea, and this the Tank that I have told you of, but it changeth thus the Name for the Names of the Cities that sit beside him.

Upon that Sea went our Lord dry Feet; and there He took up Saint Peter, when he began to drown within the Sea, and said to him, "*Modice Fidei, quare dubitasti?*" ("*O thou of little Faith, wherefore didst thou doubt?*") And after His resurrection our Lord appeared on that Sea to His Disciples and bade them fish, and filled all the Net full of great Fishes. In that Sea rowed our Lord often-time; and there He called to Him Saint Peter, Saint Andrew, and Saint James and Saint John, the Sons of Zebedee.

In that City of Tiberias is the Table upon the which our Lord ate with His Disciples after His Resurrection; and they knew Him in breaking of Bread, as the Gospel saith : "*Et cognoverunt Eum in Fractione Panis.*" And nigh that City of Tiberias is the Hill, where our Lord fed 5000 Persons with 5 Barley Loaves and 2 Fishes.

In that City a Man cast a burning Dart in Wrath after our Lord. And the Head smote into the Earth and waxed green ; and it grew to a big Tree. And it groweth yet, and the Bark thereof is all like Coals.

Also in the Head of that Sea of Galilee, toward the Septentrion (or South) is a strong Castle and an high that is hight Saphor. And fast beside it is Capernaum. Within the Land of Promise is not so strong a Castle. And there is a good Town beneath that is clept Saphor. In that Castle Saint Anne our Lady's Mother was born. And there beneath, was the Centurion's House. That Country is clept the Galilee of Folk (or the Gentiles) that were taken to Tribute of Zebulon and Napthali.

And in again coming from that Castle, a 30 Mile, is the City of Dan that sometime was clept Belinas or Cesarea Philippi ; that sits at the Foot of the Mount of Lebanon, where the River Jordan beginneth. There beginneth the Land of Promise and endureth unto Beersheba in Length, going from North to South. And it containeth well a 180 Miles. And of Breadth, that is to say, from Jericho unto Jaffa, it containeth a 40 Mile of Lombardy, or of our Country, that be also little Miles ; these be not Miles of Gascony nor of the Province of Germany, where be great Miles. And wit ye well, that

the Land of Promise is in Syria. For the Realm of
Syria endureth from the Deserts of Arabia unto
Cilicia, and that is Armenia the Great; that is to
say, from the South to the North. And, from the
East to the
West, it endur-
eth from the
great Deserts of
Arabia unto the
West Sea. But
in that Realm of

"AND THEY LET THE CULVER FLEE"

Syria is the Kingdom of Judea and many other
Provinces, as Palestine, Galilee, Little Cilicia, and
many others.

In that Country and other Countries beyond they
have a Custom, when they shall use War, and when
Men hold Siege about a City or Castle, and they
within dare not send out Messengers with Letters
from Lord to Lord to ask Succour, they make

their Letters and bind them to the Neck of a Culver, and let the Culver flee. And the Culvers be so taught, that they flee with those Letters to the very Place that Men would send them to. For the Culvers be nourished in those Places where they be sent to, and they send them thus, to bear their Letters. And the Culvers return again where-to they be nourished; and so they do commonly.

And ye shall understand that amongst the Saracens, in one Part and another, dwell many Christian Men of many Manners and diverse Names. And all be baptized and have diverse Laws and diverse Customs. But all believe in God the Father and the Son and the Holy Ghost; but always fail they in some Articles of our Faith. Some of these be clept Jacobites, for Saint James converted them and Saint John baptized them. They say that a Man shall make his Confession only to God, and not to a Man; for only to Him should Man yield Him guilty of all that he hath misdone. Neither God ordained, nor ever devised, nor the Prophet either, that a Man should shrive him to another, as they say, but only to God. As Moses writeth in the Bible, and as David saith in the Psalter Book; "*Confitebor Tibi, Domine, in toto Corde meo*," ("*I will confess to Thee, O Lord, in my whole Heart*";) and, "*Delictum meum Tibi cognitum feci*," ("*I acknowledge my Sin unto Thee*";) and, "*Deus meus es Tu, et confitebor Tibi*," ("*Thou art my God, and I will confess unto Thee*";) and, "*Quoniam Cogitatio*

Hominis confitebitur Tibi," ("*Since the Thoughts of Man shall confess to Thee*",) &c. For they know all the Bible and the Psalter. And therefore quote they so the Letter. But they quote not the Authorities thus in Latin, but in their Language full openly, and say well, that David and other Prophets say it.

Nevertheless, Saint Augustin and Gregory say thus :—Augustinus : "*Qui Scelera sua cogitat, et conversus fuerit, Veniam sibi credat,*" ("*Let him that would consider his Sins, and would be converted, believe that for him there is Forgiveness.*") Gregorius : "*Dominus potius Mentem quam Verba respicit,*" ("*The Lord looketh rather on the Purpose than on the Letter.*"). And Saint Hillary saith : "*Longorum Temporum Crimina, in Ictu Oculi pereunt, si Cordis nata fuerit Compunctio,*" ("*Sins of long Duration perish in the Twinkling of an Eye, if Repentance be born of the Heart.*") And before such Authorities they say, that only to God shall a Man acknowledge his Defaults, yielding himself guilty and crying Him Mercy, and vowing to Him to amend his Ways. And therefore, when they will shrive them, they take Fire and set it beside them, and cast therein Powder of Frankincense ; and in the Smoke thereof they shrive them to God, and cry Him Mercy. But Sooth it is, that this Confession was first and natural. But Saint Peter the Apostle, and they that came after him, have ordained to make their Confession to Man, and by good Reason ; for they perceived well that no Sickness

was curable by good Medecine to lay thereto, but if
Men knew the Nature of the Malady ; and also no
Man may give suitable Medecine, but if he know
the Quality of the Deed. For one Sin may be
greater in one Man than in another ; and therefore
it behoveth him that he know the Kind of the Deed,
and thereupon to give him Penance.

There be other, that be clept Syrians ; and they
hold the Belief held amongst us, and of them of
Greece. And they all use Beards, as Men of Greece
do. And they make the Sacrament of Therf (or
Unleavened) Bread. And in their Language they
use the Letters of the Saracens. But in the Mysteries of Holy Church they use Letters of Greece.
And they make their Confession, right as the
Jacobites do.

There be others, that Men call Georgians, that
Saint George converted ; and him they worship
more than any other Saint, and to him they cry
for Help. And they came out of the Realm of
Georgia. These Folk use shaven Crowns. The
Clerks have round Crowns, and the Laymen have
Crowns all square. And they hold Christian Laws,
as do they of Greece ; of whom I have spoken of
before.

Other there be that Men call Christian Men of
Girding, for they be all girt above. And there be
others that Men call Nestorians. And some are
Aryans, some Nubians, some of Greece, some of
Ind, and some of Prester John's Land. And all
these have many Articles of our Faith, but to some

they be variant. And of their Variance were too long to tell, and so I will leave, for the Time, without more speaking of them.

THE ROUND CROWN AND THE SQUARE

CHAPTER XI

*Of the City of Damascus. Of 3 Ways to
Jerusalem; one, by Land and by Sea;
another, more by land than by sea; and
the 3rd Way to Jerusalem, all by Land.*

NOW that I have told you of
some Part of the Folk in the
Countries before, now will I
turn again on my Way, to turn
again to this half of my Travels.
Then whoso will go from the Land of Galilee, that
I have spoke of, to come again on this half, Men
come again by Damascus, that is a full fair City
and full noble, and full of all Merchandises, and a
3 Days' Journey long from the Sea, and a 5 Days'

Journey from Jerusalem.   But upon Camels, Mules, Horses, Dromedaries and other Beasts, Men carry their Merchandise thither.   And thither come Merchants with Merchandise by Sea from India, Persia, Chaldea, Armenia, and from many other Kingdoms.

This City founded Eliezer Damascus, that was Yeoman and Dispenser (or Steward) of Abraham before that Isaac was born.   For he thought to have been Abraham's Heir, and he named the Town after his Surname.   And in that Place, where Damascus was founded, Cain slew Abel his Brother. And beside Damascus is the Mount Seir.   In that City of Damascus there is great Plenty of Wells. And within the City and without be many fair Gardens of diverse Fruits.   None other City is like in comparison to it for fair Gardens, and for fair Diversions.   The City is great and full of People, and walled with double Walls.   And there be many Physicians.   And Saint Paul himself was there a Physician to keep Men's Bodies in Health, before he was converted.   And after that he was Physician of Souls.   And Saint Luke the Evangelist was Disciple of Saint Paul to learn Physic, and many others ; for Saint Paul held then a School of Physic.   And near beside Damascus was he converted.   And after his Conversion he dwelt in that City 3 Days, without Sight and without Meat or Drink ; and in those 3 Days he was ravished to Heaven, and there he saw many Privities of our Lord.

And fast by Damascus is the Castle of Arkes that is both fair and strong.

From Damascus Men come again by our Lady of Sardenak, that is a 5 Mile on this side Damascus. And it is set upon a Rock, and it is a full fair Place; and it seemeth a Castle, for there was wont to be a Castle, but it is now a full fair Church. And there within be Monks and Nuns Christian. And there is a Vault under the Church, where that Christian Men dwell also. And they have many good Vines. And in the Church, behind the high Altar, in the Wall, is a Table of black Wood, on the which sometime was painted an Image of our Lady that turneth into Flesh: but now the Image sheweth but little, but evermore, through the Grace of God, that Table droppeth as it were of Olive; and there is a Vessel of Marble under the Table to receive the Oil; thereof they give unto Pilgrims, for it healeth of many Sicknesses. And he that keepeth it cleanly a Year, after that Year it turneth into Flesh and Blood.

Between the City of Dark and the City of Raphan is a River that Men call Sabbatoria;* for on the Saturday it runneth fast, and all the Week else it standeth still, and runneth nought or little. And there is another River, that in the Night freezeth wondrous fast, and in the Day is no Frost seen.

And so go Men by a City that Men call Beirout, and there Men go on to the Sea, that shall go unto Cyprus. And they arrive at the Port of Sur or

* Sabbatum, Latin for Saturday.

of Tyre, and then go unto Cyprus.   Or else Men
may go from the Port of Tyre right well and come
not unto Cyprus, and arrive at some Haven of
Greece.   And then come Men unto these Countries
by Ways that I have spoken of before.

Now I have told you of Ways by the which Men
go farthest and longest, as by Babylon and Mount
Sinai and other Places many, through the which
Lands Men turn again to the Land of Promise.

Now will I tell you the straight Way to Jerusalem : for some Men will not pass it ; some for the
Expense, some for they have no Company, and other
many reasonable Causes.   And therefore I tell you
shortly how a Man may go with little Cost and
short Time.

A Man that cometh from the Lands of the West,
he goeth through France, Burgundy and Lombardy
and to Venice and to Genoa, or to some other
Haven of the Borders ; and taketh a Ship there and
goes by Sea to the Isle of Gryffle (? Corfu), and so
arriveth in Greece, or in Port Muroch, or Valon or
Duras, or at some other Haven, and goes to Land
to rest him ; and goes again to Sea, and arrives in
Cyprus, and cometh not to the Isle of Rhodes, but
arrives at Famagosta that is the chief Haven of
Cyprus, or else at Lamaton ; and then entereth into
the Ship again and goes beside the Haven of Tyre
but cometh not to Land, and so passeth he by all
the Havens of that Coast until he come to Jaffa that
is the nighest Haven unto Jerusalem, whence it is
27 Mile.   And from Jaffa Men go to the City

of Ramleh, and that is but little thence, and it is a fair City. And beside Ramleh is a fair Church of our Lady, where our Lord shewed Him to our Lady in the Likeness that betokeneth the Trinity. And there, fast by, is a Church of Saint George, where that his Head was smitten off. And then unto the Castle Emmaus. And then unto Mount Joy; and from thence Pilgrims may first see unto Jerusalem. And then to Mount Modein. And then to Jerusalem. And at the Mount Modein lieth the Prophet Maccabeus. And over Ramleh is the Town of Tekoa, where-of Amos the good Prophet was.

Another Way. Forasmuch as many Men may not suffer the Savour of the Sea, but had as lief go by Land, though that it be more Pain, a Man shall so go unto one of the Havens of Lombardy, as Venice or another. And he shall pass into Greece through Port Moroch or another, and so he shall go unto Constantinople. And he shall so pass the Water that is clept the Brace of Saint George, that is an Arm of the Sea. And from thence he shall come to Pulverall and then unto the Castle of Cinopolis. And from thence shall he go unto Cappadocia that is a great Country, where there be many great Hills. And he shall go through the City of Nyke (Nicea,) the which they won from the Emperor of Constantinople; and it is a fair City and wondrous well walled; and there is a River that Men call the Laye. And then Men go by the Alps of Aryoprynant, and by the Vales of Mallebrinez, and eke the

"THE GREAT BRIDGE UPON THE RIVER OF FERNE"

Vale of Ernax; and so unto Antioch the Less that sitteth on the River Reclay. And thereabout be many good Hills and fair, and many fair Woods, and eke wild Beasts.

And he that will go by another Way, he must go by the Plain of Roumania, coasting the Roumanian Sea. Upon that Coast is a wondrous fair Castle that men call Florathe. And when a Man is out of those same Hills, Men pass then through a City, that is called Marioch and Arteis, where there is a great Bridge upon the River of Ferne that Men call Fassar; and it is a great River bearing Ships. And beside the City of Damascus is a River that cometh from the Mountain of Lebanon that Men call Abana: at passing of this River Saint Eustace lost his 2 Sons, when that he had lost his Wife; and it goeth through the Plain of Arthadoe, and so unto the Red Sea. And so Men may go unto the City of Phenne, and so unto the City of Ferne.

And Antioch is a full fair City and well walled. For it is 2 Mile long. And each Pillar of the Bridge there is a good Tower. And this is the best City of the Kingdom of Syria.

And from Antioch Men may so go forth unto the City of Latakia, and then unto Gabala, and then unto Tartus; and there-by is the Land of Cambre, where there is a strong Castle that Men call Maubeke. And from Tartus Men go unto Tripoli upon the Sea. And upon the Sea Men go unto Acre; and thence be 2 Ways unto Jerusalem. Upon the left Way, Men go first unto Damascus by River

Jordan. Upon the right Side, Men go through the Land of Flagam, and so unto the City of Caiaphas, of the which Caiaphas was Lord, and some call it the Castle of Pilgrims (Athlêt). And from thence is 4 Days' Journey unto Jerusalem, and they go through Cesarea Philippi, and Jaffa, and Ramleh and Emmaus, and so unto Jerusalem.

Now have I told you some of the Ways by the Land and eke by Water how that Men may go unto Jerusalem ; though that it be so, that there be many other Ways that Men go by, according to the Countries that they come from ; nevertheless, they turn all unto one End. Yet is there a Way all by Land unto Jerusalem and passing over no Sea. That is from France or Flanders. But that Way is full long and perilous, and of great Travail ; and therefore few go that same Way. And whoso goeth that Way, he must go through Germany and Prussia, and so unto Tartary.

This Tartary is held of the great Chan, of whom I shall speak more afterward, for thither lasteth his Lordship. And the Lords of Tartary yield unto the great Chan Tribute. This is a full ill Land and a sandy, and bearing but little Fruit. For there groweth little good of Corn or Wine, neither Beans nor Peas. But Beasts be there enough, and that full great Plenty. And there eat they nought but Flesh without Bread, and they sup the Broth thereof. And also they drink the Milk. And all Manner of wild Beasts they eat, Hounds, Cats, Rats, and all other wild Beasts. And they have no Wood, or else little; and therefore they warm and seethe their Meat with Horse-dung and Cow-dung and that of other Beasts, dried against the Sun.   And Princes and others eat not but once in the Day, and that but little.   And they be right foul Folk and of evil Kind.

PRINCE BATHO

And in Summer, by all the Countries, fall many Tempests and many hideous Thunders and Light-nings and slay much People and Beasts also full often-time.   And suddenly is it there passing hot, and suddenly also passing cold; and it is the foulest Country and the most cursed and the poorest that Men know.   And their Prince, that governeth that

Country, that they call Batho, dwelleth at the City of Orda. And truly no good Man should dwell in that Country, for the Land and the Country is not worthy of Hounds to dwell in. It were a good Country to sow in Thistle and Briars and Broom and Thorns; and for no other Thing is it good. Nevertheless, there is good Land in some Places, but it is very little, as Men say.

I have not been in that Country, nor by those Ways. But I have been at other Lands that march with those Countries, and in the land of Russia, and in the Land of Nyfland (Livonia), and in the Realm of Cracow and of Letto (Lithuania), and in the Realm of Daristan, and in many other Places that march with the Borders. But I went never by that Way to Jerusalem, wherefore I may not well tell you the Manner.

But, if this Matter please any worthy Man that hath gone by that Way, he may tell it if it like him ; to that Intent, that those, that will go by that Way and make their Voyage by those Borders, may know what Way is there. For no Man may pass by that Way goodly, but in Time of Winter, for the perilous Waters and wicked Morasses, that be in those Countries, that no Man may pass but if it be strong Frost and Snow above. For if there were no Snow, Men might not go upon the Ice, nor Horse nor Car either.

And it is well a 3 Days' Journey of such Way to pass from Prussia to the Land of Saracens that is habitable. And it behoveth to the Christian Men, that shall war against them every Year, to bear their Victuals with them ; for they shall find there none good. And then must they make carry their Victual upon the Ice with Cars that have no Wheels, that they call Sleighs. And as long as their Victuals last they may abide there, but no longer ; for there shall

AND CRY WITH A LOUD VOICE, " KERRA ! KERRA ! KERRA ! '

they find no Person that will sell them any Victual or anything. And when the Spies see any Christian Men come upon them, they run to the Towns, and cry with a loud Voice ; " *Kerra, Kerra, Kerra.*" And then anon they arm them and assemble them together.

And ye shall understand that it freezeth more strongly in those Countries than on this Half. And therefore hath every Man Stoves in his House, and on those Stoves they eat and do their Occupations all that they may. For that is at the North Parts that Men call the Septentrional where it is cold. For the Sun is but little or none toward those Countries.   And therefore in the Septentrion, that is very North, is the Land so cold, that none may dwell there.   And, on the contrary, toward the South it is so hot, that no Man may dwell there, because that the Sun, when he is upon the South, casteth his Beams all straight upon that Part.

CHAPTER XII

Of the Customs of Saracens, and of their Law. And how the Sultan questioned me, the Author of this Book ; and of the beginning of Mohammet

SARACEN AND FLAG

NOW, because that I have spoken of Saracens and of their Country — now, if ye will know a Part of their Law and of their Belief, I shall tell you what their Book that is clept "*Al Koran*" telleth. And some Men call that Book "*Meshaf.*" And some Men call it "*Harmc,*" after the diverse Languages of the Country. The which Book Mohammet took them. In the which Book, among other Things, is written, as I have often-time seen and read, that the Good shall go to Paradise, and the Evil to Hell ; and that believe all Saracens. And if a Man ask them what Paradise they mean, they say, to Paradise that is a Place of Delights

where Men shall find all Manner of Fruits in all
Seasons, and Rivers running of Milk and Honey,
and of Wine and of sweet Water; and that they
shall have fair Houses and noble, every Man after
his Desert, made of precious Stones and of Gold
and of Silver; and that every Man shall have 80
Wives* all Maidens, and he shall have ado every
Day with them, and yet he shall find them always
Maidens.

Also they believe and speak gladly of the Virgin
Mary and of the Incarnation. And they say that
Mary was taught of the Angel; and that Gabriel
said to her, that she was for-chosen from the
Beginning of the World; and that he showed to
her the Incarnation of Jesu Christ; and that she,
a Maiden, conceived and bare Child; and that witnesseth their Book.

And they say also, that Jesu Christ spake as soon
He was born; and that He was an Holy Prophet
and a true in Word and Deed, and meek and
merciful and righteous and without any Vice.

And they say also, that when the Angel showed
the Incarnation of Christ unto Mary, she was young
and had great Dread. For there was then an
Enchanter in the Country that dealt with Witchcraft, that Men called Taknia, that by his Enchantments could make him in Likeness of an Angel, and
went oftentimes and lay with Maidens. And therefore Mary dreaded lest it had been Taknia, that

* Three of the English MSS. and one of the Latin give 10; and
the two French MSS. 90.

came to deceive the Maidens.   And therefore
she conjured the Angel, that he should tell her
if it were he or no.   And the Angel answered and
said that she should have no Dread of him, for he

TAKNIA

was the very Messenger of Jesu Christ.   Also their
Book saith, that when that she had childed under
a Palm Tree she had great Shame that she had a
Child ; and she greet and said that she would
she had been dead.   And anon the Child spake to
her and comforted her, and said, "*Mother, dismay*

thee nought, for God hath hid in thee His Secrets, for the Salvation of the World." And in other many Places saith their *Al Koran*, that Jesu Christ spake as soon as He was born. And that Book saith also that Jesu was sent from God Almighty to be Mirror and Example and Token to all Men.

And the *Al Koran* saith also of the Day of Doom how God shall come to doom all Manner of Folk. And the Good He shall draw on His side and put them into Bliss, and the Wicked He shall condemn to the Pains of Hell. And among all Prophets Jesu was the most excellent and the most worthy next God, and that He made the Gospels in which is good Doctrine and heal-ful, full of Charity and Truthfastness and true Preaching to them that believe in God. And that He was a very Prophet and more than a Prophet, and lived without Sin, and gave Sight to the Blind, and healed the Lepers, and raised dead Men, and ascended to Heaven.

And when they hold the written Book of the Gospels of our Lord called *Missus est Angelus Gabriel,* that Gospel they, those that be lettered, say often-times in their Orisons, and they kiss it and worship it with great Devotion.

They fast an whole Month in the Year and eat nought but by Night. And they keep them from their Wives all that Month. But the Sick Men be not constrained to that Fast.

Also this Book speaketh of Jews and saith that they be cursed; for they would not believe that Jesu Christ was come of God. And that they lied

falsely of Mary and of her Son Jesu Christ, saying
that they had crucified Jesu the Son of Mary ; for
He was never crucified, as they say, but that God
made Him to ascend up to Him without Death and
without Annoy.   But He transfigured His Likeness
into Judas Iscariot, and him crucified the Jews, and
wot that it had been Jesus.   But Jesus ascended to
Heaven all alive.   And therefore they say, that the
Christian Men err and have no good Knowledge of
this, and that they believe foolishly and falsely that
Jesu Christ was crucified.   And they say also,
that had He been crucified, that God had done
against His Righteousness to suffer Jesu Christ that
was innocent to be put upon the Cross without
Guilt.   And in this Article they say that we fail and
that the great Righteousness of God might not
suffer so great a Wrong : and in this faileth their
Faith.   For they acknowledge well, that the Works
of Jesu Christ be good, and His Words and His
Deeds and His Doctrines by His Gospels were
true, and His Miracles also true ; and the Blessed
Virgin Mary is good, and holy Maiden before and
after the Birth of Jesu Christ ; and that all those
that believe perfectly in God shall be saved.   And
because that they go so nigh our Faith, they be
lightly converted to Christian Law when Men preach
to them and show them distinctly the Law of Jesu
Christ, and tell them of the Prophecies. ·

And also they say, that they know well by the
Prophecies that the Law of Mohammet shall fail, as
the Law of the Jews did ; and that the Law of

Christian People shall last to the Day of Doom.
And if any Man ask them what is their Belief, they
answer thus, and in this Form : " We believe in
God, Maker of Heaven and Earth and of all other
Things that He made.   And without Him is Nothing made.   And we believe in the Day of Doom,
and that every Man shall have his Merit, after that
he hath deserved.   And, we believe it for Truth,
all that God hath said by the Mouths of His
Prophets."

Also Mohammet commanded in his *Al Koran,*
that every Man should have 2 Wives, or 3 or 4 ; but
now they take unto 9, and of Lemans as many as they
may sustain.   And if any of their Wives mis-behave
them against their Husband, he may cast her out of
his House, and depart from her and take another ;
but he shall part with her his Goods.

Also, when Men speak to them of the Father and
of the Son and of the Holy Ghost, they say, that
they be 3 Persons, but not one God ; for their *Al
Koran* speaketh not of the Trinity.   But they say
well, that God hath Speech, and else were He dumb.
And God hath also a Spirit they know well, for else
they say, He were not alive.   And when Men
speak to them of the Incarnation how that by the
Word of the Angel God sent His Wisdom on to
Earth and enshadowed Him in the Virgin Mary, and
that by the Word of God shall the Dead be raised
at the Day of Doom, they say, that it is Truth and
that the Word of God hath great Strength.   And
they say that whoso knoweth not the Word of God

he should not know God.   And they say also that
Jesu Christ is the Word of God : and so saith their
Al Koran, where it saith that the Angel spake to
Mary and said : " Mary, God shall preach the Gos-
pel by the Word of His Mouth and His Name shall
be clept Jesu Christ."

And they say also, that Abraham was Friend to
God, and that Moses was a familiar Speaker with
God, and Jesu Christ was the Word and the Spirit of
God, and that Mohammet was the right Messenger
of God.   And they say, that of these 4, Jesu was
the most worthy and the most excellent and the
most great.   So that they have many good Articles
of our Faith, albeit that they have no perfect Law and
Faith as Christian Men have ; and therefore be they
lightly converted, especially those that understand
the Scriptures and the Prophecies.   For they have
Gospels and the Prophecies and the Bible written
in their Language ; wherefore they know much of
Holy Writ, but they understand it not but after the
Letter.   And so do the Jews, for they understand
not the Letter ghostly (or spiritually), but bodily ;
and therefore be they reproved of the Wise, that
ghostly understand it.   And therefore saith Saint
Paul: " *Litera occidit ; Spiritus vivificat* " (" *The
Letter killeth ; the Spirit quickeneth* ").   Also the
Saracens say, that the Jews be cursed ; for they
have be-fouled the Law that God sent them by
Moses : and the Christians be cursed also, as they
say ; for they keep not the Commandments and the
Precepts of the Gospel that Jesu Christ taught them.

And, therefore, I shall tell you what the Sultan told me upon a Day in his Chamber. He made void out of his Chamber all manner of Men, Lords and others, for he would speak with me in Counsel. And there he asked me how the Christian Men governed themselves in our Country. And I said, " Right well, thanked be God!"

And he said to me, " Truly Nay! For ye Christian Men reck not, right nought, how untruly ye serve God! Ye should give Ensample to the Lay People to do well, and ye give them Ensample to do evil. For the Commoners, upon Festival Days, when they should go to Church to serve God, then go to Taverns, and be there in Gluttony all the Day and all Night, and eat and drink as Beasts that have no Reason, and wist not when they have had enough. And also the Christian Men strengthen themselves, in all Manners that they may, to fight and deceive the one the other. And therewithal they be so proud, that they know not how to be clothed ; now long, now short, now strait, now large, now sworded, now daggered, and in all manner of Guises. They should be simple, meek and true, and full of Alms-deeds, as Jesu was, in whom they trow ; but they be all the contrary, and ever inclined to Evil, and to do Evil. And they be so covetous, that, for a little Silver, they sell their Daughters, their Sisters and their own Wives to put them to Lechery. And one withdraweth the Wife of another, and none of them holdeth Faith to another ; but they be-foul their Law that Jesu

Christ gave them to keep for their Salvation.   And thus, for their Sins, have they lost all this Land that we hold.   For, for their Sins there, God hath given them into our Hands, not only by Strength of ourselves, but for their Sins.   For we know well, in very Sooth, that when ye serve God, God will help you; and when He is with you, no Man may be against you.   And that know we well by our Prophecies, that Christian Men shall win again this Land out of our Hands, when they serve God more devoutly; but as long as they be of foul and of unclean Living, as they be now, we have Dread of them in no kind, for their God will not help them in any wise."

And then I asked him, how he knew the State of Christian Men.   And he answered me, that he knew all the State of the Commoners also by his Messengers that he sent to all Lands, in manner as though they were Merchants of precious Stones, of Cloths of Gold and of other Things, to know the Manner of every Country amongst Christian Men.

And then he let call in all the Lords that he made void first out of his Chamber, and then he shewed me 4 that were great Lords in the Country, that told me of my Country and of many other Christian Countries, as well as if they had been of the same Countries; and they spake French right well, and the Sultan also; whereof I had great Marvel.

Alas! it is great Slander to our Faith and to our Law, when Folk that be without Law shall reprove us and chide us for our Sins, and that they that should

be converted to Christ and to the Law of Jesu by
our good Ensamples and by our acceptable Life to
God, and so converted to the Law of Jesu Christ,
be, through our Wickedness and evil Living, far from
us and Strangers from the holy and true Belief,
and should thus charge us and hold us for wicked
Livers and cursed.   And truly they say Sooth, for
the Saracens be good and faithful; for they keep
entirely the Commandment of the Holy Book *Al
Koran* that God sent them by His Messenger
Mohammet, to the which, as they say, Saint Gabriel
the Angel oftentime told the Will of God.

And ye shall understand, that Mohammet was
born in Arabia, that was first a poor Knave that
kept Camels, that went with Merchants for Merchandise.   And it so befell, that he went with the
Merchants into Egypt; and they were then Christian in those Parts.   And at the Deserts of Arabia,
he went into a Chapel where a Hermit dwelt.   And
when he entered into the Chapel that was but a
little and low Thing and had but a little Door and a
low, then the Entry began to wax so great, and so
large and so high as though it had been of a great
Minster or the Gate of a Palace.   And this was the
first Miracle, the Saracens say, that Mohammet did
in his Youth.

After began he to wax wise and rich.   And he
was a great Astronomer.   And after, he was Gover-
nor and Prince of the Land of Cozrodane; and he
governed it full wisely, in such manner, that when
the Prince was dead, he took his Lady to Wife that

"THE ENTRY BEGAN TO WAX SO GREAT"

hight Kadija.   And Mohammet fell often in the great Sickness that Men call the Falling Evil; wherefore the Lady was full sorry that ever she took him to Husband.   But Mohammet made her to believe, that all Times, when he fell so, Gabriel the Angel came to speak with him, and for the great Light and Brightness of the Angel he might not sustain him from falling.   And therefore the Saracens say, that Gabriel came often to speak with him.

This Mohammet reigned in Arabia, the Year of our Lord Jesu Christ 610, and was of the Generation of Ishmael that was Abraham's Son, that he gat upon Hagar his Hand-maiden.   And therefore there be Saracens that be clept Ishmaelites; and some Hagarenes, from Hagar.   And other be properly clept Saracens, from Sarah.   And some be clept Moabites and some Ammonites, from the 2 Sons of Lot, Moab and Ammon, that he begat on his Daughters, that were afterward great earthly Princes.

And also Mohammet loved well a good Hermit that dwelled in the Deserts a Mile from Mount Sinai, in the Way that Men go from Arabia toward Chaldea and toward Ind, one Day's Journey from the Sea, where the Merchants of Venice come often for Merchandise.   And so often went Mohammet to this Hermit, that all his Men were wroth; for he would gladly hear this Hermit preach and make his Men wake all Night.   And therefore his Men thought to put the Hermit to Death.   And so it befell upon a Night, that Mohammet was drunken of good Wine, and he fell asleep. And his **Men** took Mohammet's Sword out of his Sheath, whiles he slept, and therewith they slew this Hermit, and put his Sword all bloody in his Sheath again. And

THE GOOD HERMIT

at the Morrow, when he found the Hermit dead, he was full sorry and wroth, and would have done his Men to Death. But they all, with one Accord, said that he himself had slain him, when he was drunk, and shewed him his Sword all bloody. And he trowed that they had said Truth. And then he cursed the Wine and them that drink it. And therefore Saracens that be devout drink never any Wine. But some drink it privily ; for if they drunk it openly, they should be reproved. But they drink good Beverage and sweet and nourishing that is made of Gallamelle and that is what Men make Sugar of, that is of right good Savour, and it is good for the Breast.

Also it befalleth some-time, that Christian Men become Saracens, either for Poverty or for Simpleness, or else for their own Wickedness.   And therefore the Archflamen or the Flamen, like our Archbishop or Bishop, when he receiveth them saith thus; "*La ellec Sila, Machomete Rores alla*,"* that is to say, "*There is no God but one, and Mohammet is His Messenger.*"

* Maundevile's version for "*Lá ildha illá 'llah, Muhammadun rasúlu 'llah !*"

THE FAIR LADY OF
FAERIE AND THE SPARROW-HAWK

CHAPTER XIII

*Of the Lands of Albania and of Libia.   Of the Wishings
for Watching the Sparrow-hawk ; and of
Noah's Ship*

Now, since I have told you before of the Holy
Land and of the Country about, and of many Ways
to go to that Land and to the Mount Sinai, and of
Babylon the Greater and the Less, and other Places

that I have spoken of before,—now is Time, if it like you, to tell you of the Borders and Isles and divers Beasts, and of divers Folk beyond these Borders.

For in those Countries beyond be many diverse Countries and many great Kingdoms, that be parted by the 4 Rivers that come from terrestrial Paradise. For Mesopatamia and the Kingdom of Chaldea and Arabia be between the 2 Rivers of Tigris and of Euphrates. And the Kingdom of Media and Persia be between the Rivers of Nile and of Tigris. And the Kingdom of Syria, whereof I have spoken before, and Palestine and Phœnicia be between Euphrates and the Sea Mediterranean, the which Sea endureth in Length from Morocco upon the Sea of Spain unto the great Sea, so that it lasteth beyond Constantinople 3040 Lombardy Miles.

And toward the Sea Ocean is the Kingdom of Scythia that is all closed with Hills. And after, under Scythia, and from the Sea of Caspian unto the River Thainy, is Amazonia, that is the Land of Females, where that no Man is, but only all Women. And after is Albania, a full great Realm ; and it is clept Albania, because the Folk be whiter there than in any other Borders there-about : and in that Country be so great Hounds and so strong, that they assail Lions and slay them. And then after is Hircania, Bactria, Hiberia and many other Kingdoms.

And between the Red Sea and the Sea Ocean, toward the South is the Kingdom of Ethiopia and of Lybia the Higher, the which Land of Lybia, that is to say, Lybia the Low beginneth at the Sea of Spain from thence where the Pillars of Hercules be, and endureth unto anent Egypt and toward Ethiopia. In that Country of Lybia is the Sea more high than the Land, and it seemeth that it would cover the Earth, and nevertheless it passeth not his Marks. And Men see in that Country a Mountain to which no Man cometh. In this Land of Lybia whoso turneth toward the East, the Shadow of himself is on the right Side; and here, in our Country, the Shadow is on the left Side. In that Sea of Lybia is no Fish; for they may not live nor endure for the great Heat of the Sun, because that the Water is evermore boiling for the great Heat. And many other Lands there be that it were too long to tell or to number. But of some Parts I shall speak more plainly hereafter.

Whoso will then go toward Tartary, toward Persia, toward Chaldea and toward Ind, he must enter the Sea at Genoa or at Venice or at some other Haven that I have told you before. And then Men pass the Sea and arrive at Trebizond that is a good City; and it was wont to be the Haven of Pontus. There is the Haven of Persians and of Medians and of the Borders there beyond. In that City lieth Saint Athanasius that was Bishop of Alexandria, that made the Psalm " *Quicunque vult.*"

This Athanasius was a great Doctor of Divinity. And, because that he preached and spake so deeply of Divinity and of the Godhead, he was accused

to the Pope of Rome that he was an Heretic.
Wherefore the Pope sent after him and put him in
Prison.   And whiles he was in Prison he made that
Psalm and sent it to the Pope, and said, that if he
were an Heretic, that was the Heresy, for that, he
said, was his Belief.   And when the Pope saw it,
and had examined it that it was perfect and good,
and verily our Faith and our Belief, he made him
to be delivered out of Prison, and commanded that
Psalm to be said every Day at Prime, (6 o'clock
A.M.); and so he held Athanasius a good Man.
But he would never go to his Bishopric again, because that they accused him of Heresy.

Trebizond was wont to be held of the Emperor of
Constantinople; but a great Man, that he sent to
keep the Country against the Turks, usurped the
Land and held it to himself, and called himself
Emperor of Trebizond.

And from thence Men go through Little Armenia.
And in that Country is an old Castle that stands
upon a Rock; the which is clept the Castle of the
Sparrow-hawk, that is beyond the City of Layays
beside the Town of Pharsipee, that belongeth to the
Lordship of Cruk, that is a rich Lord and a good
Christian Man; where Men find a Sparrow-hawk
upon a Perch right fair and right well made, and a
Fair Lady of Faerie that keepeth it.   And who
that will watch that Sparrow-hawk 7 Days and 7
Nights, or, as some Men say, 3 Days and 3 Nights,
without Company and without Sleep, that fair Lady
shall give him, when he hath done, the first Wish

M

that he will wish of earthly Things ; and that hath been proved often-times.

And one Time it befell, that a King of Armenia, that was a worthy Knight and doughty Man, and a noble Prince, watched that Hawk some time. And at the End of 7 Days and 7 Nights the Lady came to him and bade him wish, for he had well deserved it. And he answered that he was great Lord enough, and well in Peace, and had enough of worldly Riches ; and therefore he would wish none other Thing, but the Body of that fair Lady, to have it at his Will. And she answered him, that he knew not what he asked, and said that he was a Fool to desire that he might not have ; for she said that he should not ask but an earthly Thing, for she was none earthly Thing, but a ghostly Thing. And the King said that he would ask none other Thing. And the Lady answered ; "Since that I may not withdraw you from your lewd Courage, I shall give you without Wishing, and to all them that shall come of your Lineage. Sir King! ye shall have War without Peace, and always to the 9th Generation ye shall be in Subjection of your Enemies, and ye shall be in Need of all Goods." And never since then, neither the King of Armenia nor the Country were ever in Peace ; neither had they ever since then Plenty of Goods ; and they have been since then always under Tribute of the Saracens.

Also the Son of a poor Man watched that Hawk and wished that he might achieve well, and be

happy in Merchandise.   And the Lady granted it
him.   And he became the most rich and the most
famous Merchant that might be on Sea or on
Earth.   And he became so rich that he knew not
the 1000th Part of that he had.   And he was wiser
in Wishing than was the King.

Also a Knight of the Temple watched there, and
wished a Purse evermore full of Gold.   And the
Lady granted it him.   But she said to him that he
had asked the Destruction of their Order (the
Templars) for the Trust and Affiance of that
Purse, and for the great Pride that they should
have.   And so it was.

And therefore look that he keep him well, that
shall watch.   For if he sleep he is lost, that never
Man shall see him more.

This is not the right Way to go to the Parts that
I have named before, but to see the Marvel that I
have spoken of.   And therefore whoso will go the
right way, Men go from Trebizond toward Armenia
the Great unto a City that is clept Erzeroum, that
was wont to be a good City and a plenteous ; but
the Turks· have greatly wasted it.   There-about
groweth no Wine nor Fruit, or else little or none.
In this Land is the Earth more high than in any
other, and that maketh great Cold.   And there be
many good Waters and good Wells that come
under Earth from the River of Paradise, that is
clept Euphrates, that is a Day's Journey from that
City.   And that River cometh towards Ind under
Earth, and cometh out into the Land of Altazar.

And so pass Men by this Armenia and enter the Sea of Persia.

From that City of Erzeroum go Men to an Hill that is clept Sabissocolle. And there beside is another Hill that Men call Ararat, but the Jews call it Taneez, where Noah's Ship rested, and yet is upon that Mountain. And Men may see it afar in clear Weather. And that Mountain is well a 7 Mile high. And some Men say that they have seen and touched the Ship, and put their Fingers in the Parts where the Fiend went out, when that Noah said, "*Benedicite.*" But they that say such Words, say their Will.* For a Man may not go up the Mountain, for great Plenty of Snow that is always on that Mountain, either Summer or Winter. So that no Man may go up there. Nor never Man did, since the Time of Noah, save a Monk that, by the Grace of God, brought one of the Planks down, that yet is in the Minster at the Foot of the Mountain.

And beside is the City of Dain that Noah founded. And fast by is the City of Any in the which were a 1000 Churches.

But upon that Mountain to go up, this Monk had great Desire. And so upon a Day, he went up. And when he was upward the 3rd Part of the Mountain he was so weary that he might no further, and so he rested him, and fell asleep. And when he awoke he found himself lying at the Foot of the Mountain. And then he prayed devoutly to God

* That is, their wish is father to their speech.

that He would vouchsafe to suffer him go up. And
an Angel came to him, and said that he should go
up. And so he did. And since that Time never none.
Wherefore Men should not believe such Words.

From that Mountain go Men to the City of Thauriso
(Tabreez) that was wont to be clept Faxis, that is a
full fair City and a great, and one of the best that is
in the World for Merchandise; and it is in the Land
of the Emperor of Persia. And Men say that the
Emperor taketh more good in that City for Custom
from Merchandise than doth the richest Christian
King that liveth of all his Realm. For the Toll and

the Custom of his Merchants is without Estimation to be numbered. Beside that City is a Hill of Salt, and of that Salt every Man taketh what he will to salt with, to his Need. There dwell many Christian Men under Tribute of Saracens.

And from that City, Men pass by many Towns and Castles in going toward Ind unto the City of Sadonia, that is a 10 Days' Journey from Thauriso, and it is a full noble City and a great. And there dwelleth the Emperor of Persia in Summer; for the Country is cold enough. And there be good Rivers bearing Ships.

After go Men the way toward Ind by many Days' Journeys, and by many Countries, unto the City that is clept Cassak, that is a full noble City, and a plenteous of Corns and Wines and of all other Goods. This is the City where the 3 Kings met together when they went to seek our Lord in Bethlehem to worship Him and to present Him with Gold, Incense, and Myrrh. And it is from that City to Bethlehem 53 Days' Journey. From that City Men go to another City that is clept Gethe, that is a Day's Journey from the Sea that Men call the Gravelly Sea. That is the best City that the Emperor of Persia hath in all his Land. And they call it there Chardabago* and others call it Vapa. And the Paynims say that no Christian Man may long dwell or endure with his Life in that City, but dieth within short Time; and no Man knoweth the Cause.

* "La Char d'Abago," in the French MS.

After go Men by many Cities and Towns and great Countries that it were too long to tell unto the City of Cornaa that was wont to be so great that the Walls about hold 25 Mile. The Walls shew yet, but it is not all inhabited.

From Cornaa go Men by many Lands and many Cities and Towns unto the Land of Job. And there endeth the Land of the Emperor of Persia.

And if ye will know the Letters of the Persians, and what Names they have, they be such as I last advised you of, but not in sounding of their Words.

THE EMPEROR OF PERSIA

JOB, AS KING OF IDUMEA

CHAPTER XIV

Of the Land of Job; and of his Age. Of the Array of
Men of Chaldea. Of the Land where Women
dwell without Company of Men. Of
the Knowledge and Virtues of
the true Diamond

AFTER the departing from Cornaa, Men enter into
the Land of Job that is a full fair Country and a
plenteous of all Goods. And Men call that Land
the Land of Susiana. In that Land is the City of
Theman.

Job was a Paynim, and he was Son of Aram of Gosre, and held that Land as Prince of that Country. And he was so rich that he knew not the 100th Part of his Goods. And although he were a Paynim, nevertheless he served well God after his Law. And our Lord took his Service to His Pleasure. And when he fell in Poverty he was 78 Year of Age. And after, when God had proved his Patience that it was so great, He brought him again to Riches and to higher Estate than he was before. And after that he was King of Idumea after King Esau, and when he was King he was clept Jobab. And in that Kingdom he lived after that 170 Year.* And so he was of Age, when he died, 248 Year.

In that Land of Job there is no Default of anything that is needful to Man's Body. There be Hills, when Men get great Plenty of Manna in greater Abundance than in any other Country. This Manna is clept Bread of Angels. And it is a white Thing that is full sweet and right delicious, and more sweet than Honey or Sugar. And it cometh of the Dew of Heaven that falleth upon the Herbs in that Country. And it congealeth and becometh all white and sweet. And Men put it in Medicines for the rich to make the Womb lax, and to purge evil Blood. For it cleanseth the Blood and putteth out Melancholy. This Land of Job marcheth with the Kingdom of Chaldea.

This Land of Chaldea is full great. And the Language of that Country is more great in sounding

* Job xlii. 16; 140 years.

than it is in other Parts beyond the Sea. Men pass
to go beyond by the Tower of Babylon the Great,
of the which I have told you before, where that all

the Languages were first
changed. And that is a
4 Days' Journey from
Chaldea. In that Realm
be fair Men, and they go
full n o b l y arrayed in
Clothes of Gold, orfrayed
and apparelled with great
Pearls and precious Stones
full nobly. And the
Women be right foul and

"AND THE WOMEN BE RIGHT FOUL"

evil arrayed.   And they go all bare-foot and clothed
in evil Garments large and wide, but short to the
Knees, and long Sleeves down to the Feet like a
Monk's Frock, and their Sleeves be hanging about
their Shoulders.   And they be black Women foul
and hideous, and truly they be as foul as they be
evil.

In that Kingdom of Chaldea, in a City that is
clept Ur, dwelled Terah, Abraham's Father.   And
there was Abraham born.   And that was in that
Time that Ninus was King of Babylon, of Arabia
and of Egypt.   This Ninus made the City of
Nineveh, the which Noah had begun before.   And
because that Ninus performed it, he called it Nine-
veh after his own Name.   There lieth Tobit the
Prophet, of whom Holy Writ speaketh.   And
from that City of Ur Abraham departed, by the
Commandment of God, from thence, after the Death
of his Father, and led with him Sarah his Wife and
Lot his Brother's Son, because that he had no
Child.   And they went to dwell in the Land of
Canaan in a Place that is clept Shechem.   And this
Lot was he that was saved, when Sodom and
Gomorrah and the other Cities were burnt and
sunken down to Hell, where that the Dead Sea is
now, as I have told you before.   In that Land of
Chaldea they have their own Languages and their
own Letters.

Beside the Land of Chaldea is the Land of
Amazonia.   And in that Realm are all Women
and no Men ; not, as some Men say, that Men may

not live there, but because that the Women will not suffer any Men amongst them to be their Sovereigns.

For sometime there was a King in that Country. And Men married, as in other Countries. And so it befell that the King had War with them of Scythia, the King of which hight Colopeus, that was slain in Battle, and all the good Blood of his Realm. And when the Queen and all the other noble Ladies saw that they were all Widows, and that all royal Blood was lost, they armed them and, as Creatures out of their Wit, they slew all the Men of the Country that were left; for they would that all the Women were Widows as the Queen and they were. And from that Time hitherwards they never would suffer Man to dwell amongst them longer than 7 Days and 7 Nights; nor that any Child that were Male should dwell amongst them longer than he were weaned; and thereon be sent to his Father. And when they will have any Company of Man then they draw them towards the Lands marching next to theirs. And then they have Lovers that use them; and they dwell with them an 8 Days or 10, and then go Home again. And if they have any Boy Child they keep it a certain Time, and then send it to the Father when he can go alone and eat by himself; or else they slay it. And if it be a Female they do away one Pap with an hot Iron. And if it be a Woman of great Lineage they do away the left Pap that they may the better bear a Shield. And if it be a Woman of simple Blood they do away the right Pap, so as to shoot Turkeys with Bows; for they shoot well with Bows.

In that Land they have a Queen that governeth all that Land, and they all be obeissant to her. And always they make her Queen by Election that is most worthy in Arms; for they be right good Warriors and wise, noble and worthy. And they go oftentime in Pay to help other Kings in their Wars, for Gold and Silver as other Soldiers do; and they maintain themselves right rigourously. This Land of Amazonia is an Isle, all environed with the Sea save in 2 Places, where be 2 Entries. And beyond that water dwell the Men that be their Paramours and their Lovers, where they go to solace them when they will.

Beside Amazonia is the Land of Tarmegyte that is a great Country and a full delectable. And for the Goodness of the Country King Alexander first had made there the City of Alexandria, and yet he made 12 Cities of the same Name; but that City is now clept Celsite.

And from that other Coast of Chaldea, toward the South, is Ethiopia, a great Country that stretcheth to the End of Egypt. Ethiopia is parted in 2 principal Parts, that is the East Part and the Meridional Part; the which Meridional Part is clept Mauritania, and the Folk of that Country be black enough and more black than in the tother Part, and they be clept Moors. In that Part is a Well, that in the Day it is so cold, that no Man may drink thereof; and in the Night it is so hot, that no Man may suffer his Hand therein. And beyond that Part, toward the South, to pass by the Sea Ocean, is a great Land and a great Country; but Men may not dwell there for the fervent Burning of the Sun, so passing hot is it in that Country.

In Ethiopia all the Rivers and all the Waters be troubled, and they be somewhat salt for the great Heat that is there. And the Folk of that Country be lightly drunk and have but little Appetite for Meat. And they have commonly the Flux of the Womb. And they live not long. In Ethiopia be many diverse Folk; and Ethiope is clept Cusis. In that Country be Folk that have but one Foot, and they go so fast that it is a Marvel. And the Foot is so large, that it shadoweth all the Body against the Sun, when they will lie and rest them. In Ethiopia, when the Children be young and little, they be all yellow; and, when that they wax of Age, that Yellowness turneth to be all black. In Ethiopia is the City of Saba, and the Land of the which was King one of the 3 Kings that presented Gifts to our Lord in Bethlehem.

From Ethiopia Men go to Ind by many diverse Countries. And Men call the high Ind, Emlak. And Ind is divided in 3 principal Parts; that is, the Greater, that is a full hot Country; and Ind the Less, that is a full temperate Country, that stretcheth to the Land of Media; and the third Part toward the Septentrion is full cold, so that, for pure Cold and continual Frost, the Water becometh Crystal. And upon the Rocks of Crystal grow the

THE FOLK THAT HAVE BUT ONE FOOT

good Diamonds that be of troubled Colour. Yellow Crystal draweth Colour like Oil. And they be so hard, that no Man may polish them. And Men call them Diamonds in that Country, and "*Hamese*" in another Country. Other Diamonds Men find in Arabia that be not so good, and they be more brown and more tender. And other Diamonds also Men find in the Isle of Cyprus, that be yet more tender, and them Men may well polish. And in the Land of Macedonia Men find Diamonds also. But the best and the most precious be in Ind.

And Men find many times hard Diamonds in a Mass that cometh out of Gold, when Men purify it and refine it out of the Mine ; when Men break that Mass in small Pieces, and sometime it happens that Men find some as great as Peas and some less, and they be as hard as those of Ind.

And albeit that Men find good Diamonds in Ind, yet nevertheless Men find them more commonly upon the Rocks in the Sea and upon Hills where the Mine of Gold is. And they grow many together, one little, another great. And there be some of the Greatness of a Bean and some as great as an Hazel Nut. And they be square and pointed of their own Nature, both above and beneath, without Working of Man's Hand. And they grow together, Male and Female. And they be nourished with the Dew of Heaven. And they engender commonly and bring forth small Children, that multiply and grow all the Year. I have often-times assayed, that if a Man keep them with a little of the Rock and wet them with May-dew oft since, they shall grow every Year, and the small will wax great. For right as the fine Pearl congealeth and waxeth great of the Dew of Heaven, right so doth the true Diamond ; and right as the Pearl of his own Nature taketh Roundness, right so the Diamond, by Virtue of God, taketh Squareness. And Men shall bear the Diamond on their left Side, for it is of greater Virtue then, than on the right Side ; for the Strength of their Growing is toward the North, that is the Left side of the World, and the left Part of Man, when he turneth his Face toward the East.

And if you like to know the Virtues of the Diamond, (as Men may find in the " Lapidary,"* that many Men know not), I shall tell you, as they beyond the Sea say and affirm, of whom all Science and all Philosophy cometh. He that beareth the Diamond upon him, it giveth him Hardiness and Manhood, and it keepeth the Limbs of his Body whole. It giveth him Victory of his Enemies in Pleading and in War, if his Cause be rightful. And it keepeth him that beareth it in good Wit. And it keepeth him from Strife and Riot, from Sorrows and from Enchantments, and from Fantasies and Illusions of wicked Spirits. And if any cursed Witch or Enchanter would bewitch him that beareth the Diamond, all that Sorrow and Mischance shall turn to himself through Virtue of that Stone. And also no wild Beast dare assail the Man that beareth it on

* The " Liber Lapidarius," a popular treatise of the Middle Ages on the virtue of precious stones.

him. Also the Diamond should be given freely,
without Coveting and without Buying, and then it
is of greater Virtue.   And it maketh a Man more
strong and more stalwart against his Enemies. And
it healeth him that is lunatic, and him that the Fiend
pursueth or travaileth.   And if Venom or Poison be
brought in Presence of the Diamond, anon it beginneth to wax moist and to sweat.

There be also Diamonds in Ind that be clept
" Violastres," for their Colour is like Violet, or more
brown than Violets, that be full hard and full
precious.   But yet some Men love not them so well
as the other ; but, in sooth, for me, I would love
them as much as the other, for I have seen them
assayed.

Also there is another Manner of Diamonds that
be all white as Crystal, but they be a little more
troubled.   And they be good and of great Virtue,
and they all be square and pointed of their own
Nature.   And some be 6 squared, some 4 squared,
and some 3 as Nature shapeth them.   And therefore when great Lords and Knights go to seek
Worship in Arms, they bear gladly the Diamond
upon them.

I shall speak a little more of the Diamonds,
although I tarry my Matter for a Time, to the End,
that they that know them not, be not deceived
by Charlatans who go through the Country and sell
them.   For whoso will buy Diamonds it is needful
to him that he know them.   Because that Men
counterfeit them often of Crystal that is yellow and

of Sapphires of citron Colour that is yellow also, and of the Sapphire Loupe and of many other Stones. But I tell you these Counterfeits be not so hard; and also the Points will break lightly, and Men may easily polish them. But some Workmen,

"AND MEN LAY THE DIAMOND UPON THE ADAMANT"

for Malice, will not polish them; to that Intent, to make Men believe that they may not be polished. But Men may assay them in this Manner. First cut with them or write with them on Sapphires or Crystals or on other precious Stones. After that, Men take the Adamant that is the Shipman's Stone that draweth the Needle to him, and lay the Needle

before the Adamant; and, if the Diamond be good and virtuous, the Adamant draweth not the Needle to him, whiles the Diamond is there present. And this is the Proof that they beyond the Sea make.

Nevertheless it befalleth often-time, that the good Diamond loseth his Virtue by Sin, and for Incontinence of him that beareth it. And then it is needful to make it recover his Virtue again, or else it is of little Value.

CHAPTER XV

Of the Customs of Isles about Ind. Of the
Difference betwixt Idols and Simulacres. Of
3 Manners of Pepper growing upon one Tree.
Of the Well that changeth his Odour every
Hour of the Day; and that is a Marvel.

N Ind be full many diverse Coun-
tries. And it is clept Ind, from a
River that runneth throughout the
Country that is clept Indus. In
that River Men find Eels of 30
Foot long and more. And the
Folk that dwell nigh that Water be of evil Colour,
green and yellow.

In Ind and about Ind be more than 5000 Isles
good and great that Men dwell in, without those
that be uninhabitable, and without other small Isles.
In every Isle is great Plenty of Cities, of Towns,
and of Folk without Number. For Men of Ind

have this Condition of Nature, that they never go out of their own Country, and therefore is there great Multitude of People. But they be not stirring or movable, because that they be in the First Climate that is of Saturn ; and Saturn is slow and little moving, for he tarryeth to make his Turn by the 12 Signs 30 Year. And the Moon passeth through the 12 Signs in one Month. And because that Saturn is of so late (or tardy) Stirring, therefore the Folk of that Country that be under his Climate have of Nature no Will to move nor stir to seek strange Places. And in our Country is all the contrary ; for we be in the 7th Climate, that is of the Moon. And the Moon is lightly moving, and the Moon is a Planet of Way (or Progression), and for that Reason it giveth us Will of Nature to move lightly and to go divers Ways, and to seek strange Things and Diversities of the World ; for the Moon environeth the Earth more hastily than any other Planet.

Also Men go through Ind by many divers Countries to the great Sea Ocean. And after, Men find there an Isle that is clept Ormuz. And thither come Merchants of Venice and Genoa, and of other Coasts, to buy Merchandises. But there is so great Heat in those Coasts, and especially in that Isle, that, for the great Distress of the Heat, Men suffer from the great Dissolution of the Body. And Men of that Country, that know the Manner, let bind themselves up, or else might they not live, and anoint themselves with Ointments made therefore.

In that Country and in Ethiopia, and in many other Countries, the Folk lie all naked in Rivers and Waters, Men and Women together, from Un-

"THITHER COME MERCHANTS OF VENICE"

durn (9 o'clock) of the Day till it be past the Noon. And they lie all in the Water save the Visage for the great Heat that there is. And the Women have no Shame of the Men, but lie all together, Side to Side, till the Heat be past. There may

Men see many foul Figures assembled, and especially nigh the good Towns.

In that Isle be Ships without Nails of Iron or Bonds, because of the Rocks of the Adamants, of which that Sea is all full thereabout, that it is a Marvel to speak of. And if a Ship passed by those Coasts that had either Iron Bonds or Iron Nails anon he should be perished; for the Adamant of his Nature draweth the Iron to him. And so would it draw to him the Ship because of the Iron, that it should never depart from him, nor ever go thence.

From that Isle Men go by Sea to another Isle that is clept Chana, where is great Plenty of Corn and Wine. And it was wont to be a great Isle, and a great Haven and a good; but the Sea hath greatly wasted it and overcome it. The King of that Country was wont to be so strong and so mighty that he held War against King Alexander.

The Folk of that Country have diverse Laws. For some of them worship the Sun, some the Moon, some the Fire, some Trees, some Serpents, or the first Thing that they meet of a Morning. And some worship Simulacres and some Idols. But between Simulacres and Idols is a great Difference. For Simulacres be Images made after Likeness of Men or of Women, or of the Sun, or of the Moon, or of any Beast, or of any natural Thing. And an Idol is an Image made of lewd Will of Man, that Man may not find among natural Things, as an Image that hath 4 Heads, one of a

Man, another of an Horse or of an Ox, or of some other Beast that no Man hath seen after natural Disposition.

And they that worship Simulacres, they worship them for some worthy Man that was sometime, as Hercules, and many other that did many Marvels in their Time. For they say well that they be not Gods; for they know well that there is a God of Nature that made all Things, the which is in Heaven. But they know well that such an one might not do the Marvels that he made, but if it had been by the special Gift of God; and therefore they say that he was well with God, and because he was so well with God, therefore they worship him. And so say they of the Sun, because that it changeth the Time, and giveth Heat, and nourisheth all Things upon Earth; and because it is of so great Profit, they know well that that might not be, but that God loveth it more than any other Thing, and, for that Reason, God hath given it more great Virtue in the World. Therefore, it is good Reason, as they say, to do it Worship and Reverence. And so say they, that make their Reasons, of other Planets, and of the Fire also, because it is so profitable.

And of Idols they say also that the Ox is the most holy Beast that is in the Earth and most patient, and more profitable than any other. For he doth Good enough and doth no Evil; and they know well that it may not be without special Grace of God. And therefore make they their God of an

Ox the one Part, and the other Half End of a Man.
Because that Man is the most noble Creature in
Earth, and also because he hath Lordship above all
Beasts, therefore make they the Half End of the
Idol a Man upwards ; and the tother Half they make
of an Ox downwards, and of Serpents, and of other
Beasts and divers Things, that they worship, that
they meet first of a Morning.

And they worship also specially all those that
they have good Meeting of when, after their
Meeting, they speed well on their Journey, and
specially such as they have proved and assayed by
Experience of long Time ; for they say that this
same good Meeting may not come but of the Grace
of God. And therefore they make Images like to
those Things that they have Belief in, to behold
them and worship them first of a Morning, ere they
meet any contrarious Things. And there be also
some Christian Men that say, that some Beasts
have good Meeting, that is to say to meet with them
first of a Morning, and some Beasts wicked Meeting, and that they have proved oft-time that the
Hare hath full evil Meeting, and Swine and many
other Beasts. And the Sparrow-hawk and other
Fowls of Rapine, when they fly after their Prey and
take it before Men of Arms, it is a good Sign ; and
if they fail of taking their Prey, it is an evil Sign.
And also to such Folk, it is an evil Meeting of
Ravens.

In these Things and in such other, there be many
Folk that believe, because it happeneth so often-

time to fall after their Fantasies. And also there be Men enough that have no Belief in them. And, since that Christian Men have such Belief, that be informed and taught all Day by holy Doctrine, wherein they should believe, it is no Marvel then, that the Paynims, that have no good Doctrine but only of their Nature, believe more largely for their Simpleness. And truly I have seen Paynims and Saracens that Men call Augurs, that, when we rode in Arms in divers Countries upon our Enemies, they would tell us by the Flying of Fowls the Prognostications of Things that fell after; and so they did full oftentimes, and proffered their Heads to Pledge, that it would fall as they said. But nevertheless, therefore should not a Man put his Belief in such Things, but always have full Trust and Belief in God our Sovereign Lord.

This Isle of Chana the Saracens have won and hold. In that Isle be many Lions and many other wild Beasts. And there be Rats in that Isle as great as Hounds here; and Men take them with great Mastiffs, for Cats may not take them. In this Isle and many others Men bury not any dead Men, for the Heat is there so great, that in a little Time the Flesh will consume from the Bones.

From thence Men go by Sea toward Ind the More to a City, that Men call Sarche, that is a fair City and a good. And there dwell many Christian Men of good Faith. And there be many religious Men, and especially Mendicants.

· After go Men by Sea to the Land of Lomb. In

that Land groweth the Pepper in the Forest that
Men call Combar.   And it groweth nowhere else in
all the World, but in that Forest, and that endureth
well an 18 Days' Journey in Length.   In the
Forest be 2 good Cities ; the one is hight Fladrine
and the other Zinglantz, and in each of them dwell
Christian Men and Jews, great Plenty.   For it is a
good Country and a plentiful, but there is overmuch
passing Heat.

And ye shall understand, that the Pepper groweth
in manner as doth a wild Vine and is planted near
by the Trees of that Wood to sustain it, and hangeth
as doth the Vine.   And the Fruit thereof hangeth
in the manner of Raisins.   And the Tree is so thick
charged, that it seemeth that it would break.   And
when it is ripe it is all green, as it were Ivy Berries.
And then Men cut them, as Men do the Vines, and
then they put them upon an Oven, and there they
wax black and crisp.   And there are 3 Manners of
Pepper all upon one Tree ; Long Pepper, Black Pepper and White Pepper.   The Long Pepper Men call
" *Sorbotin*," and the Black Pepper is clept " *Ful-
fulle*," and the White Pepper is clept " *Bano*."   The
Long Pepper cometh first when the Leaf beginneth
to come, and it is like the Catkins of Hazel that
come before the Leaf, and it hangeth low.   And
after cometh the Black with the Leaf, in manner of
Clusters of Raisins, all green.   And when Men have
gathered it, then cometh the White that is somewhat
less than the Black.   And of that Men bring but little
into this Country ; for they beyond withhold it for

themselves, because it is better and more temperate in its Nature than the Black. And therefore is there not so great Plenty as of the Black.

In that Country be many manner of Serpents and of other Vermin for the great Heat of the Country and of the Pepper. And some Men say, that when they will gather the Pepper, they make Fires, and burn thereabout to make the Serpents and the Cockodrills to flee. But save their Grace of all that say so.* For if they burnt about the Trees that bear, the Pepper would be burnt, and it would dry up all the Virtue, as of any other Thing ; and then would they do themselves much Harm, and they would never quench the Fire. But thus they do: they anoint their Hands and their Feet with a Juice made of Limes and of other Things made therefore, of the which the Serpents and the venomous Beasts hate and dread the Savour ; and that maketh them flee before them, because of the Smell, and they gather the Pepper surely enough.

And toward the Head of that Forest is the City of Polombe. And above the City is a great Mountain that also is clept Polombe. And of that Mount the City hath his Name.

And at the Foot of that Mount is a fair Well and a great, that hath Odour and Savour of all Spices. And at every Hour of the Day he changeth his Odour and his Savour diversely. And whoso drinketh 3 Times fasting of that Water of that Well he is whole of all Manner of Sickness that he

* Maundevile apologises for denying this statement.

hath.   And they that dwell there and drink often of that Well they never have Sickness; and they seem always young.   I have drunken thereof 3 or 4 Times, and, methinketh, I fare the better yet.   Some Men call it the "Well of Youth." For they that often drink thereof seem always young-like, and live without Sickness.   And Men say, that that Well cometh out of Paradise, and therefore it is so virtuous.

By all that Country groweth good Ginger, and therefore thither go the Merchants for Spicery.

In that Land Men worship the Ox for his Simpleness and for his Meekness, and for the Profit that cometh of him.   And they say, that he is the holiest Beast on Earth.   For it seemeth them, that whosoever be meek and patient, he is holy and profitable; for then, they say, he hath all Virtues in him.   They make the Ox to labour 6 Year or 7, and then they eat him.   And the King of the Country hath alway an Ox with him.   And he that keepeth him hath every Day great Fees, and keepeth every Day his Dung and his Urine in 2 Vessels of Gold, and brings it before their Prelate that they call " Archi-proto-papaton."   And he beareth it before the King and maketh there over a great Blessing.   And then the King wetteth his Hands there, in that they call Gall, and anointeth his Fore-head and his Breast. And after, he fretteth him with the Dung and with the Urine with great Reverence, to be filled full of Virtues of the Ox and made holy by the Virtue of that holy Thing that is worth Nought.   And when the King hath done, then do so the Lords; and after them their Ministers and other Men, if they have any remaining.

In that Country they make Idols, half Man half Ox. And in those Idols evil Spirits speak and give

THE ARCHI-PROTOPAPATON

Answer to Men of what is asked them. Before these Idols Men many times slay their Children, and sprinkle the Blood upon the Idols ; and so they make their Sacrifice.

And when any Man dieth in the Country they burn his Body in Name of Penance ; to that Intent, that he suffer no Pain on Earth to be eaten of Worms. And if his Wife have no Child they burn her with him, and say, that the Reason is, that she shall make him Company in that other World as she did in this. But and she have Children by him, they let her live with them, to bring them up if she will. And if that she love more to live with her Children than to die with her Husband, Men hold her for false and cursed ; nor shall she ever be loved or trusted of the People. And if the Woman die before the Husband, Men burn him with her, if that he will ; and if he will not, no Man constraineth him thereto, but he may wed another time without Blame and Reproof.

In that Country grow many strong Vines. And the Women drink Wine, and Men not. And the Women shave their Beards, and the Men not.

"AND THE WOMEN DRINK WINE"

CHAPTER XVI

Of the Judgments made by St. Thomas. Of Devotion and Sacrifice made to Idols there, in the City of Calamye; and of the Procession in the going about the City

THE HAND OF ST. THOMAS

ROM that Country Men pass by many Borders toward a Country, a 10 Days' Journey thence, that is clept Mabaron; and it is a great Kingdom, and it hath many fair Cities and Towns.

In that Kingdom lieth the Body of Saint Thomas the Apostle in Flesh and Bone, in a fair Tomb in the City of Calamye; for there he was martyred and buried. But Men of Assyria bare his Body into Mesopotamia into the City of Edessa, and after, he was brought thither again. And the Arm and the Hand that he put in our Lord's Side, when He appeared to him after His Resurrection and said to him, "*Noli*

THE GREAT IDOL OF MABARON

esse incredulus, set fidelis," (*Be not faithless, but believing,*") are yet lying in a Vessel without the Tomb. And by that Hand they make all their Judgments in the Country, whoso hath Right or Wrong. For when there is any Dissension between 2 Parties, and each of them maintaineth his Cause, and one saith that his Cause is rightful, and that other saith the contrary, then both Parties write their Causes on 2 Bills and put them in the Hand of Saint Thomas. And anon he casteth away the Bill of the wrong Cause and holdeth still the Bill with the right Cause. And therefore Men come from far Countries to have Judgment of doubtable Causes. And other Judgment use they not there.

Also the Church, where Saint Thomas lieth, is both great and fair, and all full of great Simulacres, and those be great Images that they call their Gods, of the which the least is as great as 2 Men.

And, amongst these, there is an Image more great than any of the other, that is all covered with fine gold and precious Stones and rich Pearls ; and that Idol is the God of false Christians that have denied their Faith. And it sitteth in a Chair of Gold, full nobly arrayed, and he hath about his Neck large Girdles wrought of Gold and precious Stones and Pearls. And this Church is full richly wrought and, all over, gilt within. And to that Idol go Men on Pilgrimage, as commonly and with as great Devotion as Christian Men go to Saint James, or on other holy Pilgrimages. And many Folk that come from far Lands to seek that Idol for the great Devotion

that they have, they look never upward, but evermore down to the Earth, for Dread to see anything about them that should hinder them of their Devotion. And some there be that go on Pilgrimage to this Idol, that bear Knives in their Hands, that be made full keen and sharp; and always, as they go, they smite themselves in their Arms and in their Legs and in their Thighs with many hideous Wounds; and so they shed their Blood for Love of that Idol. And they say, that he is blessed and holy, that dieth so for Love of his God. And other there be that lead their Children to slay, to make Sacrifice to that Idol; and after they have slain them they sprinkle the Blood upon the Idol. And some there be that come from far; and in going toward this Idol, at every 3rd Pace that they go from their House, they kneel; and so continue, till they come thither: and when they come there, they take Incense and other aromatic Things of noble Smell, and perfume the Idol, as we would do here God's precious Body. And so come Folk to worship this Idol, some from an 100 Mile, and some from many more.

And before the Minster of this Idol, is a Vivary (or Fish Pool), in manner of a great Lake, full of Water. And therein Pilgrims cast Gold and Silver, Pearls and precious Stones without Number, instead of Offerings. And when the Ministers of that Church need to make any Reparation of the Church or of any of the Idols, they take Gold and Silver, Pearls and precious Stones out of the Vivary, to acquit the Cost of such Thing as they make or repair; so that nothing is faulty, but anon it shall be amended.

And ye shall understand, that when be great Feasts and Solemnities of that Idol, such as the Dedication of the Church and the Throning of the Idol, all the Country about meet there together. And they set this Idol upon a Chariot with great Reverence, well arrayed with Cloths of Gold, of rich Cloths of Tartary, of Camaka, and other precious Cloths. And they lead him about the City with great Solemnity. And before the Chariot go first in Procession all the Maidens of the Country 2 and 2 together full orderly. And after those Maidens go the Pilgrims. And some of them fall down under the Wheels of the Chariot, and let the Chariot go over them, so that they be dead anon. And some have their Arms or their Limbs all broken, and some the Sides. And all this they do for Love of their God, in great Devotion. And they think, that the more Pain, and the more Tribulation that they suffer for Love of their God, the more Joy they shall have in another World. And, shortly to tell you, they suffer so great Pains, and so hard Martyrdoms for Love of their Idol, that a Christian Man, I trow, durst not take upon him the 10th Part of the Pain for Love of our Lord Jesu Christ. And after, I say to you, before the Chariot, go all the Minstrels of the Country without Number, with divers Instruments, and they make all the Melody that they can.

And when they have gone all about the City,

then they return again to the Minster, and put the
Idol again into his Place. And then for the Love
and in Worship of that Idol, and for the Reverence
of the Feast, they slay themselves, a 200 or 300
Persons, with sharp Knives, and bring the Bodies
before the Idol. And then they say that those be
Saints, because that they slew themselves of their
own good Will for Love of their Idol. And as
Men here that had an holy Saint of their Kin would
think that it were to them an high Worship, right
so they think there. And as Men here devoutly
would write holy Saints' Lives and their Miracles,
and make Suit to have them canonised, right so do
they there for them that slay themselves wilfully
for Love of their Idol, and say, that they be
glorious Martyrs and Saints, and put them in their
Writings and in their Litanies, and vaunt them
greatly, one to another, of their holy Kinsmen that
so become Saints, and say, "I have more holy
Saints in my Kindred, than thou in thine!"

And the Custom also there is this, that when he
that hath such Devotion and Intent will slay himself
for Love of his God, they send for all their Friends,
and have great Plenty of Minstrels; and they go
before the Idol leading him that will slay himself for
such Devotion between them, with great Reverence.
And he, all naked, hath a full sharp Knife in his
Hand, and he cutteth a great Piece of his Flesh, and
casteth it in the Face of his Idol, saying his Orisons,
recommending himself to his God. And then he
smiteth himself and maketh great Wounds and

deep, here and there, till he fall down dead.   And
then his Friends present his Body to the Idol.
And then say, singing, " Holy God! behold what
thy true Servant hath done for thee.   He hath forsaken his Wife and his Children and his Riches,
and all the Goods of the World and his own Life
for the Love of thee, and to make the Sacrifice of
his Flesh and of his Blood.   Wherefore, Holy God,
put him among thy best beloved Saints in the Bliss
of Paradise, for he hath well deserved it."   And
then they make a great Fire, and burn the Body.
And then every one of his Friends takes a Quantity
of the Ashes, and keeps them instead of Relics, and
saith that it is a holy Thing.   And they have no
Dread of any Peril whiles they have those holy
Ashes upon them.   And they put his Name in their
Litanies as a Saint.

THE FOLK OF LAMARY SCOFFING
AT SIR JOHN

CHAPTER XVII

*Of the evil Customs used in the Isle of Lamary. And how
the Earth and the Sea be of round Form and Shape,
by Proof of the Star that is clept Antarctic,
that is fixed in the South*

FROM that Country go Men by the Sea Ocean, and
by many divers Isles and by many Countries that
were too long to tell of.

And a 52 Days' Journey from this Land that I have spoken of, there is another Land, that is full great, that Men call Lamary. In that Land is full great Heat. And the Custom there is such, that Men and Women go all naked. And they scorn when they see any strange Folk going clothed. And they say, that God made Adam and Eve all naked, and that no Man should be ashamed of what is after Nature. And they say, that they that be clothed be Folk of another World, or they be Folk that trow not in God. And they say, that they believe in God that formed the World, and that made Adam and Eve and all other Things. And they wed there no Wives, for all the Women there be common and they deny no Man. And they say they sin if they refuse any Man; and so God commanded to Adam and Eve and to All that come of Him, when He said, " *Crescite et multiplicamini, et replete Terram,*" ("*Increase and multiply, and replenish the Earth.*") And therefore may no Man in that Country say, " This is my Wife "; nor no Woman may say, " This my Husband." And when they have Children, they may give them to what Man they will that hath companied with them. And also all the Land is common; for all that a Man holdeth one Year, another Man hath it another Year; and every Man taketh what Part that it liketh him. And also all the Goods of the Land, Corn and all other Things, be common : for nothing there is kept enclosed, nor nothing there is under Lock, and every Man there taketh what he will without

any Contradiction, and one Man there is as rich as another.

But in that Country there is a cursed Custom, for they eat more gladly Man's Flesh than any other Flesh; and yet is that Country abundant of Flesh, of Fish, of Corn, of Gold and Silver, and of all other Goods. Thither go Merchants and bring with them Children to sell to them of the Country, and they buy them. And if they be fat they eat them anon. And if they be lean they feed them till they be fat, and then they eat them. And they say, that it is the best Flesh and the sweetest of all the World.

In that Land, and in many other beyond that, no Man may see the Star Transmontane (or Polar Star,) that is clept the Star of the Sea, that is un-movable and that is toward the North, that we call the Lode-star. But Men see another Star, the contrary (or opposite) to it, that is toward the South, that is clept Antarctic. And right as the Ship-men here take their Advice and govern them by the Lode-star, right so do Ship-men beyond these Parts govern them by the Star of the South, the which Star appeareth not to us. And this Star that is toward the North, that we call the Lode-star, ap-peareth not to them. For which Cause Men may well perceive, that the Land and the Sea be of round Shape and Form; for the Part of the Fir-mament showeth in one Country that sheweth not in another Country. And Men may well prove by Experience and subtle Compassing of Wit, that if a Man found Passages by Ships that would go to search the World, he might go by Ship all about the World and above and beneath.

The which Thing I prove thus after what I have seen. For I have been toward the Parts of Brabant, and beheld by the Astrolabe that the Star that is clept the Transmontane is 53 Degrees high ; and more further in Germany and Bohemia it hath 58 Degrees ; and more further toward the Septentrional (or Northern) Parts it is 62 Degrees of Height and certain Minutes ; for I myself have measured it by the Astrolabe. Now shall ye know, that over against the Transmontane is the tother Star that is clept Antarctic, as I have said before. And those 2 Stars move never, and on them turneth all the Firmament right as doth a Wheel that turneth on his Axle-tree. So that those Stars bear the Firmament in 2 equal Parts, so that it hath as much above as it hath beneath. After this, I have gone toward the Meridional Parts, that is, toward the South, and I have found that in Lybia Men see first the Star Antarctic. And so the more further I have gone in those Countries, the more high I have found that Star ; so that toward the High Lybia it is 18 Degrees of Height and certain Minutes (of the which 60 Minutes make a Degree). After going by Sea and by Land toward this Country of which I have spoken, and to other Isles and Lands beyond that Country, I have found the Star Antarctic 33 Degrees of Height and some Minutes. And if I had had Company and Shipping to go more beyond, I trow well, as certain, that we

should have seen all the Roundness of the Firmament all about. For, as I have said to you before,
the Half of the Firmament is between those 2 Stars,
the which Half-part I have seen. And of the tother
Half-part I have seen, toward the North under the
Transmontane, 62 Degrees and 10 Minutes, and
toward the Meridional Part I have seen under the
Antarctic, 33 Degrees and 16 Minutes. And then,
the Half-part of the Firmament holdeth in all but
180 Degrees. And of those 180, I have seen 62 on
that one Part and 33 on that other Part; in all, 95
Degrees and nigh the Half-part of a Degree. And
so, there faileth not but that I have seen all the
Firmament, save 84 Degrees and the Half·part of a
Degree, and that is not the 4th Part of the Firmament; for the 4th Part of the Roundness of the
Firmament holds 90 Degrees, so there faileth but
5 Degrees and an Half of the 4th Part. And so I
have seen 3 Parts of all the Roundness of the
Firmament and more yet by 5 Degrees and a Half.

By the which I say to you certainly that Men
may environ all the Earth of all the World, as well
underneath as above, and return again to their
Country, if that they had Company and Shipping
and Conduct. And always they should find Men,
Lands and Isles, as well as in this Country. For
wit ye well, that they that be toward the Antarctic,
be straight, Feet against Feet, to them that dwell
under the Transmontane; as well as we and they
that dwell under us be Feet against Feet. For all
the Parts of Sea and of Land have their Opposites,

habitable or passable, and also they of this Half and the beyond Half.

And wit well, that, after what I can perceive and comprehend, the Lands of Prester John, Emperor of Ind, be under us. For in going from Scotland or from England toward Jerusalem Men go upward always. For our Land is in the low Part of the Earth toward the West, and the Land of Prester John is in the low Part of the Earth toward the East. And they have there the Day when we have the Night; and also, on the contrary, they have the Night when we have the Day. For the Earth and the Sea be of round Form and Shape, as I have said before; and as men go upward to one Side, so Men go downward to another Side.

Also ye have heard me say that Jerusalem is in the Midst of the World. And that may Men prove, and shew there by a Spear, that is fixed into the Earth, that sheweth no Shadow on any Side upon the Hour of Midday, when it is Equinox. And that it should be in the Midst of the World, David witnesseth in the Psalter, where he saith, "*Deus operatus est Salutem in Medio Terræ*," ("*God working Salvation in the Midst of the Earth.*") They, then, that depart from the Parts of the West to go toward Jerusalem, as many Days' Journeys as they go upward to go thither, in so many Days' Journeys may they go from Jerusalem unto other Confines of the Superficiality of the Earth beyond. And when Men go beyond those Journeys toward Ind and to the foreign Isles, they are environing

the Roundness of the Earth and of the Sea under
our Country on this Half.

And therefore hath a Thing befallen, as I have
heard recounted many times when I was young,
how a worthy Man departed some-time from our
Countries to go search the World. And so, he
passed Ind and the Isles beyond Ind, where be
more than 5000 Isles. And so long he went by
Sea and Land, and so environed the World by
many Seasons, that he found an Isle where he
heard Folk speak his own Language, calling on
Oxen at the Plough, such Words as Men speak to
Beasts in his own Country; whereof he had great
Marvel, for he knew not how it might be. But I
say, that he had gone so long by Land and by Sea,
that he had environed all the Earth; and environing. that is to say, going about, he was come again
unto his own Borders; and if he would have passed
further, he had found his Country and Things
well-known. But he turned again from thence,
from whence he was come. And so he lost much
painful Labour, as he himself said a great while
after, when that he was come Home. For it befell
after, that he went unto Norway. And there a
Tempest of the Sea took him, and he arrived in an
Isle. And, when he was in that Isle, he knew well
that it was the Isle, where he had heard speak his
own Language before and the calling of the Oxen
at the Plough; and that was a possible Thing.

But now it seemeth to simple Men unlearned,
that Men may not go under the Earth, and also that

HE HEARD FOLK CALLING ON OXEN

Men should fall toward the Heaven from under.
But that may not be, any more than we may fall
toward Heaven from the Earth where we be. For
on whatever Part of the Earth that Men dwell,
either above or beneath, it seemeth always to them,
that they go more up-right than any other Folk.
And right as it seemeth to us that they be under us,
right so it seemeth to them that we be under them.
For if a Man might fall from the Earth unto the
Firmament, by greater Reason the Earth and the
Sea that be so great and so heavy should fall to the
Firmament: but that may not be, and therefore
saith our Lord God, "*Non timeas Me, qui suspendi
Terram ex Nihilo*," ("*Have no Dread of Me, that
hanged the Earth from Nought.*)

And albeit that it be a possible Thing that Men
may so environ all the World, nevertheless, of a
1000 Persons, not one might happen to return to
his Country. For, for the Greatness of the Earth
and of the Sea, Men may go by a 1000 and a 1000
other Ways, so that no Man could return perfectly
toward the Parts that he came from, but if it were
by Adventure and Hap, or by the Grace of God.
For the Earth is full large and full great, and
holds in Roundness and Environment about, by
above and by beneath, 20425 Miles, after the
Opinion of the old wise Astronomers; and their
Sayings I reprove nought. But, after my little
Wit, it seemeth me, saving their Reverence, that it
is more.

And to have better Understanding I say thus.

Be there imagined a Figure that hath a great Compass. And, about the Point of the great Compass that is clept the Centre, be made another little Compass. Then after, be the great Compass divided by Lines in many Parts, and let all the Lines meet at the Centre. So, that in as many Parts as the great Compass shall be parted, in so many shall be parted the little Compass that is about the Centre, albeit that the Spaces be less. Now then, let the great Compass represent the Firmament, and the little compass represent the Earth. Now then, the Firmament is divided by Astronomers into 12 Signs, and every Sign is divided into 30 Degrees; that is, 360 Degrees that the Firmament hath above. Also, be the Earth divided into as many Parts as the Firmament, and let every Part answer to a Degree of the Firmament. And wit well, that, after the Authors of Astronomy, 700 Furlongs of the Earth answer to a Degree of the Firmament, and those be 87 Miles and 4 Furlongs. Now be that multiplied by 360 Times, and then they be 31,500 Miles of 8 Furlongs, after the Miles of our Country. So much hath the Earth in Roundness and in going round about, after mine Opinion and mine Understanding.

And ye shall understand, that after the Opinion of old wise Philosophers and Astronomers, neither our Country nor Ireland nor Wales nor Scotland nor Norway nor the other Isles coasting to them be in the Superficiality counted above the Earth, as it sheweth by all the Books of Astronomy. For the

The Old Wise Astronomers

Superficiality of the Earth is parted in 7 Parts for the 7 Planets, and those Parts be clept Climates. And our Parts be not of the 7 Climates, for they be descending toward the West. And also these Isles of Ind which be evenly over against us be not reckoned in the Climates. For they be over against us that be in the low Country. And the 7 Climates environing stretch them round the World.

AN OLD WISE PHILOSOPHER

CHAPTER XVIII

Of the Palace of the King of the Isle of Java. Of the
Trees that bear Meal, Honey, Wine, and Venom;
and of other Marvels and Customs used in
the Isles marching thereabout

WOMAN OF SUMOBOR

ESIDE that Isle that I have spoken of, there is another Isle that is clept Sumobor that is a great Isle. And the King thereof is right mighty. The Folk of that Isle make them always to be marked in the Visage with an hot Iron, both Men and Women, for great Noblesse, to be known from other Folk; for they hold themselves most noble and most worthy of all the World. And they have War always with the Folk that go all naked.

And fast beside is another Isle, that is clept Betemga, that is a good Isle and a plentiful. And many other Isles be thereabout, where there be many divers Folk, of the which it were too long to speak of all.

But fast beside that Isle, to pass by Sea, is a great Isle and a great Country that Men call Java. And it is nigh 2000 Mile in Circuit. And the King of that Country is a full great Lord and a rich and a mighty, and hath under him 7 other Kings of 7 other Isles about him. This Isle is full well inhabited, and full well manned. There groweth all manner of Spicery, more plentifully than in any other Country, as Ginger, Cloves-gilofre, Cinnamon, Seedwall, Nutmegs and Maces. And wit well, that the Nutmeg beareth the Maces; for right as the Nut of the Hazel hath an Husk without, that the Nut is closed in till it be ripe and that after falleth out, right so it is with the Nutmeg and with the Maces. Many other Spices and many other Goods grow in that Isle. For of all things there is Plenty, save only of Wine. But there is Gold and Silver, great Plenty.

And the King of that Country hath a Palace full noble and full marvellous, and more rich than any in the World. For all the Steps to go up into the Halls and Chambers be, one of Gold, another of Silver. And also, the Pavements of Halls and Chambers be all in Squares, one of Gold, and another of Silver. And all the Walls within be covered with Gold and Silver in fine Plates, and in those Plates

be Stories and Battles of Knights inlaid, and the
Crowns and the Circles about their Heads be made
of precious Stones and rich Pearls and great. And
the Halls and the Chambers of the Palace be all
covered within with Gold and Silver, so that no
Man would believe the Riches of that Palace but he
had seen it. And wit well, that the King of that
Isle is so mighty, that he hath many times overcome
the great Chan of Cathay in Battle, that is the most
great Emperor that is under the Firmament either
beyond the Sea or on this Half. For they have
had often-time War between them, because that the
great Chan would constrain him to hold his Land of
him ; but that other at all times defendeth him well
against him.

After that Isle, in going by Sea, Men find another
Isle, good and great, that Men call Pathen that is a
great Kingdom full of fair Cities and full of Towns.
In that Land grow Trees that bear Meal, whereof
Men make good Bread and white and of good
Savour ; and it seemeth as it were of Wheat, but it
is not altogether of such Savour. And there be
other Trees that bear Honey good and sweet, and
other Trees that bear Venom, against the which
there is no Medicine but one ; and that is to take
their own Leaves and stamp them and temper them
with Water and then drink it, and else shall a Man
die ; for Triacle* will not avail, nor any other Medicine.
For this Venom the Jews had made one of their

* A particular composition in ancient Medicine ; French, Theri-
aque ; of which Triacle is a corruption.

Friends seek to em-poison all Christianity, as I have heard them say in their Confession before they die : but thanked be Almighty God! they failed

" MEN HEW THE TREES WITH AN HATCHET "

of their Purpose ; but always they make great Mor- tality of People.   And other Trees there be also that bear Wine of noble Scent.   And if you like to hear how the Meal cometh out of the Trees I shall tell you.   Men hew the Trees with an Hatchet, all about the Foot of the Tree, till that the Bark be

parted in many Parts, and then cometh out thereof
a thick Liquor, the which they receive in Vessels,
and dry it at the Heat of the Sun; and then they
take it to a Mill to grind and it becometh fair Meal
and white. And the Honey and the Wine and the
Venom be drawn out of other Trees in the same
Manner, and put in Vessels to keep.

In that Isle is a dead Sea, that is a Lake that
hath no Bottom; and if anything fall into that Lake
it shall never come up again. In that Lake grow
Reeds, that be Canes, that they call " Thaby," that be
30 Fathoms long; and of these Canes Men make
fair Houses. And there be other Canes that be
not so long, that grow near the Land and have so
long Roots that they endure well a 4th of a Furlong
or more; and at the Knots of those Roots Men find
precious Stones that have great Virtues. And he
that beareth any of them upon him, Iron and Steel
may not hurt him nor draw any Blood from him;
and therefore, they that have those Stones upon
them fight full hardily both on Sea and Land, for
Men may not harm them in any Part. And therefore, they that know the Manner, and shall fight
with them, they shoot at them Arrows and Cross-
bow Bolts without Iron or Steel, and so they hurt
them and slay them. And also of those Canes they
make Houses and Ships and other Things, as we do
here, making Houses and Ships of Oak or of any
other Trees. And deem no Man that I say it for
Trifling, for I have seen the Canes with mine own
Eyes, full many times, lying upon the River of that

Lake, of the which 20 of our Fellows might not lift
up nor bear one to the Earth.

After this Isle Men go by Sea to another Isle that
is clept Calonak.   And it is a fair Land and plentiful
of Goods.   And the King of that Country hath as
many Wives as he will.   For he maketh Search all
the Country to get him the fairest Maidens that may
be found, and maketh them to be brought before
him.   And he taketh one one Night, and another
another Night, and so forth continually following;
so that he hath a 1000 Wives or more.   And he
lieth never but one Night with one of them, and
another Night with another ; unless that one happen
to be more lusty to his Pleasure than another.   And
therefore the King getteth full many Children,
some-time an 100, some-time a 200, and some-time
more.   And he hath also up to 14,000 Elephants
or more that he maketh to be brought up amongst
his Villains (or Serfs) in all his Towns.   For in
Case that he had any War against any other King
about him, then he maketh certain Men of Arms to
go up into the Castles of Tree made for the War,
that craftily be set upon the Elephants' Backs, to
fight against their Enemies.   And so do other Kings
there-about.   For the Manner of War is not there
as it is here or in other Countries, nor the Ordinance of War neither.   And Men call the Elephants
" *Warkes.*"

And in that Isle there is a great Marvel, more to
speak of than in any other Part of the World.   For
all Manner of Fishes, that be there in the Sea about

them, come once in the Year—each Manner of diverse Fishes, one Manner of Kind after another. And they cast themselves on to the Sea Bank of that Isle in so great Plenty and Multitude, that a Man can scarcely see ought but Fish. And there they abide 3 Days. And every Man of the Country taketh of them as many as he liketh. And after, that Manner of Fish after the 3rd day departeth and goeth into the Sea. And after them come another Multitude of Fish of another Kind and do in the same Manner as the first did, another 3 Days. And after them another, till all the diverse Manner of Fishes have been there, and that Men have taken of them what they like. And no Man knoweth the Cause wherefore it may be. But they of the Country say that it is to do Reverence to their King, that is the most worthy King that is in the World as they say ; because that he fulfilleth the Commandment that God bade to Adam and Eve, when God said, *" Crescite et multiplicamini et replete Terram "* (*Increase and multiply, and replenish the Earth."*) And because he multiplies the World so with Children, therefore God sendeth him so the Fishes of diverse Kinds of all that be in the Sea, to take at his Will for him and all his People. And therefore all the Fishes of the Sea come to make him Homage as the most noble and excellent King of the World, and that is best beloved of God, as they say. I know not the Reason, why it is, but God knoweth; but this, me-seemeth, is the most great Marvel that ever I saw. For this Marvel is against

Nature and not with Nature, that the Fishes that have Freedom to environ all the Coasts of the Sea at their own List, come of their own Will to proffer themselves to the Death, without Constraining of Man.   And therefore, I am sure that this may not be, unless it be a great Token.

There be also in that Country a Kind of Snails that be so great, that many Persons may lodge them in their Shells, as Men would do in a little House. And other Snails there be that be full great but not so huge as the other.   And of these Snails, and of great white Worms that have black Heads that be as great as a Man's Thigh, and of some less great Worms that Men find there in Woods, Men make Royal Viaunds for the King and for other great Lords.   And if a Man that is married die in that Country, Men bury his Wife with him all alive ; for Men say there, that it is reasonable that she make him Company in that other World as she did in this.

From that Country Men go by the Sea Ocean by an Isle that is clept Caffolos.   Men of that Country when their Friends be sick hang them upon Trees, and say that it is better that Birds, that be Angels of God, eat them, than the foul Worms of the Earth.

From that Isle Men go to another Isle, where the Folk be of full cursed Nature.   For they nourish great Dogs and teach them to strangle their Friends when they be sick.   For they will not that they die of a natural Death.   For they say, that they should suffer

too great Pain if they wait to die by themselves, as
Nature would.   And, when they be thus strangled,
they eat their Flesh instead of Venison.

Afterward Men go by many Isles by Sea unto an
Isle that Men call Milke.   And there is a full cursed
People.   For they delight in nothing more than to
fight and to slay Men.   And they drink gladliest
Man's Blood, the which they call " Dieu."   And the
more Men that a Man may slay, the more Worship
he hath amongst them.   And if 2 Persons be at
Debate and, peradventure, make Accord with their
Friends or with some of their Alliance, it behoveth
that every one of them, that shall be of Accord,
shall drink of the other's Blood : and else neither
the Accord nor the Alliance is worth ought ; neither
shall there be any Blame to him that breaks the
Alliance and the Accord, unless every one of them
drink of the others' Blood.

And from that Isle Men go by Sea, from Isle to
Isle, unto an Isle that is clept Tracoda, where the
Folk of that Country be as Beasts, and unreasonable,
and dwell in Caves that they make in the Earth ;
for they have no Wit to make them Houses.   And
when they see any Man passing through their
Countries they hide them in their Caves.   And they
eat Flesh of Serpents, and they eat but little.   And
they speak Nought, but they hiss as Serpents do.
And they set no Price on any Riches, but only on a
precious Stone, that is amongst them, that is of 60
Colours.   And from the Name of the Isle, they call
it Tracodon.   And they love more that Stone than

THE DOG-HEADED FOLK ELECTING THEIR KING.

anything else ; and yet they know not the Virtue thereof, but they covet it and love it only for the Beauty.

After that Isle Men go by the Sea Ocean, by many Isles, unto an Isle that is clept Nacumera, that is a great Isle and good and fair. And it is in Compass about, more than a 1000 Mile. And all the Men and Women of that Isle have Hounds' Heads, and they be clept Cunocephali. And they be full reasonable and of good Understanding, save that they worship an Ox for their God. And also every one of them beareth an Ox of Gold or of Silver in his Forehead, in Token that they love well their God. And they go all naked save a little Clout, that they cover them with to their Knees. They be great Folk and well-fighting. And they have a great Targe that covereth all the Body, and a Spear in their Hand to fight with. And if they take any Man in Battle, anon they eat him.

The King of that Isle is full rich and full mighty and right devout after his Law. And he hath about his Neck 300 orient Pearls, good and great and knotted, as Pater-nosters here of Amber. And in manner as we say our *Pater Noster* and our *Ave Maria*, counting the *Pater Nosters*, right so this King saith every Day devoutly 300 Prayers to his God, ere that he eat. And he beareth also about his Neck an orient Ruby, noble and fine, that is a Foot of Length and 5 Fingers large. And, when they choose their King, they take him that Ruby to bear in his Hand ; and so they lead him, riding all about the City. And from thence-forward they be all obeissant to him. And that Ruby he shall bear always about his Neck, for if he had not that Ruby upon him Men would not hold him for King. The great Chan of Cathay hath greatly coveted that Ruby, but he might never have it for War, nor for any manner of Goods. This King is so rightful and of such Equity in his Judgments, that Men may go securely throughout all his Country and bear with them what they list; so that no Man shall be so hardy as to rob them, and if he were, the King would judge him anon.

From this Land Men go to another Isle that is clept Silha (Ceylon). And it is well an 800 Mile about. In that Land is full much Waste, for it is full of Serpents, of Dragons and of Cockodrills, so that no Man dare dwell there. These Cockodrills be Serpents, yellow and rayed above, and have 4 Feet and short Thighs, and great Nails like Claws or Talons. And there be some that have 5 Fathoms of Length, and some of 6 and of 8 and of 10. And when they go by Places that be gravelly, it seemeth as though Men had drawn a great Tree through the gravelly Place. And there be also many wild Beasts, and especially Elephants.

In that Isle is a great Mountain. And in mid Place of the Mount is a great Lake in a full fair Plain; and there is great Plenty of Water. And they of the Country say, that Adam and Eve wept upon that Mount an 100 Year, when they were driven out of Paradise, and that Water, they

say, is of their Tears; for so much Water they
wept, that they made the aforesaid Lake.   And in
the Bottom of that Lake Men find many precious
Stones and great Pearls.   In that Lake grow many
Reeds and great Canes; and there within be many
Cockodrills and Serpents and great Water-leeches.
And the King of that Country, once every Year,
giveth Leave to poor Men to go into the Lake to
gather them precious Stones and Pearls, by way of
Alms, for the Love of God that made Adam.   And
every Year Men find enough.   And because of the
Vermin that is within, they anoint their Arms and
their Thighs and Legs with an Ointment made of a
Thing that is clept Limes, that is a manner of
Fruit like small Pease; and then have they no
Dread of Cockodrills, or of any other venomous
Vermin.   This Water runneth, flowing and ebbing,
by a Side of the Mountain, and in that River Men
find precious Stones and Pearls, great Plenty.
And Men of that Isle say commonly, that the
Serpents and the wild Beasts of that Country will
do no Harm nor touch with Evil any strange Man
that entereth into that Country, but only Men that
be born of the same Country.

In that Country and others thereabout there be
Wild Geese that have 2 Heads.   And there be
Lions, all white and as great as Oxen, and many
other diverse Beasts and Fowls also that be not
seen amongst us.

And wit well, that in that Country and in other
Isles thereabout, the Sea is so high, that it seemeth

as though it hangs on the Clouds, and that it would cover all the World. And that is a great Marvel that it might be so, save only that by the Will of God, the Air sustaineth it. And therefore saith David in the Psalter, "*Mirabiles Elationes Maris*" ("*The wonderful Upliftings of the Sea*").

THE FLAT FACED FOLK

AND THEY HAVE BUT ONE EYE

CHAPTER XIX

How Men know by the Idol, if the Sick shall die or not.
Of Folk of diverse Shape and marvellously dis-
figured. And of the Monks that give their
Leavings to Baboons, Apes and Mar-
mosets, and to other Beasts

FROM that Isle, in going by the Sea toward the
South, is another great Isle that is clept Dondun.
In that Isle be Folk of diverse Kinds, so that the
Father eateth the Son, the Son the Father, the
Husband the Wife, and the Wife the Husband.
And if it so befall, that the Father or Mother or any
of their Friends be sick, anon the Son goeth to the
Priest of their Law and prayeth him to ask the Idol

if his Father or Mother or Friend shall die of that Evil or not. And then the Priest and the Son go together before the Idol and kneel full devoutly and ask of the Idol their Demand. And if the Devil that is within answer that he shall live, they keep him well; and if he say that he shall die, then the Priest goeth with the Son, with the Wife of him that is sick, and they put their Hands upon his Mouth and stop his Breath, and so they slay him. And after that, they chop all the Body in small Pieces, and pray all his Friends to come and eat of him that is dead. And they send for all the Minstrels of the Country and make a solemn Feast. And when they have eaten the Flesh, they take the Bones and bury them, and make great Melody. And all those that be of his Kin or pretend themselves to be his Friends, and who come not to that Feast, they be reproved for ever and ashamed, and make great Dole, for never after shall they be holden as Friends. And they say also, that Men eat their Flesh to deliver them out of Pain; for if the Worms of the Earth eat them the Soul should suffer great Pain, as they say. And especially when the Flesh is tender and meagre, then say their Friends, that they do great Sin to let them have so long Languor to suffer so much Pain without Reason. And when they find the Flesh fat, then they say, that it is well done to send him soon to Paradise, and that they have not suffered him too long to endure in Pain.

The King of this Isle is a full great Lord and a mighty, and hath under him 54 great Isles that give

Tribute to him.   And in every one of these Isles is a King crowned ; and all be obeissant to that King. And he hath in those Isles many divers Folk.

In one of these Isles be Folk of great Stature, as Giants.   And they be hideous to look upon.   And

"THEIR EYES AND THEIR MOUTHS BE BEHIND IN THEIR SHOULDERS"

they have but one Eye, and that is in the Middle of the Forehead.   And they eat nothing but raw Flesh and raw Fish.

And in another Isle toward the South dwell Folk of foul Stature and of cursed Nature that have no Heads.   And their Eyes be in their Shoulders, and their Mouths be round shapen, like an Horse-shoe, amidst their Breasts.

And in another Isle be Men without Heads, and

their Eyes and their Mouths be behind in their Shoulders.

And in another Isle be Folk that have the Face all flat, all plain, without Nose and without Mouth. But they have 2 small Holes, all round, instead of their E y e s, and their Mouth is flat also without Lips.

THE BIG-LIPPED FOLK

And in another Isle be Folk of foul Fashion and Shape that have the Lip above the Mouth so great, that when they sleep in the Sun they cover all the Face with that Lip.

And in another Isle there be Little Folk, as Dwarfs. And they be so small as the Pigmies. And they have no Mouth; but instead of their Mouth they have a little round Hole, and when they shall eat or drink, they take through a Pipe or Pen or such a Thing. and suck it in, for they have no Tongue; and therefore they speak not, but they make a manner of Hissing as an Adder doth, and they make Signs to one another as Monks do, by the which every one of them understandeth the other.

And in another Isle be Folk that have great Ears and long that hang down to their Knees.

And in another Isle be Folk that have Horses' Feet. And they be strong and mighty, and swift

"THEY HAVE GREAT EARS"

Runners; for they take wild Beasts with Running, and eat them.

And in another Isle be Folk that go upon their Hands and their Feet as Beasts. And they be all skinned and feathered, and they would leap as lightly into Trees, and from Tree to Tree, as it were Squirrels or Apes.

And in another Isle be Folk that be both Man
and Woman, and they have the Nature of the one
and of the other. And they have but one Pap on
the one Side, and on the other none. And they be
both Men and Women when they list, at one Time
the one, and another Time the other. And they
beget Children, when they be Men ; and they bear
Children, when they be Women.

And in another Isle be Folk that go always upon
their Knees full marvellously. And at every Pace
that they go, it seemeth that they would fall. And
they have in every Foot 8 Toes.

Many other diverse Folk of diverse Natures be
there in other Isles about, of the which it were too
long to tell, and therefore I pass over shortly.

From these Isles, in passing by the Sea Ocean
toward the East by many Days' Journeys, Men find
a great Country and a great Kingdom that Men call
Mancy. And that is in Ind the More. And it is
the best Land and one of the fairest that may be in
all the World, and the most delectable and the most
plentiful of all Goods that is in the Power of Man.
In that Land dwell many Christian Men and
Saracens, for it is a good Country and a great.
And there be therein more than 2000 great Cities
and rich, besides other great Towns. And there is
more Plenty of People there than in any other Part
of Ind, for the Bountifulness of the Country. In
that Country is no needy Man, nor any one that
goeth a-begging. And they be full fair Folk, but
they be all pale. And the Men have thin Beards

and few Hairs, but they be long ; but scarcely hath any Man passing 50 Hairs in his Beard, and one Hair sits here, another there, as the Beard of a Leopard or of a Cat.   In that Land be many fairer Women than in any other Country beyond the Sea, and therefore Men call that Land Albany, because that the Folk be white.

And the chief City of that Country is clept Latorin, and it is a Day's Journey from the Sea, and it is much greater than Paris.   In that City is a great River bearing Ships that go to all the Coasts in the Sea.   No City of the World is so well stored of Ships as is that.   And all those of the City and of the Country worship Idols.   In that Country be double times more Birds than be here.   There be white Geese, red about the Neck, and they have a great Crest as a Cock's Comb upon their Heads ; and they be much more great there than they be here, and Men buy them there all alive, right greatly cheap.   And there is Plenty of Adders of whom Men make great Feasts and eat them at great Solemnities ; and he that maketh there a Feast be it never so costly, if he have no Adders he hath no Thank for his Travail.

Many good Cities there be in that Country and Men have great Plenty and great Cheapness of all Wines and Victuals.   In that Country be many Churches of religious Men, and of their Law.   And in those Churches be Idols as great as Giants ; and to these Idols they give to eat at great Festival Days in this Manner.   They bring before them

Meats all sodden, as hot as they come from the Fire, and they let the Smoke go up towards the Idols ; and then they say that the Idols have eaten ; and then the religious Men eat the Meat afterwards.

In that Country be white Hens without Feathers, but they bear white Wool as Sheep do here. In that Country Women that be unmarried, they have Tokens on their Heads like Garlands to be known for unmarried. Also in that Country there be Beasts taught of Men to go into Waters, into Rivers and into deep Tanks to take Fish ; the which Beast is but little, and Men call them Loirs. And when Men cast them into the Water, anon they bring up great Fishes, as many as Men would. And if Men will have more, they cast them in again, and they bring up as many as Men list to have.

And from that City, passing by many Days' Journeys is another City, one of the greatest in the World, that Men call Cassay ; * that is to say, the "City of Heaven." That City is well a 50 Mile about, and it is strongly inhabited with People, insomuch that in one House Men make 10 Households. In that City be 12 principal Gates ; and before every Gate, a 3 Mile or a 4 Mile in Length therefrom, is a great Town or a great City. That City sits upon a great Lake on the Sea, as doth Venice. And in that City be more than 12,000 Bridges. And upon every Bridge be strong Towers and good, in the which dwell the Wardens to keep

* Called by Marco Polo, " Kinsai," the capital of Southern China under the Song Dynasty.

the City from the great Chan. And on the one Side
of the City runneth a great River all along the City.
And there dwell Christian Men and many Merchants
and other Folk of divers Nations, because that
the Land is so good and so plentiful. And there
groweth full good Wine that Men call "Bigon," that
is full mighty, and gentle in drinking. This is a
Royal City where the King of Mancy was wont to
dwell. And there dwell many religious Men, as it
were of the Order of Friars, for they be Mendicants.

From that City Men go by Water, solacing and
disporting them, till they come to an Abbey of
Monks that is fast by, that be good religious Men
after their Faith and Law. In that Abbey is a
great Garden and a fair, where be many Trees of
diverse Manner of Fruits. And in this Garden is a
little Hill full of delectable Trees. In that Hill and
in that Garden be many diverse Beasts, as Apes,
Marmosets, Baboons and many other diverse
Beasts. And every Day, when the Convent of this
Abbey hath eaten, the Almoner makes bear the
Leavings to the Garden, and he smiteth on the
Garden Gate with a Clicket of Silver that he
holdeth in his Hand; and anon all the Beasts of
the Hill and of diverse Places of the Garden come
out a 3000, or a 4000; and they come in Guise of
poor Men, and Men give them the Leavings in fair
Vessels of Silver, cleanly over-gilt. And when
they have eaten, the Monk smiteth eftsoons on the
Garden Gate with the Clicket, and then anon all

the Beasts return again to their Places that they come from. And they say that these Beasts be Souls of worthy Men that resemble in Likeness the Beasts that be fair, and therefore they give them Meat for the Love of God; and the other Beasts that be foul, they say be Souls of poor Men and of rude Common-folk. And thus they believe, and no Man may put them out of this Opinion. These Beasts above-said they take when they be young, and nourish them so with Alms, as many as they may find. And I asked them if it had not been better to have given those Leavings to poor Men, rather than to the Beasts. And they answered me and said, that they had no poor Men amongst them in that Country; and though it had been so that poor Men had been among them, yet were it greater Alms to give it to those Souls that do there their Penance. Many other Marvels be in that City and in the Country thereabout, that were too long to tell you.

From that City go Men by the Country a 6 Days' Journey to another City that Men call Chilenfo, of the which City the Walls be 20 Mile about. In that City be 60 Bridges of Stone, so fair that no Man may see fairer. In that City was the first Siege of the King of Mancy, for it is a fair City and plentiful of all Goods.

After, pass Men overthwart a great River that Men call Dalay. And that is the greatest River of fresh Water that is in the World. For there, where it is most narrow, it is more than 4 Mile of Breadth.

And then enter Men again into the Land of the great Chan.

That River goeth through the Land of Pigmies, where that the Folk be of little Stature, and be but 3 Span long, and they be right fair and gentle, after their Size, both the Men and the Women. And they marry them when they be half a Year of Age and get Children. And they live not but 6 Year or 7 at the most ; and he that liveth 8 Year, Men hold him there right passing old. These Men be Workers of Gold, Silver, Cotton, Silk and of all such Things, the best of any other that be in the World. And they have often-times War with the Birds of that Country that they take and eat. This Little Folk neither labour in Lands nor in Vines ; but they have great Men amongst them of our Stature that till the Land and labour amongst the Vines for them. And of those Men of our Stature have they as great Scorn and Wonder as we would have among us of Giants if they were amongst us. There is a good City, amongst others, where there is dwelling great Plenty of those Little Folk, and it is a great City and a fair. And there be great Men that dwell amongst them, but when they get any Children they be as little as the Pigmies. And therefore they be, all for the most part, all Pigmies ; for the Nature of the Land is such. The great Chan makes keep this City full well, for it is his. And albeit, that the Pigmies be little, yet they be full reasonable according to their Age, and know enough both of Good and of Evil.

From that City go Men by the Country by many Cities and many Towns unto a City that Men call Jamchay; and it is a noble City and a rich and of great Profit to the Lord thereof, and thither go Men to seek Merchandise of all manner of Thing. That City is full much worth yearly to the Lord of the Country. For he hath every Year as Rent of that City, as they of the City say, 50,000 Cumants of Florins of Gold: for they count there all by Cumants, and every Cumant is 10,000 Florins of Gold. Now Men may well reckon how much that it amounteth to. The King of that Country is full mighty, and yet he is under the great Chan. And the great Chan hath under him 12 such Provinces. In that Country in the good Towns is a good Custom: for there be certain Inns in every good Town, and whoso will make a Feast to any of his Friends, he that will make the Feast will say to the Hosteler (or Innkeeper), "Array for me to-morrow a good Dinner for so many Folk," and telleth him the Number, and deviseth him the Viands; and he saith also, "Thus much will I spend and no more." And anon the Hosteler arrayeth for him so fair and so well and so honestly, that there shall lack nothing; and it shall be done sooner and with less Cost than if a Man made it in his own House.

And a 5 Mile from that City, toward the Head of the River of Dalay, is another City that Men call Menke. In that City is a strong Navy of Ships. And all be as white as Snow like the Trees that they be made of. And they be full great Ships and fair,

THE MARVELLOUS NAVY OF MENKE

and well-ordained, and made with Halls and Chambers and other Easements, as though it were on the Land.

From thence go Men, by many Towns and many Cities, through the Country, unto a City that Men call Lanterine. And it is an 8 Days' Journey from the City above-said. This City sits upon a fair River, great and broad, that Men call Caramaron. This River passeth throughout Cathay. And it doth often-time Harm, and that full great, when it is over great.

CHAPTER XX

Of the great Chan of Cathay. Of the Royalty of his Palace, and how he sits at Meat; and of the great Number of Officers that serve him

NOBLE OF CATHAY

CATHAY is a great-Country and a fair, noble and rich, and full of Merchants. Thither go Merchants every Year to seek Spices and all manner of Merchandises, more commonly than in any other Part. And ye shall understand, that Merchants that come from Genoa or from Venice or from Romania or other Parts of Lombardy, they go by Sea and by Land 11 Months or 12, or more some-time, ere they may come to the Isle of Cathay that is the principal Region of all Parts beyond; and it is of the great Chan.

From Cathay go Men toward the East by many Days' Journeys. And then Men find a good City between these others, that Men call Sugarmago.

That City is one of the best stored of Silk and other Merchandises that is in the World.

After go Men to yet another old City toward the East. And it is in the Province of Cathay. And beside that City the Men of Tartary have made another City that is clept Caydon. And it hath 12 Gates, and between 2 Gates there is always a great Mile; so that the 2 Cities, that is to say, the old and the new, have in Circuit more than 20 Mile.

In this City is the Seat of the great Chan in a full great Palace and the most passing fair in all the World, of the which the Walls be in Circuit more than 2 Mile. And within the Walls it is all full of other Palaces. And in the Garden of the great Palace there is a great Hill, upon the which there is another Palace; and it is the most fair and the most rich that any Man may devise. And all about the Palace and the Hill be many Trees bearing many diverse Fruits. And all about that Hill be Ditches great and deep, and beside them, on the one Side and on the other, be great Vivaries. And there is a full fair Bridge to pass over the Ditches. And in these Vivaries be so many wild Geese and Ganders and wild Ducks and Swans and Herons that they are without Number. And all about these Ditches and Vivaries is the great Garden full of wild Beasts. So that when the great Chan will have any Sport therein, to take any of the wild Beasts or of the Fowls, he will make chase them and take them at the Windows without going out of his Chamber.

This Palace, where his Seat is, is both great and

passing fair. And within the Palace, in the Hall, there be 24 Pillars of fine Gold. And all the Walls be covered within with red Skins of Beasts that Men call Panthers, that be fair Beasts and well smelling; so that for the sweet Odour of those Skins no evil Air may enter into the Palace. Those Skins be as red as Blood, and they shine so bright against the Sun, that scarcely may a Man behold them. And many Folk worship those Beasts, when they meet them first of a Morning, for their great Virtue and for the good Smell that they have. And those Skins they prize more than though they were Plates of fine Gold.

And in the Midst of this Palace is the Mountour (or Dais) for the great Chan, that is all wrought of Gold and of precious Stones and great Pearls. And at the 4 Corners of the Mountour be 4 Serpents of Gold. And all about there are made large Nets of Silk and Gold and great Pearls hanging all about the Mountour. And under the Mountour be Conduits of Beverage that they drink in the Emperor's Court. And beside the Conduits be many Vessels of Gold, by the which they that be of the Household drink at the Conduit.

And the Hall of the Palace is full nobly arrayed, and full marvellously attired on all Parts in all Things that Men apparel any Hall with. And first, at the Head of the Hall is the Emperor's Throne, full high, where he sitteth at Meat. And that is of fine precious Stones, bordered all about with purified Gold and precious Stones and great Pearls. And the

Noise. And whether it be by Craft or by Necromancy I wot never; but it is a good Sight to behold,
and a fair; and it is a great Marvel how it may be.
But I have the less Marvel, because that they be the
most subtle Men in all Sciences and in all Crafts that
be in the World; for of Subtlety and of Malice and
of Forecasting they pass all Men under Heaven.
And therefore they themselves say, that they see
with 2 Eyes and the Christian Men see but with
one, because that they be more subtle than they.
For all other Nations, they say, be but blind in
knowing and working in Comparison to them. I did
great Business to have learned that Craft, but the
Master told me that he had made a Vow to his God
to teach it to no Creature, but only to his eldest
Son.

Also above the Emperor's Table and the other
Tables, and above a great Part of the Hall, is a Vine
made of fine Gold. And it spreadeth all about the
Hall. And it hath many Clusters of Grapes, some
white, some green, some yellow and some red and
some black, all of precious Stones. The white be of
Crystal and of Beryl and of Iris; the yellow be of
Topazes; the red be of Rubies and of Garnets and
of Alabrandines; the green be of Emeralds of
Perydoz and of Chrysolites; and the black be of
Onyx and Garnets. And they be all so properly
made that it seemeth a veritable Vine bearing
natural Grapes.

And before the Emperor's Table stand great
Lords and rich Barons and others that serve the

Emperor at Meat. And no Man is so hardy to speak a Word, but if the Emperor speak to him; unless it be Minstrels that sing Songs and tell Jests or other Disports, to solace the Emperor with. And all the Vessels that Men be served with in the Hall or in Chambers be of precious Stones, and especially at great Tables either of Jasper or of Crystal or of Amethysts or of fine Gold. And the Cups be of Emeralds and of Sapphires, or of Topazes, of Perydoz and of many other precious Stones. Vessel of Silver is there none, for they set no Price thereon to make Vessels; but they make thereof Stairs and Pillars and Pavements to Halls and Chambers, And before the Hall Door stand many Barons and Knights fully armed to keep it that no Man enter, but if it be the Will or the Commandment of the Emperor, or if they be Servants or Minstrels of the Household; and none other is so hardy as to draw nigh the Hall Door.

And ye shall understand, that my Fellows and I with our Yeomen, we served this Emperor, and were his Soldiers 15 Months against the King of Mancy, that held War against him. And the Cause was that we had great Lust to see his Noblesse and the Estate of his Court and all his Governance, to wit if it were such as we heard say that it was. And truly we found it more noble and more excellent, and richer and more marvellous, than ever we heard speak of, insomuch that we would never have believed it had we not seen it. For I trow, that no Man would believe the Noblesse, the Riches

A SOLDIER OF THE GREAT CHAN

nor the Multitude of Folk that be in his Court, but he had seen it; for it is not there as it is here. For the Lords here have Folk of a certain Number as it may suffice them; but the great Chan hath every Day Folk at his Cost and Expense without Number. But neither the Ordinance, nor the Expenses in Meat and Drink, nor the Honesty, nor the Cleanness, is so arrayed there as it is here; for all the Commons there eat without Cloth upon their Knees, and they eat all manner of Flesh and little of Bread, and after Meat they wipe their Hands upon their Skirts, and

they eat not but once a Day.   But the Estate of
Lords is full great, rich and noble.

And albeit that some Men will not believe me,
but hold it for Fable to tell them the Noblesse of
his Person and of his Estate and of his Court and of
the great Multitude of Folk that he holds, nevertheless I shall tell you somewhat of him and of his Folk,
and the Manner and the Ordinance, after that I have
seen full many a Time.   And whoso that will may
believe me if he will, and whoso will not, may so
choose.   For I wot well, if any Man hath been in
those Countries beyond, though he have not been in
that Place where the great Chan dwelleth, he shall
hear speak of him so many marvellous Things, that
he shall not believe it lightly.   And truly, no more
did I myself, till I saw it.   And those that have
been in those Countries and in the great Chan's
Household know well that I say Truth.   And therefore I will not spare my words because of them,
that know nought nor believe nought, but that
which they see, but will tell you somewhat of him
and of his Estate that he holds, when he goeth from
Country to Country, and when he maketh solemn
Feasts.

CHAPTER XXI

Wherefore he is clept the great Chan. Of the Style of his Letters ; and of the Superscription about his great Seal and his Privy Seal

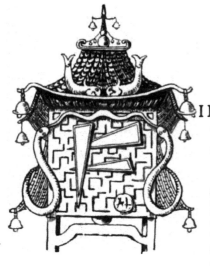

FIRST I shall say to you why he was clept the great Chan.

Ye shall understand, that all the World was destroyed by Noah's Flood, save only Noah and his Wife and his Children. Noah had 3 Sons, Shem, Cham (Ham) and Japhet. This Cham was he that saw his Father's Nakedness when he slept, and scorned him, and shewed him with his Finger to his Brethren in scorning Wise. And therefore he was cursed of God. And Japhet turned his Face away and covered him.

These 3 Brethren seized all the Land. And this Cham, for his Cruelty, took the greater and the best Part, toward the East, that is clept Asia, and Shem took Africa, and Japhet took Europe. And therefore is all the Earth parted in these 3 Parts by these 3 Brethren. Cham was the greatest and the most mighty, and of him came more Generations than of the others. And of his Son Cush was engendered Nimrod the Giant, that was the first King that ever was in the World; and he began the Foundation of the Tower of Babylon. And that Time, the Fiends of Hell came many Times and lay with the Women of his Generation and engendered on them divers Folk, as Monsters and Folk disfigured, some without Heads, some with great Ears, some with one Eye, some Giants, some with Horses' Feet, and many other diverse Shapes against Nature. And of that Generation of Cham come the Paynims and divers Folk that be in Isles of the Sea by all Ind. And forasmuch as he was the most mighty, and no Man might withstand him, he called himself the Son of God and Sovereign of all the World. And from this Cham, this Emperor calleth himself " Cham," and Sovereign of all the World.

And of the Generation of Shem be come the Saracens. And of the Generation of Japhet is come the People of Israel, and we that dwell in Europe. This is the Opinion, that the Syrians and the Samaritans have amongst them. And that they told me, before that I went toward Ind, but I found it otherwise. Nevertheless, the Truth is this; that the Tartars and they that dwell in the great Asia, they came of Cham; but the Emperor of Cathay calleth himself not "Cham," but "Chan," and I shall tell you how.

It is but little more than 8 Score Year that all Tartary was in Subjection and in Servage to other Nations about. For they were but Beast-herding Folk and did nothing but kept Beasts and led them to Pastures. But among them they had 7 principal Nations that were Sovereigns of them all. Of the which, the first Nation or Lineage was clept Tartar, and that is the most noble and the most prized. The 2nd Lineage is clept Tanghot, the 3rd Eurache, the 4th Valair, the 5th Semoche, the 6th Megly, the 7th Coboghe.

Now befell it so that of the first Lineage succeeded an old worthy Man that was not rich, that had to Name Ghengis. This Man lay upon a Night in his Bed. And he saw in a Vision, that there came before him a Knight armed all in White. And he sat upon a White Horse, and said to him, "Chan, sleepest thou? The Immortal God hath sent me to thee, and it is His Will, that thou go to the 7 Lineages and say to them that thou shalt be their Emperor. For thou shalt conquer the Lands and the Countries that be about, and they that march upon you shall be under your Subjection, as ye have been under theirs, for that is God's Will immortal!"

And when it became Morning, Ghengis rose, and went to the 7 Lineages, and told them how the

Knight had said.   And they scorned 'him, and said
that he was a Fool.   And so he departed from them
all ashamed.   And on the Night ensuing, this
White Knight came to the 7 Lineages, and
commanded them on Immortal God's Behalf, that
they should make this Ghengis their Emperor, and
they should be out of Subjection, and they should
hold all other Regions about them in their Servage
as they had been to them before.   And on the
Morrow, they chose him to be their Emperor.
And they set him upon a black Litter, and after
that they lifted him up with great Solemnity.   And
they set him in a Chair of Gold and did him all
manner of Reverence, and they called him " Chan,"
as the White Knight called him.

And when he was thus chosen, he would assay if
he might trust in them or not, and whether they
would be obeissant to him or not.   And then he
made many Statutes and Ordinances that they
called " *Ysya Chan.*"   The first Statute was, that
they should believe in and obey Immortal God, that
is Almighty, that would cast them out of Servage,
and at all Times call to Him for Help in Time of
Need.   The tother Statute was, that all manner of
Men that might bear Arms should be numbered,
and to every 10 should be a Master, and to every
100 a Master, and to every 1000 a Master, and to
every 10,000 a Master.   After he commanded to
the Principals of the 7 Lineages, that they should
leave and forsake all that they had in Goods and
Heritage, and from thenceforth hold them paid of

"AND THEY SAW AN OWL ABOVE HIM"

what he would give them of his Grace. And they did so anon. After he commanded to the Principals of the 7 Lineages, that every one of them should bring his eldest Son before him, and with their own Hands smite off their Heads without tarrying. And anon his Commandment was performed.

And when the Chan saw that they made no Obstacle to perform his Commandment, then he thought well that he might trust in them, and commanded them anon to make them ready and to follow his Banner. And after this, Chan put in Subjection all the Lands about him.

Afterward it befell upon a Day, that the Chan rode with a few Companies to behold the Strength of the Country that he had won. And so it befell, that a great Multitude of his Enemies met with him. And to give good Example of Hardiness to his People, he was the first that fought, and encountered his Enemies in the Midst, and there he was cast from his Horse, and his Horse slain. And when his Folk saw him on the Earth, they were all abashed, and thought he had been dead, and fled every one. And their Enemies followed after and chased them, but they wist not that the Emperor was there. And when they were come again from the Chase, they went and sought the Woods if any of them had been hid in the Thick of the Woods; and many they found and slew them anon. So it happened as they went searching toward the Place where that the Emperor was, they saw an Owl sitting upon a Tree above him; and then they said amongst them, that no Man was there because that they saw that Bird there, and so they went their Way ; and thus escaped the Emperor from Death. And then he went privily all by Night, till he came to his Folk that were full glad of his coming, and made great Thankings to Immortal God, and to that Bird by whom their Lord was saved. And therefore principally above all Fowls of the World they worship the Owl ; and when they have any of their Feathers, they keep them full preciously instead of Relics, and bear them upon their Heads with great Reverence ; and they hold themselves blessed and safe from all Perils while that they have them upon them, and therefore they bear their Feathers upon their Heads.

After all this the Chan put his Affairs in Order and assembled his People, and went against them that had assailed him before, and destroyed them, and put them in Subjection and Servage.

And when he had won and put all the Lands and Countries on this Side the Mount Belian in Subjection, the White Knight came to him again in his Sleep, and said to him, "Chan ! the Will of Immortal God is that thou pass the Mount Belian. And thou shalt win the Land and thou shalt put many Nations in Subjection. And as thou shalt find no good Passage to go toward that Country, go to the Mount Belian that is upon the Sea, and kneel there 9 Times toward the East in the Worship of Immortal God. And He shall shew the Way to pass by." And the Chan did so. And anon the Sea that touched and was fast by the Mount began to withdraw himself, and shewed a fair Way of 9 Foot broad large; and so he passed with his Folk, and won the Land of Cathay that is the greatest Kingdom of the World.

And for the 9 Kneelings and for the 9 Foot of Way the Chan and all the Men of Tartary have the Number of 9 in great Reverence. And therefore who that will make the Chan any Present, be it of Horses, or of Birds, or of Arrows, or of Fruit, or of any other Thing, always he must make it of the Number 9. And so then be the Presents of greater Pleasure to him; and more benignly he will receive them than though he were presented with an 100 or 200. For to him seemeth the Number of 9 so holy, because the Messenger of Immortal God so devised it.

Also, when the Chan of Cathay had won the Country of Cathay, and put in Subjection and under Foot many Countries about, he fell sick. And when he felt that he should well die, he said to his 12 Sons, that every one of them should bring him one of his Arrows. And so they did anon. And then he commanded that Men should bind them together in 3 Places. And then he took them to his eldest Son, and bade him break them all together. And he strove with all his Might to break them, but he might not. And then the Chan bade his 2nd Son to break them; and so, shortly, to all, each after the other; but none of them might break them. And then he bade the youngest Son dissever every one from the other, and break every one by itself. And so he did. And then said the Chan to his eldest Son and to all the others, "Wherefore might ye not break them?" And they answered, that they might not, because they were bound together. "And wherefore," quoth he, "hath your little youngest Brother broken them?" "Because," quoth they, "that they were parted each from the other." And then said the Chan, "My Sons," quoth he, "truly thus will it fare by you. For as long as ye be bound together in 3 Places, that is to say, in Love, in Truth and in good Accord, no Man shall be of Power to grieve you. But and ye be dissevered from these 3 Places, that the one help not the other, ye shall be destroyed and brought to Nought. And if each of you love the other and help the other, ye shall be Lords and Sovereigns of all others." And when he had made his Ordinances, he died.

And then after him reigned Oktai Chan, his eldest Son. And his other Brethren went to win them many Countries and Kingdoms, unto the Land of Prussia and of Russia, and made themselves to be clept Chans ; but they were all obeissant to their elder Brother, and therefore was he clept the great Chan.

After Oktai reigned Gaiouk Chan.

And after him Mango Chan that was a good Christian Man and baptized, and gave Letters of perpetual Peace to all Christian Men, and sent his Brother Halaon with great Multitude of Folk to

win the Holy Land and to put it into Christian Mens' Hands, and to destroy Mohammet's Law, and to take the Caliph of Bagdad that was Emperor and Lord of all the Saracens. And when this Caliph was taken, Men found him of so high Worship, that in all the Rest of the World, a Man might not find a more reverend Man, nor a higher in Worship. And then Halaon made him come before him, and said to him, "Why," quoth he, "haddest thou not taken with thee more Soldiers and Men enough, hired for a little Quantity of Treasure, to defend thee and thy Country, that art so abundant of Treasure and so high in all Worship?" And the Caliph answered him, that he well trowed that he had enough ·of his own proper Men. And then said Halaon, "Thou wert as a

HALAON

God of the Saracens. And it is convenient to a God to eat no Meat that is mortal. And therefore, thou shall not eat but precious Stones, rich Pearls and Treasure, that thou lovest so much." And then he commanded him to Prison, and all his Treasure about him. And so he died for Hunger and Thirst. And then after this, Halaon won all the Land of Promise, and put it into Christian Men's

Hands. But the great Chan, his Brother, died; and that was great Sorrow and Loss to all Christian Men.

After Mango Chan reigned Houlagou Chan that was also a Christian Man. And he reigned 42 Year. He founded the great City Izonge in Cathay, that is a great deal larger than Rome.

The tother great Chan that came after him became a Paynim, and all the others after him.

The Kingdom of Cathay is the greatest Realm of the World. And also the great Chan is the most mighty Emperor of the World and the greatest Lord under the Firmament. And so he calleth himself in his Letters, right thus: "*Chan! Filius Dei Excelsi, Omnium universam Terram colentium summus Imperator, et Dominus omnium Dominantium!*" ("*Chan! Son of Almighty God, High Emperor of all that till the whole Earth, and Lord of all Lordships!*") And the Letter of his Great Seal, written about, is this; "*Deus in Cœlo, Chan super Terram, ejus Fortitudo! Omnium Hominum Imperatoris Sigillum!*" ("*God in Heaven, Chan upon Earth, his Strength! The Seal of the Emperor of all Men!*") And the Superscription about his Little Seal is this; "*Dei Fortitudo! omnium Hominum Imperatoris Sigillum!*" ("*God of Strength! the Seal of the Emperor of all Men!*")

And albeit that they be not christened, yet nevertheless the Emperor and all the Tartars believe in Immortal God. And when they will menace

any Man, then they say, "God knoweth well that I shall do thee such a Thing," and telleth his Menace.

And thus have ye heard, why he is clept the great Chan.

MAN OF CATHAY

CHAPTER XXII

*Of the Governance of the great Chan's Court, and when
he maketh solemn Feasts.   Of his Philosophers.
And of his Array, when he rideth
by the Country*

 OW shall I tell you the Govern-
ance of the Court of the great
Chan, when he maketh solemn
Feasts ; and that is principally
4 Times in the Year.

The first Feast is of his Birth,
the next is of his Presentation
in their Temple that they call
their Mosque, where they make a manner of Circumcision, and the tother 2 Feasts be of his Idols.
The first Feast of the Idol is when he is first put
into their Temple and throned ; the tother Feast
is when the Idol beginneth first to speak, or to
work Miracles. More be there not of solemn Feasts,
but and if he will marry any of his Children.

Now understand, that at every one of these Feasts
he hath great Multitude of People, well ordained
and well arrayed, by thousands, by hundreds, and
by tens. And every Man knoweth well what Service

he shall do, and every Man giveth so good Heed
and so good Attendance to his Service that no Man
findeth any Default. And there be first ordained
4000 Barons, mighty and rich, to govern and to
make Ordinance for the Feast, and to serve the
Emperor. And these solemn Feasts be made
without in Halls and Tents made of Cloths of Gold
and of Tartarins,* full nobly. And all those Barons
have Crowns of Gold upon their Heads, full noble
and rich, full of precious Stones and great orient
Pearls. And they be all clothed in Cloths of Gold
or of Tartarins or of Camakas, so richly and so
perfectly, that no Man in the World can amend it,
nor better devise it. And all those Robes be orfrayed all about, and dubbed full of precious Stones
and of great orient Pearls, full richly. And they
may well be so, for Cloths of Gold and of Silk be
more cheap there a great deal than be Cloths of
Wool. And these 4000 Barons be devised in 4
Companies, and every 1000 is clothed in Cloths all
of one Colour, and that so well arrayed and so richly,
that it is a Marvel to behold.

The 1st 1000, that is of Dukes, of Earls, of
Marquises and of Admirals, is all clothed in Cloths
of Gold, with Tissues of green Silk, and bordered
with Gold full of precious Stones in manner as I
have said before. The 2nd 1000 is all clothed in
diapered Cloths of red Silk, all wrought with Gold,
and the Orfrays set full of great Pearls and precious
Stones, full nobly wrought. The 3rd 1000 is clothed

* A kind of silk.

in Cloths of Silk, of purple or of Ind. And the 4th 1000 is in Cloths of yellow. And all their Cloths be so nobly and richly wrought with Gold and precious Stones and rich Pearls, that if a Man of this Country had but only one of their Robes, he might well say that he should never be poor ; for the Gold and the precious Stones and the great orient Pearls be of greater Value on this side the Sea than they be beyond the Sea in those Countries.

And when they be thus apparelled, they go 2 and 2 together, full orderly, before the Emperor, without Speech of any Word, save only inclining to him. And every one of them beareth a Tablet of Jasper or of Ivory or of Crystal, the Minstrels going before them, sounding their Instruments of divers Melody. And when the 1st 1000 is thus passed and hath made its Muster, it withdraweth itself

" MANY PHILOSOPHERS THAT BE PROVED
TO BE FOR WISE MEN "

on the one Side; and then entereth that other 2nd 1000, and doth right so, in the same Manner of Array and Countenance, as did the 1st; and after, the 3rd; and then, the 4th; and none of them saith any one Word.

And at one Side of the Emperor's Table sit many Philosophers that be proved for wise Men in many diverse Sciences, as of Astronomy, Necromancy, Geomancy, Pyromancy, Hydromancy, of Augury and of many other Sciences. And every one of them hath before them Astrolabes of Gold, or Spheres, and some the Brain Pan of a dead Man, some Vessels of Gold full of Gravel or Sand, some Vessels of Gold full of Coals burning, some Vessels of Gold full of Water and of Wine and of Oil, and some Horologes of Gold, made full nobly and richly wrought, and many other Manner of Instruments after their Sciences.

And at certain Hours, when they think Time, they say to certain Officers that stand before them or-dained for the Time to fulfil their Commandments; "Make Peace!"

And then say the Officers; "Now Peace lis-teneth!"

And after that, saith another of the Philosophers; "Every Man do Reverence and incline to the Emperor, that is God's Son and Sovereign Lord of all the World! For now is Time!" And then every Man boweth his Head toward the Earth.

And then commandeth the same Philosopher again; "Stand up!" And they do so.

And at another Hour, saith another Philosopher ; " Put your little Finger in your Ears ! " And anon they do so.

And at another Hour, saith another Philosopher ; " Put your Hand before your Mouth ! " And anon they do so.

And at another Hour, saith another Philosopher ; " Put your Hand upon your Head ! " And after that he biddeth them to put their Hand away. And they do so.

And so, from Hour to Hour, they command certain Things ; and they say, that those Things have diverse Significations. And I asked them privily what those Things betokened. And one of the Masters told me, that the Bowing of the Head at that Hour betokened this ; that all those that bowed their Heads should evermore after be obeissant and true to the Emperor, and never, for Gifts nor for Promise of any Kind, be false nor Traitor unto him for Good nor Evil. And the putting of the little Finger in the Ear betokeneth, as they say, that none of them shall hear speak any contrarious Thing of the Emperor but that he shall tell it anon to his Council or discover it to some Men that will make Relation thereof to the Emperor, though he were his Father or Brother or Son. And so forth, of all other Things that be done by the Philosophers, they told me the Causes of many diverse Things. And trust right well in certain, that no Man doth anything for the Emperor and what belongeth to him, neither Clothing nor Bread nor Wine nor Bath nor any

other Thing that belongeth to him, but at certain
Hours that his Philosophers will devise. And if
there fall War on any Side to the Emperor, anon
the Philosophers come and say their Advice after
their Calculations, and counsel the Emperor of their
Advice by their Sciences; so that the Emperor doth
nothing without their Counsel.

And when the Philosophers have done and performed their Commandments, then the Minstrels
begin to do their Minstrelsy, every one on their
Instruments, each after the other, with all the
Melody that they can devise. And when they have
done this a good while, one of the Officers of the
Emperor goeth up on a high Stage wrought full
curiously, and crieth and saith with a loud Voice;
"Make Peace!" And then every Man is still.

And then, anon after, all the Lords that be of the
Emperor's Lineage, nobly arrayed in rich Cloths of
Gold and royally apparelled on white Steeds, as
many as may well follow him at that time, be ready
to make Presents to the Emperor. And then saith
the Steward of the Court to the Lords, by Name;
"N. of N.!" and nameth first the most noble and
the worthiest by Name, and saith; "Be ye ready
with such a Number of white Horses, to serve the
Emperor, your Sovereign Lord!" And to another
Lord he saith; "N. of N., be ready with such a
Number, to serve your Sovereign Lord!" And to an-
other, right so, and to all the Lords of the Emperor's
Lineage, each after the other, as they be of Estate.
And when they be all called, they enter each after

the other, and present the white Horses to the
Emperor, and then go their Way. And then after,
all the other Barons every one of them, give him
Presents or Jewels or some other Thing, after that
they be of Estate. And then after them, all the
Prelates of their Law, and religious Men and others ;
and every Man giveth him something. And when
that all Men have thus presented to the Emperor,
the greatest of Dignity of the Prelates giveth him
a Blessing, saying an Orison of their Law.

And then begin the Minstrels to make their
Minstrelsy on divers Instruments with all the
Melody that they can devise. And when they have
done their Craft, then they bring before the
Emperor, Lions, Leopards and other divers Beasts,
and Eagles and Vultures and other divers Fowls,
and Fishes and Serpents, to do him Reverence.
And then come Jugglers and Enchanters, that do
many Marvels ; for they make, by seeming, the
Sun and the Moon to come in the Air, to every
Man's Sight. And after they make the Night, and
so dark that no Man may see anything. And after
they make the Day to come again, fair and pleasant
with bright Sun, to every Man's Sight. And then
they bring in Dances of the fairest Damsels of the
World, and richest arrayed. And after they make
to come in other Damsels bringing Cups of Gold
full of Milk of divers Beasts, that give Drink to
Lords and to Ladies. And then they make
Knights to joust in Arms full lustily ; and they run
together at great Speed, and they dash head-long

together full fiercely, and they break their Spears so rudely that the Fragments fly in Splinters and Pieces all about the Hall. And then they make to come in an Hunting for the Hart and for the Boar, with Hounds running with open Mouth. And many other Things they do by Craft of their Enchantments, that it is marvellous to see. And such Plays of Disport they make till the taking up of the Boards of the Tables. This great Chan hath full many People to serve him, as I have told you before. For he hath of Minstrels the Number of 13 Cumants (130,000), but they abide not always with him. For all the Minstrels that come before him, of whatever Nation that they be of, they be withheld by him as of his Household, and entered in his Books as his own Men. And after that, where that ever they go, they claim to be Minstrels of the great Chan ; and under that Title, all Kings and Lords cherish them the more with Gifts and all Things. And therefore he hath so great a Multitude of them.

And he hath of certain Men as though they were Yeomen, to the Amount of 15 Cumants (150,000) of Yeomen, that keep Birds, as Ostriches, Gerfalcons, Sparrowhawks, Falcons fine, Laner-hawks, Sakers (or Peregrine-hawks), Sakrets, well speaking Popinjays (or Parrots), and singing Birds ; and also wild Beasts, as Elephants tame and other, Baboons, Apes, Marmosets, and other divers Beasts.

And of Christian Physicians he hath 200, and of Leeches that be Christian he hath 210, and of

Leeches and Physicians that be Saracens 20, but he trusteth more in the Christian Leeches than in the Saracen. And his other common Household is without Number, and they have all Necessaries and all that they need from the Emperor's Court. And he hath in his Court many Barons as Servitors, that be Christian and converted to good Faith by the Preaching of religious Christian Men that dwell with him ; but there be many more, that will not that Men know that they be Christian.

This Emperor may spend as much as he will without Estimation ; for he spendeth and maketh no Money but of imprinted Leather or of Paper. And of that Money some is of greater Price and some of less Price, after the Diversity of his Statutes. And when that Money hath run so long that it beginneth to waste, then Men bear it to the Emperor's Treasury and then they take new Money for the old. And that Money goeth throughout all the Country and throughout all his Provinces, for there and beyond them they make no Money either of Gold or of Silver ; and therefore he may spend enough, and outrageously. And of Gold and Silver that Men have in his Country he maketh Colours, Pillars and Pavements in his Palace, and other divers Things what he liketh.

This Emperor hath in his Chamber, in one of the Pillars of Gold, a Ruby and a Carbuncle of half a Foot long, that in the Night giveth so great Lustre and Shining, that it is as light as Day. And he hath many other precious Stones and many other

Rubies and Carbuncles; but those be the greatest and the most precious.

This Emperor dwelleth in Summer in a City that is toward the North that is clept Saduz; and there it is cold enough. And in the Winter he dwelleth in a City that is clept Camaaleche, and that is in an hot Country. But the Country, where he dwelleth in most commonly, is in Gaydo or in Jong, that is a good Country and a temperate, going by what the Country is there; but to Men of this Country it were passing hot.

And when this Emperor will ride from one Country to another he ordaineth 4 Hosts of his Folk, of the which the first Host goeth before him a Day's Journey. For that Host shall be lodged the Night where the Emperor shall lie upon the Morrow. And there shall every Man have all Manner of Victual and Necessaries that be needful, at the Emperor's Costs. And in this first Host the Number of People is 50 Cumants, either of Horse or of Foot, of the which every Cumant amounts to 10,000, as I have told you before. And another Host goeth on the right Side of the Emperor, nigh half a Day's Journey from him. And another goeth on the left Side of him, in the same Wise. And in every Host is as much Multitude of People as in the first Host. And then after cometh the 4th Host, that is much more than any of the others, and that goeth behind him, the Amount of a Bow's Draw. And every Host hath its Journey ordained to certain Places, where they shall be lodged at Night, and there shall they have all that they need. And if it befall that any one of the Host die, anon they put another in his Place, so that the Number shall evermore be complete.

And ye shall understand, that the Emperor, in his own Person, rideth not as other great Lords do beyond, but if he list to go privily with few Men, to be unknown. Else, he rides in a Chariot with 4 Wheels, upon the which is made a fair Chamber, and it is made of a certain Wood, that cometh out of Terrestrial Paradise, that Men call Lignum Aloes, that the Rivers of Paradise bring out at divers Seasons, as I have told you here before. And this Chamber is full well smelling because of the Wood that it is made of. And all this Chamber is covered within with Plates of fine Gold dubbed with precious Stones and great Pearls. And 4 Elephants and 4 great Dromedaries, all white and covered with rich Coverlets, go leading the Chariot. And 4, or 5, or 6, of the greatest Lords ride about this Chariot, full richly arrayed and full nobly, so that no Man shall draw nigh the Chariot, but only those Lords, unless that the Emperor call any Man to him that he list to speak withal. And above the Chamber of this Chariot that the Emperor sitteth in be set upon a Perch 4 or 5 or 6 Gerfalcons, to that Intent, that when the Emperor seeth any Wild Fowl, he may take them at his own List, and have the Sport and the Play of the Flight, first with one, and after with another; and so he taketh his Sport passing by the Country.

And no Man rideth before him of his Company, but all after him. And no Man dare come nigh the Chariot, by a Bow's Draw, but those Lords only that be about him. And all the Host cometh fairly after him in a great Multitude.

And also such another Chariot with such Hosts ordained and arrayed go with the Empress upon another Way, every one by itself, with 4 Hosts, right as the Emperor did; but not with so great Multitude of People. And his eldest Son goeth by another Way in another Chariot, in the same Manner. So that there is between them so great Multitude of Folk that it is marvellous to tell it. And no Man should believe the Number, but he had seen it. And sometime it haps that when he will not go far, and that it liketh him to have the Empress and his Children with him, then they go altogether, and their Folk be all mingled in company, and divided in 4 Parties only.

And ye shall understand, that the Empire of this great Chan is divided in 12 Provinces; and every Province hath more than 2000 Cities, and Towns without Number. This County is full great, for it hath 12 principal Kings in 12 Provinces, and every one of those Kings have many Kings under them, and they all be obeissant to the great Chan. And his Land and his Lordship endureth so far, that a Man may not go from one End to another, neither by Sea nor Land, in the Space of 7 Year. And through the Deserts of his Lordship, there where Men may find no Towns, there be Inns ordained

by every Day's Journey, to receive both Man and
Horse, in the which they shall find Plenty of
Victual, and of all Things that they need to go by
the Country.

And there is a marvellous Custom in that
Country, but it is profitable, that if there be any
contrarious Thing that should be Prejudice or
Grievance to the Emperor in any kind, anon the
Emperor hath Tidings thereof and full Knowledge
in a Day, though it be 3 or 4 Days' Journeys from
him or more. For his Ambassadors take their
Dromedaries or their Horses, and they spur all that
ever they may toward one of the Inns. And when
they come there, anon they blow an Horn. And
anon they of the Inn know well enough that there
be Tidings to warn the Emperor of some Rebellion
against him. And then anon they make other
Men ready, in all Haste that they may, to bear
Letters, and spur all that ever they may, till they
come to the other Inns with their Letters. And
then they make fresh Men ready, to spur forth with
the Letters toward the Emperor, while that the last
Bringer rests him, and baits his Dromedary or his
Horse. And so, from Inn to Inn, till it come to the
Emperor. And thus anon hath he hasty Tidings
of anything that beareth Weight, by his Couriers,
that run so hastily throughout all the Country.
And also when the Emperor sendeth his Couriers
hastily throughout his Land, every one of them
hath a large Thong full of small Bells, and when
they draw nigh near to the Inns of other Couriers

that be also ordained for the Journeys, they ring
their Bells, and anon the other Couriers make them
ready, and run their Way unto another Inn. And
thus runneth one to the other, full speedily and
swiftly, till the Emperor's Intent be served, in all

"THEY SPUR ALL THAT EVER THEY MAY"

Haste. And these Couriers be clept "*Chydydo*,"
after their Language, that is to say, a Messenger.

Also when the Emperor goeth from one Country
to another, as I have told you here before, and he
passeth through Cities and Towns, every Man
maketh a Fire before his Door, and putteth therein
Powder of good Gums that be sweet smelling, to
make good Savour to the Emperor. And all the

People kneel down over against him, and do him great
Reverence. And there, where religious Christian
Men dwell, as they do in many Cities in their Land,
they go before him in Procession with Cross and
Holy Water, and they sing, "*Veni Creator Spiritus!*"
with an high Voice, and go towards him. And
when he heareth them, he commandeth to his
Lords to ride beside him, that the religious Men
may come to him. And when they be nigh him
with the Cross, then he putteth down his Galiot (or
Head-piece) that sits on his Head in manner of a
Chaplet, that is made of Gold and precious Stones
and great Pearls, and is so rich, that Men prize it at
the Value of a Realm in that Country. And then
he kneeleth to the Cross. And then the Prelate of
the religious Men saith before him certain Orisons,
and giveth him a Blessing with the Cross ; and he
inclineth to the Blessing full devoutly. And then
the Prelate giveth him some manner of Fruit, to the
number of 9, in a Platter of Silver, with Pears or
Apples, or other manner of Fruit. And he taketh
one. And then Men give to the other Lords that
be about him. For the Custom is such, that no
Stranger shall come before him, but if he give him
some manner of Thing, after the old Law that saith,
"*Nemo accedat in Conspectu meo vacuus.*" ("*None
cometh into my Sight empty.*") And then the
Emperor saith to the religious Men, that they shall
withdraw them again, that they be neither hurt nor
harmed of the great Multitude of Horses that come
behind him. And also, in the same Manner, do the

religious Men that dwell there, to the Empresses that pass by them, and to his eldest Son. And to every one of them they present Fruit.

And ye shall understand, that the People that he hath so many Hosts of, about him and about his Wives and his Son, they dwell not continually with him. But always, when it liketh him, they be sent for. And after, when they have done, they return to their own Households, save only they that be dwelling with him in his Household to serve him and his Wives and his Sons to govern his Household. And albeit, that the others be departed from him after that they have performed their Service, yet there abideth continually with him in Court 50,000 Men at Horse and 200,000 Men at Foot, besides Minstrels and those that keep Wild Beasts and divers Birds, of the which I have told you the Number before.

Under the Firmament is not so great a Lord, nor so mighty, nor so rich as the great Chan; neither Prester John, that is Emperor of the High Ind, nor the Sultan of Babylon, nor the Emperor of Persia. All these be not in Comparison to the great Chan, neither of Might, nor of Noblesse, nor of Royalty, nor of Riches, for in all these he passeth all earthly Princes. Wherefore it is great Harm that he believeth not faithfully in God. And nevertheless he will gladly hear speak of God. And he suffereth well that Christian Men dwell in his Lordship, and that Men of his Faith be made Christian Men if they will, throughout all his Country; for he for-

biddeth no Man to hold any Law other than it liketh him.

In that Country some Men have an 100 Wives, some 60, some more, some less. And they take the next of their Kin to be their Wives, save only that they take not their Mothers, their Daughters, and their Sisters on the Mother's Side; but their Sisters on the Father's side by another Woman they may well take, and their Brothers' Wives also after their Death, and their Step-mothers also in the same Wise.

WOMAN OF SADUZ

CHAPTER XXIII

Of the Law and the Customs of the Tartars dwelling in Cathay. And how that Men do when the Emperor shall die, and how he shall be chosen

TARTAR OF CATHAY

THE Folk of that Country all use long Clothes without Furs. And they be clothed with precious Cloths of Tartary, and of Cloths of Gold. And their Clothes be slit at the Side, and they be festooned with Laces of Silk. And they clothe them also with Pilches,* the Hide without; and they use neither Cape nor Hood. And in the same Manner as the Men go, the Women go, so that no **Man** may scarcely know the Men from the Women, save only those Women that be married, that bear the Token upon their Heads of a Man's Foot, in Sign

* A winter garment of skins of fur.

that they be under Man's Foot and under Subjection of Man.

And their Wives dwell not together, but every one of them by herself; and the Husband may lie with whom of them that it liketh him. Every one hath his House, both Man and Woman. And their Houses be made round with Staves, and they have a round Window above that giveth them Light, and also serveth for Deliverance of Smoke. And the Coverings of their Houses and the Walls and the Doors be all of Wood. And when they go to War, they take their Houses with them upon Chariots, as Men do Tents or Pavilions. And they make their Fire in the Midst of their Houses.

And they have great Multitude of all manner of Beasts, save only of Swine, for these they do not breed. And they believe well in one God that made and formed all Things. And yet nevertheless have they Idols of Gold and Silver, and of Wood and of Cloth. And to their Idols they offer always their first Milk of their Beasts, and also of their Meats and of their Drinks before they eat. And they offer often-times Horses and Beasts. And they call the God of Nature, " *Yroga.*"

And their Emperor also, whatever Name that ever he have, they put evermore thereto, Chan. And when I was there, their Emperor had to Name Thiaut, so that he was clept Thiaut-Chan. And his eldest Son was clept Tossue; and when he shall be Emperor, he shall be clept Tossue-Chan. And at that Time the Emperor had 12 other Sons also, that were named Cuncy, Ordii, Chadahay, Buryr Negu, Nocab, Cadu, Siban, Cuten, Balacy, Babylar and Garegan. And of his 3 Wives, the first an principal, that was Prester John's Daughter, had t Name Serioche-Chan, and the tother Borak-Char and the tother Karanke-Chan.

The Folk of that Country begin all their Thing in the new Moon, and they worship much the Moo

" THEY WORSHIP MUCH THE MOON "

and the Sun and often-time kneel to them. And al the Folk of the Country ride commonly withou Spurs, but they bear always a little Whip in thei Hands to urge their Horses with.

And they have great Conscience and hold it for a great Sin to cast a Knife in the Fire, and to draw Flesh out of a Pot with a Knife, and to smite an Horse with the Handle of a Whip, or to smite an Horse with a Bridle, or to break one Bone with another, or to cast Milk or any Liquor that Men may drink upon the Earth, or to take and slay little

Children. And the most great Sin that any Man may do is to defile their own Houses that they dwell in, and whoso that may be found with that Sin surely they slay him. And of every one of those Sins it behoveth them to be shriven of their Priests, and to pay a great Sum of Silver for their Penance. And it behoveth also, that the Place that Men have defiled be hallowed again, and else dare no Man enter therein. And when they have paid their Penance, Men make them pass through a Fire or through 2, to cleanse them of their Sins. And also when any Messenger cometh and bringeth Letters or any Present to the Emperor, it behoveth him that he, with the Thing he bringeth, pass through 2 burning Fires to purge them, that he bring no Poison nor Venom, nor no wicked Thing that might be a Grievance to their Lord. And also if any Man or Woman be taken in Adultery or Fornication, anon they slay him.

Men of that Country be all good Archers and shoot right well, both Men and Women, as well on Horse-back, spurring, as on Foot, running. And the Women make all Things and all manner of Trades and Crafts, as of Clothes, Boots and other Things; and they drive Carts, Ploughs and Wains and Chariots; and they make Houses and all manner of Trades, except Bows and Arrows and Armours that Men make. And all the Women wear Breeches, as well as Men.

All the Folk of that Country be full obeissant to their Sovereign; neither fight they nor chide one

with another. And there be neither Thieves nor Robbers in that Country. And every Man is worshipful to the other ; but no Man doth any Reverence to any Strangers, but if they be great Princes.

And they eat Hounds, Lions, Leopards, Mares and Foals, Asses, Rats and Mice and all manner of Beasts, great and small, save only Swine and Beasts that were forbidden by the old Law. And they eat all the Beasts without and within, without casting away of anything, save only the Filth. And they eat but little Bread, but if it be in Courts of great Lords. And they have not in many Places, either Pease or Beans or any other Pottages but the Broth of the Flesh. For little eat they of anything but Flesh and the Broth. And when they have eaten, they wipe then their Hands upon their Skirts ; for they use no Napery or Towels, but if it be before great Lords ; but the common People have none. And when they have eaten, they put their Dishes unwashen into the Pot or Cauldron with the Remnant of the Flesh and of the Broth till they will eat again. And the rich Men drink Milk of Mares or of Camels or of Asses or of other Beasts. And they will be lightly made drunk with Milk or with another Drink that is made of Honey and Water boiled together ; for in that Country is neither Wine nor Ale. They live full wretchedly, and they eat but once in the Day, and that but little, either in Courts or in other Places. And in Sooth, one Man alone in this Country will eat more in a Day than one of them will eat in 3 Days. And if any strange Messenger come there to a Lord, Men make him to eat but once a Day, and that full little.

And when they war, they war full wisely and always do their Business, so as to destroy their Enemies. Every man there beareth 2 Bows or 3, and of Arrows a great Plenty, and a great Axe. And the Gentlefolk have short Spears and large and full sharp on the one Side. And they have Plates and Helmets made of Cuir-bouilli, and their Horses Coverlets of the same. And whoso fleeth from the Battle they slay him. And when they hold any Siege about Castle or Town that is walled or defensible, they promise to them that be within to do all the Profit and Good, that it is marvellous to hear; and they grant also to them that be within all that they will ask them. And after that they be yielden, anon they slay them all; and they cut off their Ears and souse them in Vinegar, and thereof they make great Service for Lords. All their Lust and all their Imagination is to put all Lands under their Subjection. And they say that they know well by their Prophecies, that they shall be overcome by Archers and by Strength of them; but they know not of what Nation nor of what Law they shall be of, that shall overcome them. And therefore they suffer that Folk of all Laws may peaceably dwell amongst them.

Also when they will make their Idols or an Image of any of their Friends to have Remembrance of him, they make always the Image all naked without any manner of Clothing. For they say that in good Love should be no Covering, that Man should not love for the fair Clothing nor for the rich Array, but only for the Body, such as God hath made it, and for the good Virtues that the Body is endowed with of Nature, and not only for fair Clothing that is not natural to Nature.

And ye shall understand that it is great Dread to pursue the Tartars if they flee in Battle. For in fleeing they shoot behind them and slay both Men and Horses. And when they will fight they will rush together in a Clump; so that if there be 20,000 Men, Men shall not think that there be a scant 10,000. And they can well, win Land of Strangers, but they cannot keep it; for they have greater Lust to lie in Tents without than to lie in Castles or in Towns. And they prize as nothing the Wit of other Nations.

And amongst them Oil of Olive is full dear, for they hold it for full noble Medicine. And all the Tartars have small Eyes and little of Beard, and be not thick haired but shaved. And they be false and Traitors; and they keep nought that they promise. They be full hardy Folk, and much Pain and Woe and Disease may suffer, more than any other Folk, for they be taught thereto in their own Country from Youth. And therefore they are spent or enfeebled as one may say, but little.

And when any Man shall die, Men set a Spear beside him. And when he draweth towards Death, every Man fleeth out of the House till he be dead. And after that they bury him in the Fields.

And when the Emperor dieth, Men set him in a Chair in the mid Place of his Tent. And Men set a Table before him cleanly covered with a Cloth, and thereupon Flesh and divers Viands and a Cup full of Mare's Milk. And Men put a Mare beside him with her Foal, and an Horse saddled and bridled. And they lay upon the Horse Gold and Silver, great Quantity. And they put about him great Plenty of Straw. And then Men make a great Pit and a large, and with the Tent and all these other Things they put him in the Earth. And they say that when he shall come into another World, he shall not be without an House, nor without Horse, nor without Gold and Silver ; and the Mare shall give him Milk, and bring him forth more Horses till he be well stored in the other World. For they believe that after their Death they shall be eating and drinking in that other World, and solacing then with their Wives, as they did here.

And after the Time that the Emperor is thus interred no Man shall be so hardy to speak of him before his Friends. And yet nevertheless, it befalleth many times that they make him to be interred privily by Night in wild Places, and put again the Grass over the Pit to grow ; or else Men cover the Pit with Gravel and Sand, that no Man shall perceive where nor know where the Pit is, to that Intent that ever after none of his Friends shall have Mind or Remembrance of him. And then they say that he is ravished to another World, where he is a greater Lord than he was here.

And then, after the Death of the Emperor, the 7 Lineages assemble them together, and choose his eldest Son, or the next after him of his **Blood.** And thus they **say** to him; "We will and **we pray** and ordain that ye be our Lord and our Emperor!"

And then he answereth, "If ye will that I **reign** over you as Lord, do every one of you that I **shall** command him, either to **abide** or to go; and **whomsoever** that I command to be **slain,** anon be he slain!"

And they answer all **with** one Voice, "Whatsoever **ye** command, it shall be done!"

Then saith the Emperor, "Now understand well, **that** my Word from henceforth **is** sharp and biting as a Sword!"

WOMAN OF CAMAKA.

After, Men set him upon a black Steed **and so** Men bring him to a Chair full richly arrayed, **and** there they crown him. And then all the Cities **and** good Towns send him rich Presents. So that, on that Day, he shall have more than 60 Chariots **charged** with Gold and Silver, besides Jewels of Gold **and** precious Stones, that Lords give him, that be without Estimation, and besides Horses, and Cloths **of** Gold, and of Camakas (Silks) and Tartarins (Silks) that be without Number.

CHAPTER XXIV

*Of the Realm of Thurse and the Lands and Kingdoms
towards the Septentrional or Northern Parts,
in coming down from the Land of Cathay*

THE KING OF THURSE

HIS Land of Cathay is in Asia the Deep; and after, on this Side, is Asia the More. The Kingdom of Cathay marcheth toward the West with the Kingdom of Thurse, of the which was one of the Kings that came to give Presents to our Lord in Bethlehem. And they that be of the Lineage of that King are, some of them, Christian. In Thurse they eat no Flesh, neither drink they any Wine.

And on this Side, toward the West, is the Kingdom of Turkestan, that stretcheth toward the West to the Kingdom of Persia, and toward the Septentrional or North to the Kingdom of Khorasan. In

the Country of Turkestan be but few good Cities ; but
the best City of that Land is hight Octorar.   There
be great Pastures, but little Corn ; and therefore, for
the most Part, they be all Herdsmen, and they lie
in Tents and they drink a Manner of Ale made of
Honey.

And after, on this Side, is the Kingdom of Khorasan, that is a good Land and a plenteous, without

"SO MANY FLIES"

Wine.   And it hath a Desert toward the East that
lasteth more than an 100 Days' Journey.   And the
best City of that Country is clept Khorasan, and
from that City the Country beareth his Name.   The
Folk of that Country be hardy Warriors.

And on this Side is the Kingdom of Comania,
wherefrom the Comanians that dwelled in Greece
sometime were chased out.   This is one of the greatest

Kingdoms of the World, but it is not all inhabited.
For at one of the Parts there is so great Cold that
no Man may dwell there ; and in another Part there
is so great Heat that no Man may endure it, and
also there be so many Flies, that no Man may know
on what Side he may turn him.   In that Country is
but little Wood or Trees that bear Fruit or others.
They lie in Tents ; and they burn the Dung of
Beasts for Default of Wood.   This Kingdom descendeth on this Side toward us and toward Prussia
and toward Russia.

And through that Country runneth the River of
Ethille that is one of the greatest Rivers of the
World.   And it freezeth so strongly every Year,
that many times Men have fought upon the Ice
with great Hosts, both Parties on Foot, and their
Horses quitted for the Time, and what with those
on Horse and on Foot, more than 200,000 Persons
on each Side.

And between that River and the great Sea Ocean,
that they call the Sea Maure, lie all these Realms.
And toward the Head, beneath, in that Realm is the
Mount Chotaz, that is the highest Mount of the
World, and it is between the Sea Maure and the
Sea Caspian.   There is a full strait and dangerous
Passage to go toward Ind.   And therefore King
Alexander made there a strong City, that Men call
Alexandria, to guard the Country that no Man
should pass without his Leave.   And now Men call
that City, the Gate of Hell.

And the principal City of Comania is clept Sarak,

that is on one of the 3 Ways to go into Ind. But
by this Way, may not pass any great Multitude of
People, but if it be in Winter. And that Passage
Men call the Derbent. The tother Way is to go
from the City of Turkestan by Persia, and by that
Way be many Days' Journey by Desert. And the
3rd Way is that which cometh from Comania and
then goes by the great Sea and by the Kingdom of
Abchaz.

And ye shall understand, that all these Kingdoms
and all these Lands above-said unto Prussia and to
Russia be all obeissant to the great Chan of Cathay,
and many other Countries that march with other
Borders. Wherefore his Power and his Lordship is
full great and full mighty.

CHAPTER XXV

*Of the Emperor of Persia, and of the Land of Darkness;
and of other Kingdoms that belong to the great
Chan of Cathay, and other Lands of
his, unto the Sea of Greece*

WOMAN OF ABCHAZ

OW, since I have advised you of the Lands and the Kingdoms toward the Septentrional or Northern Parts, in coming down from the Land of Cathay unto the Lands of the Christians, toward Prussia and Russia,— now shall I advise you of other Lands and Kingdoms coming down by other Borders, toward the right Side, unto the Sea of Greece, toward the Land of Christian Men. And, therefore, as after Ind and after Cathay the Emperor of Persia is the greatest Lord,—therefore, I shall tell you of the Kingdom of Persia first, where he hath 2 Kingdoms.

The first Kingdom beginneth toward the East, toward the Kingdom of Turkestan, and it stretcheth

toward the West unto the River of Pison, that is one of the 4 Rivers that come out of Paradise. And on another Side it stretcheth toward the Septentrion or North unto the Sea of Caspian; and also toward the South unto the Desert of Ind. And this Country is good and plenteous and full of People. And there be many good Cities. But the 2 principal Cities be these, Bokhara, and Seornergant, that Men call Samarcand. The tother Kingdom of Persia stretcheth toward the River of Pison and the Parts of the West unto the Kingdom of Media, and from the Great Armenia and toward the Septentrion to the Sea of Caspian and toward the South to the Land of Ind. That is also a good Land and a plenteous, and it hath 3 great principal Cities—Messabor, Caphon, and Sarmassan.

And then after is Armenia, in the which were wont to be 5 Kingdoms, that is a noble Country and full of Goods. And it beginneth at Persia and stretcheth toward the West in Length unto Turkey. And in Breadth it endureth to the City of Alexandria, that now is clept the Gate of Hell, that I spake of before, under the Kingdom of Media. In this Armenia be full many good Cities, but Taurizo (Tabreez) is most of Name.

After this is the Kingdom of Media, that is full long, but is not full broad, that beginneth toward the East at the Land of Persia and at Ind the Less; and it stretcheth toward the West, toward the Kingdom of Chaldea and toward the Septentrion, descending toward the Little Armenia. In that

THE MARVELLOUS DARK COUNTRY CALLED HANYSON

Kingdom of Media there be many great Hills and little of flat Earth. There dwell Saracens and another manner of Folk, that Men call Kurds. The best 2 Cities of that Kingdom be Sarras and Karemen.

After that is the Kingdom of Georgia, that beginneth toward the East, at the great Mountain that is clept Abzor, where dwell many divers Folk of diverse Nations. And Men call the Country Alamo. This Kingdom stretcheth him towards Turkey and toward the great Sea, and toward the South it marcheth with the Great Armenia. And there be 2 Kingdoms in that Country ; the one is the Kingdom of Georgia, and the other is the Kingdom of Abchaz. And always in that Country be 2 Kings ; and they be both Christians, but the King of Georgia is in Subjection to the great Chan. And the King of Abchaz hath the more strong Country and he always vigorously defendeth his Country against all those that assail him, so that no Man may make him in Subjection to any Man.

In that Kingdom of Abchaz is a great Marvel. For a Province of the Country that hath well in Circuit 3 Days' Journeys, that Men call Hanyson, is all covered with Darkness, without any Brightness or Light ; so that no Man may see there, nor no Man dare enter into him. And, nevertheless, they of the Country say, that sometimes Men hear Voices of Folk, and Horses neighing, and Cocks crowing. And Men wit well, that Men dwell there, but they know not what Men. And they say, that Darkness

befell by Miracle of God. For a cursed Emperor of Persia, that was hight Saures, pursued all Christian Men to destroy them and to compel them to make Sacrifice to his Idols, and rode with a great Host, in all that ever he might, to confound the Christian Men. And then in that Country dwelled many good Christian Men, the which left their Goods and would have fled into Greece. And when they were in a Plain that was hight Megon, anon this cursed Emperor met with them with his Host to have slain them and hewn them in Pieces. And anon the Christian Men kneeled to the Ground, and made their Prayers to God to succour them. And anon a thick Cloud came and covered the Emperor and all his Host. And so they endure in that Manner that they must not go out any Side ; and so shall they evermore abide in Darkness till the Day of Doom, by the Miracle of God. And then the Christian Men went where liked them best, at their own Pleasure, without Hindering of any Creature, their Enemies enclosed and confounded in Darkness without any Stroke.

Wherefore we may well say with David, "*A Domino factum est istud ; et est mirabile in Oculis nostris.*" ("*This is the Lord's doing, and it is marvellous in our Eyes.*") And that was a great Miracle, that God made for them. Wherefore methinketh that Christian Men should be more devout to serve our Lord God than any other Men of any other Sect. For without any Doubt, if there were not Cursedness and Sin of Christian Men, they should be Lords of all the World.   For the Banner of Jesu Christ is always displayed, and ready on all Sides to the Help of his true loving Servants. Insomuch, that one good Christian Man in good Belief should overcome and chase out a 1000 cursed misbelieving Men, as David saith in the Psalter.* *" Quoniam persequebatur unus mille, et duo fugarent decem milia ;"* (*" How should one chase a 1000, and 2 put 10,000 to Flight ;"*) and, *" Cadent a latere tuo mille, et decem milia a dextris tuis."* (*" A 1000 shall fall at thy Side, and 10,000 at thy right Hand."*)   And how that it might be that one should chase a 1000, David himself saith, following, *" Quia Manus Domini fecit hæc omnia."* (*" For the Hand of the Lord made all these Things."*)   So that we may see openly that if we be good Men, no Enemy may endure against us.

Also ye shall understand that out of that Land of Darkness goeth out a great River that sheweth well that there be Folk dwelling there by many ready Tokens ; but no Man dare enter into it.

And wit well, that in the Kingdoms of Georgia, of Abchaz and of the Little Armenia be good Christian Men and devout.   For they shrive them and housel them (take the Sacrament) evermore once or twice in the Week.   And there be many of them that housel them every Day ; and so do we not on this Side, albeit that Saint Paul commandeth it,† saying, *" Omnibus Diebus Dominicis ad Communicandum hortor "* (*" Every Lord's Day I exhort you to com-*

---

* An error.   *Vide* Deut. xxxii. 30.   † Not from St. Paul.

municate"). They keep that Commandment, but we keep it not

And after, on this Side, is Turkey, that marcheth with the Great Armenia. And there be many Provinces, as Cappadocia, Saure, Brique, Quesiton, Pytan and Gemethe. And in every one of these be good Cities. This Turkey stretcheth unto the City of Sathala that sitteth upon the Sea of Greece, and so it marcheth with Syria. Syria is a great Country and a good, as I have told you before. And also it hath, above toward Ind, the Kingdom of Chaldea, that stretcheth from the Mountains of Chaldea toward the East unto the City of Nineveh, that sitteth upon the River of Tigris ; and in Breadth it beginneth toward the North to the City of Maraga ; and it stretcheth toward the South unto the Sea Ocean. In Chaldea it is a flat Country, and few Hills and few Rivers.

After is the Kingdom of Mesopotamia, that beginneth, toward the East, at the River Tigris, at a City that is clept Mosul ; and it stretcheth toward the West to the River of Euphrates unto a City that is clept Roianz ; and in Length it goeth from the Mount of Armenia unto the Desert of Ind the Less. This is a good Country and a flat, but it hath few Rivers. It hath but 2 Mountains in that Country, of the which one is called Symar and the other Lyson. And this Land marcheth with the Kingdom of Chaldea.

Also, there be, toward the Meridional or Southern Parts, many Countries and many Regions, as the

Land of Ethiopia, that marcheth, toward the East with the great Deserts, toward the South with the Kingdom of Mauritania, and toward the North with the Red Sea.

After is Mauritania, that endureth from the Mountains of Ethiopia unto Lybia the High. And that Country lieth along from the Sea Ocean toward the South ; and toward the North it marcheth with Nubia and with the High Lybia, and the Men of Nubia be Christian ; and it marcheth from the Lands above-said with the Deserts of Egypt, and that is the Egypt that I have spoken of before.

And after is Lybia the High and Lybia the Low that descendeth down low toward the great Sea of Spain, in the which Country be many Kingdoms and many divers Folk.

Now I have advised you of many Countries on this Side the Kingdom of Cathay, of the which many be obeissant to the great Chan.

"MEN FIND WITHIN A LITTLE BEAST"

CHAPTER XXVI

*Of the Countries and Isles that be beyond the Land
of Cathay ; and of the Fruits there ; and of the
22 Kings enclosed within the Mountains*

Now shall I say to you, following, of Countries
and Isles that be beyond the Countries that I have
spoken of.

Wherefore I say to you, in passing by the Land
of Cathay toward the High Ind and toward Bacharia,
Men pass by a Kingdom that Men call Caldilhe, that
is a full fair Country.

And there groweth a manner of Fruit, as though it were Gourds. And when they be ripe, Men cut them in two, and Men find within a little Beast in Flesh and Bone and Blood, as though it were a little Lamb without Wool. And Men eat both the Fruit and the Beast. And that is a great Marvel. Of that Fruit I have eaten, although it were wonderful, but that I know well that God is marvellous in His . Works. And, nevertheless, I told them of as great a Marvel to them, that is amongst us, and that was of the Barnacle Geese. For I told them that in our Country were Trees that bear a Fruit that become Birds flying, and those that fall in the Water live, and they that fall on the Earth die anon, and they be right good to Man's Meat. And thereof had they so great Marvel, that some of them trowed it were an impossible Thing to be.

In that Country be long Apples of good Savour, whereof be more than 100 in one Cluster, and as many in another, and they have great long Leaves and large, of 2 Foot long or more. And in that Country, and in other Countries thereabout, grow many Trees that bear Gylofre-Cloves and Nutmegs, and great Nuts of Ind, and Cinnamon and many other Spices. And there be Vines that bear so great Grapes, that a strong Man should have enough to do to bear one Cluster with all the Grapes.

In that same Region be the Mountains of Caspian that Men call Uber in the Country. Between those Mountains the Jews of 10 Lineages be enclosed, that Men call Gog and Magog, and they may not

go out on any Side. There were enclosed 22 Kings with their People, that dwelled between the Mountains of Scythia. There King Alexander chased them between those Mountains, and there he thought to enclose them through Work of his Men. But when he saw that he might not do it nor bring it to an End, he prayed to the God of Nature that He would perform that he had begun. And albeit so, that he was a Paynim and not worthy to be heard, yet God of His Grace closed the Mountains together, so that they dwell there all fast locked and enclosed with high Mountains all about, save only on one Side, and on that Side is the Sea of Caspian.

Now Men may ask, "Since that the Sea is on that one Side, wherefore go they not out on the Sea Side, to go where it liketh them?"

But to this Question, I shall answer; "That Sea of Caspian goeth out by Land under the Mountains, and runneth by the Desert at one Side of the Country, and after it stretcheth unto the Ends of Persia, and although it be clept a Sea, it is no Sea, nor toucheth it to any other Sea, but it is a Lake, the greatest of the World; and though they would put them on to that Sea, they wist never where they should arrive; and also they know no Language but only their own, that no Man knoweth but they; and therefore may they not go out."

And also ye shall understand, that the Jews have no Land of their own to dwell in, in all the World, but only that Land between the Mountains. And yet they yield Tribute for that Land to the

Queen of Amazonia, the which maketh them to be kept enclosed full diligently, that they shall not go out on any Side but at the Cost of their Land ; for their Land marcheth with the Mountains.

THE QUEEN OF AMAZONIA

And often it hath befallen, that some of these Jews have gone up the Mountains and climbed down to the Valleys.   But great Number of Folk may not do so, for the Mountains be so high and so straight up, that they must abide there, maugre their Might. For they may not go out, but by a little Issue that was made by Strength of Men, and it lasteth well a 4 great Mile.

And after, is there then a Land all Desert, where Men may find no Water, neither by Digging nor by any other Thing.   Wherefore Men may not dwell in that Place, so full is it of Dragons, Serpents and other venomous Beasts, that no man dare pass, but if it be in severe Winter.   And that strait Passage Men, in that Country, call Clyron.   And that is the Passage that the Queen of Amazonia maketh to be kept.   And though it happen that some of them by Fortune go out, they know no Manner of Language but Hebrew, so that they cannot speak to the People.

And yet, nevertheless, Men say that they shall go out in the Time of Anti-Christ, and that they shall make great Slaughter of Christian Men. And therefore all the Jews that dwell in all Lands learn always to speak Hebrew, in Hope, that when the other Jews shall go out, that they may understand their Speech and lead them into Christendom to destroy the Christian People.   For the Jews say that they know well by their Prophecies, that they of Caspia shall go out, and spread throughout all the World, and that the Christian Men shall be under their Subjection, as long as they have been in Subjection to them.

And if that ye will wit, how that they shall find their Way, after that I have heard say I shall tell you.

In the Time of Anti-Christ a Fox shall make there his Lair, and mine an Hole where King Alexander made make the Gates; and so long

THE MARVELLOUS LAND OF BACHARIA

shall he mine and pierce the Earth, that he shall pass through towards that Folk. And when they see the Fox, they shall have great Marvel of him, because that they saw never such a Beast. For all other Beasts they have enclosed amongst them, save only the Fox. And then they shall chase him and pursue him so straight, till that he come to the same Place that he came from. And then they shall dig and mine so strongly, till that they find the Gates that King Alexander made make of Stones, great and passing huge, well cemented and made strong for the Mastery. And those Gates they shall break, and so go out by finding of that Issue.

From that Land go Men toward the Land of Bacharia, where be full evil Folk and full cruel. In that Land be Trees that bear Wool, as though it were of Sheep, whereof they make Clothes and all Things that may be made of Wool.

In that Country be many Hippotaynes that dwell sometime in the Water and sometime on the Land. And they be half Man and half Horse, as I have said before. And they eat Men when they may take them.

And there be Rivers of Waters that be full bitter, 3 times more than is the Water of the Sea.

In that Country be many Griffins, more Plenty than in any other Country. Some Men say that they have the Body upward as an Eagle and beneath as a Lion ; and truly they say Truth, that they be of that Shape. But one Griffin hath the Body more great and is more strong than 8 Lions,

of such Lions as be on this Side, and more great and stronger than an 100 Eagles such as we have amongst us.   For one Griffin there will bear, flying to his Nest, a great Horse if he may find him at the Place, or 2 Oxen yoked together as they go to the Plough.   For he hath Talons so long and so large and so great upon his Feet, as though they were Horns of great Oxen or of Buffaloes or of Kine, that Men make Cups of them to drink of.   And of their Ribs and of the Feathers of their Wings, Men make Bows, full strong, to shoot Arrows and Bolts with.

From thence go Men by many Days' Journey through the Land of Prester John, the great Emperor of Ind.   And Men call his Realm the Isle of Pentexoire.

CUP MADE FROM GRIFFIN'S TALON

THE ADAMANT ROCKS

CHAPTER XXVII

*Of the Royal Estate of Prester John. And of a rich
Man that made a marvellous Castle and called
it Paradise; and of his Subtlety*

THIS Emperor, Prester John, holds
full great Land, and hath many
full noble Cities and good Towns
in his Realm, and many great
divers Isles and large. For all the Country of
Ind is divided into Isles by the great Rivers
that come from Paradise, that part all the Land
into many Parts. And also in the Sea he hath
full many Isles. And the best City in the Isle of

Pentexoire is Nyse, that is a full Royal City and a noble, and full rich.

This Prester John hath under him many Kings and many Isles and many divers Folk of divers Conditions. And this Land is full good and rich, but not so rich as is the Land of the great Chan. For the Merchants come not thither so commonly to buy Merchandises, as they do in the Land of the great Chan, for it is too far to travel to. And on that other Side, in the Isle of Cathay, Men find all manner of Thing that is need-ful to Man—Cloths of Gold, of Silk, and Spicery. And therefore, albeit that Men have greater Cheapness in the Isle of Prester John, nevertheless, Men dread the long Way and the great Perils in the Sea in those Parts.

For in many Places of the Sea be great Rocks of Stones of the Adamant (or Lode-stone,) that of his own Nature draweth Iron to him. And therefore pass there no Ships that have either Bonds or Nails of Iron within them. And if they do, anon the Rocks of the Adamants draw them to them, that never they may go thence. I myself have seen afar off in that Sea as though it had been a great Isle full of Trees and Bush, full of Thorns and Briars, great Plenty. And the Shipmen told us, that all that was of Ships that were drawn thither by the Adamants, for the Iron that was in them. And from the Rotten-ness, and other Things that were within the Ships, grew such Bush, and Thorns and Briars and green Grass, and such manner of Things, and from the Masts and the Sail-yards it seemed a great Wood or a Grove. And such Rocks be in many Places thereabout. And therefore dare not the Merchants pass there, but if they know well the Passages, or else that they have good Pilots.

And also they dread the long Way. And therefore they go to Cathay, for it is more nigh. And yet it is not so nigh, but that Men must be travelling by Sea and Land, 11 Months or 12, from Genoa or Venice, ere they come to Cathay. And yet is the Land of Prester John more far by many dreadful Days' Journeys.

And the Merchants pass by the Kingdom of Persia, and go to a City that is clept Hermes (Ormuz,) for Hermes the Philosopher founded it. And after that they pass an Arm of the Sea, and then go to another City that is clept Golbache. And there they find Merchandises, and of Popinjays (or Parrots,) as great. Plenty as Men find here of Geese. And if they will pass further, they may securely enough. In that Country is but little go Wheat or Barley, and therefore they eat Rice and Honey and Milk and Cheese and Fruit.

This Emperor Prester John taketh always to Wife the Daughter of the great Chan ; and the great Chan also, in the same Wise, the Daughter of Prester John. For these 2 be the greatest Lords under the Firmament.

In the Land of Prester John be many divers Things and many precious Stones, so great and so large, that Men make of them Vessels, as Platters,

Dishes and Cups. And many other Marvels be there, that it were too cumbrous and too long to put in Writing of Books; but of the principal Isles and of his Estate and of his Law, I shall tell you some Part.

This Emperor Prester John is Christian, and a great Part of his Country also. But yet, they have not all the Articles of our Faith as we have. They believe well in the Father, in the Son and in the Holy Ghost. And they be full devout and right true to one another. And they set no Store by any Contests, nor by Tricks, nor on any Deceits.

And he hath under him 72 Provinces, and in every Province is a King. And these Kings have Kings under them, and all be Tributaries to Prester John. And he hath in his Lordships many great Marvels.

For in his Country is the Sea that Men call the Gravelly Sea, that is all Gravel and Sand, without any Drop of Water, and it ebbeth and floweth in great Waves as other Seas do, and it is never still nor at Peace, in any manner of Season. And no Man may pass that Sea by Ship, nor by any manner of Craft, and therefore may no Man know what Land is beyond that Sea. And albeit that it have no Water, yet Men find therein and on the Banks full good Fishes of other manner of Nature and Shape, than Men find in any other Sea, and they be of right good Taste and delicious for Man's Meat.

And a 3 Days' Journey long from that Sea be great Mountains, out of the which goeth out a great

"AND THERE BE MANY WILD HOUNDS, HORNED MEN, AND POPINJAYS"

River that cometh out of Paradise.   And it is full
of precious Stones, without any Drop of Water, and
it runneth through the Desert on the one Side, so
that it maketh the Sea gravelly; and it runneth
into that Sea, and there it endeth.   And that River
runneth, also, 3 Days in the Week and bringeth
with him great Stones and the Rocks also there-
· with, and that great Plenty.   And anon, as they be
entered into the Gravelly Sea, they be seen no more,
but lost for evermore.   And in those 3 Days that
that River runneth, no Man dare enter into it ; but
on other Days Men dare enter well enough.

Also beyond that River, more upward to the
Deserts, is a great Plain all gravelly, between the
Mountains.   And in that Plain, every Day at the
Sun-rising, begin to grow small Trees, and they
grow till Mid-day, bearing Fruit ; but no Man dare
take of that Fruit, for it is a Thing of Faerie.   And
after Mid-day, they decrease and enter again into
the Earth, so that at the going down of the Sun
they appear no more.   And so they do, every Day.
And that is a great Marvel.

In that Desert be many Wild Men, that be
hideous to look on ; for they be horned, and they
speak nought, but they grunt, as Pigs.   And there
is also great Plenty of wild Hounds.   And there be
many Popinjays (or Parrots,) that they call Psittakes*
in their Language.   And they speak of their own
Nature, and say, "*Salve !*" ("*God save you !*")
to Men that go through the Deserts, and speak to

* Lat.: Psittacus, parrot.

them as freely as though it were a Man that spoke.
And they that speak well have a large Tongue, and
have 5 Toes upon a Foot. And there be also some
of another Manner, that have but 3 Toes upon a
Foot, and they speak not, or but little, for they
cannot but cry.

This Emperor Prester John when he goeth into
Battle against any other Lord, he hath no Banners
borne before him ; but he hath 3 Crosses of Gold,
fine, great and high, full of precious Stones, and
every one of the Crosses be set in a Chariot, full
richly arrayed. And to keep every Cross, be
ordained 10,000 Men of Arms and more than
100,000 Men on Foot, in manner as when Men
would keep a Standard in our Countries, when that
we be in a Land of War. And this Number of Folk
is besides the principal Host and besides the Wings
ordained for the Battle. And when he hath no
War, but rideth with a private Company, then he
hath borne before him but one Cross of Tree,
without Painting and without Gold or Silver or
precious Stones, in Remembrance that Jesu Christ
suffered Death upon a Cross of Wood. And he hath
borne before him also a Platter of Gold full of Earth,
in Token that his Nobleness and his Might and his
Flesh shall turn to Earth. And he hath borne
before him also a Vessel of Silver, full of noble
Jewels of Gold full rich and of precious Stones, in
Token of his Lordship and of his Nobleness and of
his Might.

He dwelleth commonly in the City of Susa. And

there is his principal Palace, that is so rich and noble, that no Man will believe it by Estimation, but he had seen it.   And above the chief Tower of the Palace be 2 round Pommels or Balls of Gold, and in each of them be 2 Carbuncles great and large, that shine full bright upon the Night.   And the principal gates of his Palace be of precious Stone that Men call Sardonyx, and the Border and the Bars be of Ivory.   And the Windows of the Halls and Chambers be of Crystal.   And the Tables whereon Men eat, some be of Emeralds, some of Amethyst, and some of Gold, full of precious Stones ; and the Pillars that bear up the Tables be of the same precious Stones.   And of the Steps to go up to his Throne, where he sitteth at Meat, one is of Onyx, another is of Crystal, and another of green Jasper, another of Amethyst, another of Sardine, another of Cornelian, and the 7th, that he setteth his Feet on, is of Chrysolite.   And all these Steps be bordered with fine Gold, with the tother precious Stones, set with great orient Pearls.   And the Sides of the Seat of his Throne be of Emeralds, and bordered with Gold full nobly, and dubbed with other precious Stones and great Pearls.   And all the Pillars in his Chamber be of fine Gold with precious Stones, and with many Carbuncles, that give Light upon the Night to all People. And albeit that the Carbuncles give Light right enough, nevertheless, at all Times burneth a Vessel of Crystal full of Balm, to give good Smell and Odour to the Emperor, and to void away all

wicked Eyes and Corruptions. And the Form of his Bed is of fine Sapphires, bound with Gold, to make him sleep well and to refrain him from Lechery; for he will not lie with his Wives, but 4 Times in the Year, according to the 4 Seasons, and that is only to engender Children.

He hath also a full fair Palace and a noble at the City of Nyse, where that he dwelleth, when it best liketh him ; but the Air is not so temperate, as it is at the City of Susa.

And ye shall understand, that in all his Country and in the Countries there all about, Men eat not but once in the Day, as Men do in the Court of the great Chan. And so they eat every Day in his Court, more than 30,000 Persons, besides Goers and Comers. But the 30,000 Persons of his Country, and of the Country of the great Chan, spend not so much in goods as do 12,000 of our Country.

This Emperor Prester John hath evermore 7 Kings with him to serve him, and they share their Service by certain Months. And with these Kings serve always 72 Dukes and 360 Earls. And all the Days of the Year, there eat in his Household and in his Court, 12 Archbishops and 20 Bishops. And there the Patriarch of Saint Thomas is as the Pope here. And the Archbishops and the Bishops and the Abbots in that Country be all Kings. And every one of these great Lords know well enough the Attendance of their Service. The one is Master of his Household, another is his Chamberlain, another serveth him with a Dish, another with the Cup, another is Steward, another is Marshal, another is Prince of his Arms, and thus is he full nobly and royally served.   And his Land endureth verily in Breadth 4 Months' Journeys, and in Length beyond Measure, that is to say, to all the Isles under the Earth that we suppose to be under us.

Beside the Isle of Pentexoire, that is the Land of Prester John, is a great Isle, long and broad, that Men call Mistorak; and it is in the Lordship of Prester John.   In that Isle is great Plenty of Goods.

There was dwelling there, sometime, a rich Man; and it is not long since; and Men called him Gatholonabes.   And he was full of Tricks and of subtle Deceits.   And he had a full fair Castle and a strong in a Mountain, so strong and so noble, that no Man could devise a fairer cr a stronger.   And he had made wall all the Mountain about with a strong Wall and a fair.   And within those Walls he had the fairest Garden that any Man might behold. And therein were Trees bearing all manner of Fruits, that any Man could devise.   And therein were also all manner of Herbs of Virtue of good Smell, and all other Herbs also that bear fair Flowers. And he had also in that Garden many fair Wells; and beside those Wells he had made fair Halls and fair Chambers, painted all with Gold and Azure; and there were painted in that Place many divers Things, and many diverse Stories of Beasts, and of Birds that sung full delectably and moved by Craft, that it seemed that they were alive. And he had also in his Garden all manner of Fowls and of Beasts that any Man might think on, to have Play or Sport to behold them.

And he had also, in that Place, the fairest Damsels that might be found, under the Age of 15 Years, and the fairest young Striplings that Men might get, of that same Age. And they were all clothed in Cloths of Gold, full richly. And he said that those were Angels.

And he had also made 3 Wells, fair and noble, and all environed with Stone of Jasper, and of Crystal, diapered with Gold, and set with precious Stones and great orient Pearls. And he had made a Conduit under the Earth, so that the 3 Wells, at his List, should run, one Milk, another Wine and another Honey. And that Place he clept Paradise.

And when that any good Knight, that was hardy and noble, came to see this Royalty, he would lead him into his Paradise, and show him these wonderful Things for his Sport, and the marvellous and delicious Song of divers Birds, and the fair Damsels, and the fair Wells of Milk, Wine and Honey, plenteously running. And he would make divers Instruments of Music to sound in an high Tower, so merrily, that it was Joy to hear; and no Man should see the Craft thereof. And those, he said, were Angels of God, and that Place was Paradise, that God had promised to his Friends, saying, "*Dabo vobis Terram fluentem Lacte et Melle.*" ("*I shall give thee a Land flowing with Milk and*

Honey.") And then would he make them to drink of certain Drink, whereof anon they should be drunk. And then would they think it greater Delight than they had before. And then would he say

GATHOLONABES AND A HARDY KNIGHT

to them, that if they would die for him and for his Love, that after their Death they should come to his Paradise; and they should be of the Age of the Damsels, and they should play with them, and yet be Maidens. And after that should he put them in a yet fairer Paradise, where that they should see the God of Nature visibly, in His Majesty and in His Bliss. And then would he shew them his Intent, and say to them, that if they would go slay

such a Lord, or such a Man that was his Enemy or contrarious to his List, that they should not therefore dread to do it and to be slain themselves. For after their Death, he would put them in another Paradise, that was an 100-fold fairer than any of the tother ; and there should they dwell with the most fairest Damsels that might be, and play with them ever-more.

And thus went many divers lusty Bachelors to slay great Lords in divers Countries, that were his Enemies, and made themselves to be slain, in Hope to have that Paradise. And thus, often-time, he was revenged of his Enemies by his subtle Deceits and false Tricks.

And when the worthy Men of the Country had perceived this subtle Falsehood of this Gatholonabes, they assembled them with Force, and assailed his Castle, and slew him, and destroyed all the fair Places and all the Nobilities of that Paradise. The Place of the Wells and of the Walls and of many other Things be yet openly seen, but the Riches be clean voided. And it is not long ago, since that Place was destroyed.

CHAPTER XXVIII

Of the Devil's Head in the Valley Perilous. And of the Customs of Folk in diverse Isles that be about in the Lordship of Prester John

ESIDE that Isle of Mistorak upon the left Side nigh to the River of Pison is a marvellous Thing. There is a Vale between the Mountains, that endureth nigh a 4 Mile. And some call it the Vale Enchanted, some call it the Vale of Devils, and some call it the Vale Perilous. In that Vale hear Men often-time great Tempests and Thunders, and great Murmurs and Noises, all Days and Nights, and great Noise, as it were Sound of Tabors and of Nakers (Drums) and Trumps, as though it were of a great Feast. This Vale is all full of Devils, and hath been always. And Men say

there, that it is one of the Entries of Hell. In that Vale is great Plenty of Gold and Silver. Wherefore many misbelieving Men, and many Christian Men also, go in oftentime to have of the Treasure that there is ; but few come back again, and especially of the misbelieving Men, nor of the Christian Men either, for they be anon strangled of Devils.

And in mid Place of that Vale, under a Rock, is an Head and the Visage of a Devil bodily, full horrible and dreadful to see, and it sheweth not but the Head, to the Shoulders. But there is no Man in the World so hardy, Christian Man nor other, but that he would be a-dread to behold it, and that it would seem to him to die for Dread, so hideous is it to behold. For he beholdeth every Man so sharply with dreadful Eyes, that be evermore moving and sparkling like Fire, and changeth and stareth so often in diverse Manner, with so horrible Countenance, that no Man dare draw nigh towards him. And from him cometh out Smoke and Stink and Fire and so much Abomination, that scarcely any Man may there endure.

But the good Christian Men, that be stable in the Faith, enter well without Peril. For they will first shrive them, and mark them with the Token of the Holy Cross, so that the Fiends have no Power over them. But albeit that they be without Peril, yet, nevertheless, they be not without Dread, when that they see the Devils visibly and bodily all about them, that make full many diverse Assaults and Menaces, in Air and in Earth, and aghast them with

THE HORRIBLE DEVIL IN THE VALLEY PERILOUS

Strokes of Thunder-blasts and of Tempests. And the most Dread is, that God will take Vengeance then of what Men have misdone against His Will.

And ye shall understand, that when my Fellows and I were in that Vale, we were in great Thought, whether that we durst put our Bodies in Adventure, to go in or not, in the Protection of God. And some of our Fellows accorded to enter, and some not. So there were with us 2 worthy Men, Friars Minors, that were of Lombardy, that said, that if any Man would enter they would go in with us. And when they had said so, upon the gracious Trust of God and of them, we made sing Mass, and made every Man to be shriven and houseled. And then we entered 14 Persons ; but at our going out we were but 9. And so we wist never, whether that our Fellows were lost, or else turned again for Dread. But we saw them never after ; and those were 2 Men of Greece, and 3 of Spain. And our other Fellows that would not go in with us, they went by another Side to be before us ; and so they were.

And thus we passed that Perilous Vale, and found therein Gold and Silver, and precious Stones and rich Jewels, great Plenty, both here and there, as it seemed to us. But whether that it was, as it seemed to us, I wot never. For I touched none, because that the Devils be so subtle to make a Thing to seem otherwise than it is, to deceive Mankind. And therefore I touched none, and also because that I would not be put out of my Devotion ; for I was more devout then, than ever I was before or after, and all for the Dread of Fiends that I saw in diverse Figures, and also for the great Multitude of dead Bodies, that I saw there lying by the Way, by all the Vale, as though there had been a Battle between 2 Kings the mightiest of the Country, and that the greater Part had been discomfited and slain. And I trow, that scarcely should any Country have so much People within him, as lay slain in that Vale as we thought, the which was an hideous Sight to see. And I marvelled much, that there were so many, and the Bodies all whole without rotting. But I trow, that Fiends made them so seem to be whole without rotting. But it might not be to mine Advice that so many should have entered so newly, neither so many newly slain, without stinking and rotting. And many of them were in Habit of Christian Men, but I trow well, that they were of such that went in for Covetousness of the Treasure that was there, and had overmuch Feebleness in Faith; so that their Hearts might not endure in the Belief for Dread. And therefore were we the more devout a great Deal. And yet we were cast down, and beaten down many times to the hard Earth by Winds and Thunders and Tempests. But evermore God of His Grace help us. And so we passed that Perilous Vale without Peril and without Encumbrance. Thanked be Almighty God!

After this, beyond the Vale, is a great Isle, where the Folk be great Giants of 28 Foot long, or of 30 Foot long. And they have no Clothing but of

Skins of Beasts that they hang upon them. And they eat no Bread, but all raw Flesh ; and they drink Milk of Beasts, for they have Plenty of all Cattle. And they have no Houses to lie in. And they eat more gladly Man's Flesh than any other Flesh. Into that Isle dare no Man gladly enter. And if they see a Ship and Men therein, anon they enter into the Sea to take them.

And Men said to us, that in an Isle beyond that were Giants of greater Stature, some of 45 Foot, or 50 Foot long, and, as some Men say, of 50 Cubits long. But I saw none of those, for I had no Lust to go to those Parts, because that no Man cometh neither into that Isle nor into the other, but he be devoured anon. And among those Giants be Sheep as great as Oxen here, and they bear great Wool and rough. Of the Sheep I have seen many times. And Men have seen, many times, those Giants take Men in the Sea out of their Ships, and bring them to Land, 2 in one Hand and 2 in another, eating them going, all raw and all alive.

Another Isle is there toward the North, in the Sea Ocean, where that be full cruel and evil Women of Nature. And they have precious Stones in their Eyes. And they be of that Nature, that if they behold any Man with Wrath, they slay him anon with the Beholding, as doth the Basilisk.

After that is another Isle, where that Women make great Sorrow when their Children be born. And when they die, they make great Feast and great Joy and Revel, and then they cast them into a

great burning Fire. And those that love well their
Husbands, if their Husbands be dead, they cast
themselves also in the Fire with their Children, and
burn themselves. And they say that the Fire shall
cleanse them of all Filths and of all Vices, and they

" PRECIOUS STONES IN THEIR EYES "

shall go purified and clean into another World to
their Husbands, and they shall lead their Children
with them. And the Cause why that they weep,
when their Children be born is this ; that when
they come into this World, they come to Labour,
Sorrow and Heaviness. And why they make Joy
and Gladness at their Dying is because that, as they
say, then they go to Paradise where the Rivers run
Milk and Honey, where Men see them in Joy and in
Abundance of Goods, without Sorrow and Labour.

In that Isle Men make their King evermore by
Election, and they choose him not for any Nobleness or for any Riches, but such an one as is of
good Manners and of good Conditions, and there-

withal righteous, and also see that he be of great Age,
and that he have no Children.   In that Isle Men be
full righteous and they do righteous Judgments in
every Cause both of rich and poor, small and great,
after the Quantity of the Trespass that is mis-done.
And the King may no doom any Man to Death
without Assent of his Barons and other Men wise of
Counsel, and if that all the Court accord thereto.
And if the King himself do any Homicide or any
Crime, as to slay a Man, or any such Hazard, he
shall die there for.   But he shall not be slain as
another Man ; but Men shall forbid, on Pain of
Death, that any Man be so hardy as to make him
Company or to speak with him, or that any Man
give him or sell him or serve him, either with Meat
or Drink ; and so shall he die in Misfortune.   They
spare no Man that hath trespassed, neither for Love
nor for Favour nor for Riches nor for Nobleness ; but
that shall he have, according to that he hath done.

Beyond that Isle is another Isle, where is great
Multitude of Folk.   And they will not, for any
thing, eat Flesh of Hares, or of Hens, or of Geese,
and yet they breed enough, to see them and to
behold them only ; but they eat Flesh of all other
Beasts, and drink Milk.   In that Country they take
their Daughters and their Sisters to Wife, and their
other Kins-women.   And if there be 10 or 12 Men
or more dwelling in an House, the Wife of every one
of them shall be common to all them that dwell in
that House ; so that every Man may lie with whom
he will of them on one Night, and with another,

another Night. And if she have any Child, she may give it to what Man she list, that hath companied with her, so that no Man knoweth there whether the Child be his or another's. And if any Man say to them, that they nourish other Men's Children, they answer that so do other Men theirs.

In that Country and by all Ind be great Plenty of Cockodrills, that is a manner of a long Serpent, as I have said before. And in the Night they dwell in the Water, and in the Day upon the Land, in Rocks and Caves. And they eat no Meat in all the Winter, but they lie as in a Dream, as do Serpents. These Serpents slay Men, and they eat them weeping ; and when they eat they move the over Jaw, and not the nether Jaw, and they have no Tongue.

In that Country and in many others beyond that, and also in many on this Side, Men put the Seed of Cotton to work, and they sow it every Year. And then groweth it in small Trees, that bear Cotton. And so do Men every Year, so that there is Plenty of Cotton at all times. *Item;* in this Isle and in many other, there is a manner of Wood, hard and Strong. Whoso covereth the Coals of that Wood under the Ashes thereof, the Coals will dwell and abide all alive, a Year or more. And that Tree hath many Leaves, as the Juniper hath. And there be also many Trees, of that Nature that they will never burn nor rot in any manner. And there be Nut Trees, that bear Nuts as great as a Man's Head.

There also be many Beasts, that be clept Orafles (Giraffes). In Arabia, they be clept Gerfaunts. That is a dappled or spotted Beast, that is but a little more high than is a Steed, but he hath the Neck a 20 Cubits long; and his Croup and his Tail be as of an Hart; and he may look over a great high House. And there be also in that Country many Chameleons; that is a little Beast as a Goat, that is wild, and he liveth on the Air and eateth nought and drinketh nought at any time. And he changeth his Colour often-time, for Men see him often-times, now in one Colour and now in another Colour; and he may change him into all manner of Colours that he list, save only into red and white. There be also in that Country passing great Serpents, some of 120 Foot long, and they be of divers Colours, and rayed, as red, green, yellow, blue and black, and all speckled. And there be others that have Crests upon their Heads, and they go upon their Feet, upright, and they be well a 4 Fathom great, or more, and they dwell always in Rocks or in Mountains, and they have always the Throat open, from whence they drop Venom always. And there be also Wild Swine of many Colours, as great as be Oxen in our Country, and they be all spotted, as be young Fawns. And there be also Hedgehogs, as great as Wild Swine here; we call them Porcupines. And there be Lions all white, great and mighty. And there be also of other Beasts, as great and more greater than is a War-horse, and Men call them Loerancs; and some Men call them

Odenthos; and they have a black Head and 3 long Horns, trenchant, on the Forehead, sharp as a Sword, and the Body is slender; and he is a full felonious Beast, and he chaseth and slayeth the

THE BOAR-HEADED BEAR-BODIED LION-TAILED 6-LEGGED BEAST

Elephant. There be also many other Beasts, full wicked and cruel, that be not much greater than a Bear, and they have the Head like a Boar, and they have 6 Feet, and on every Foot 2 large Claws, trenchant; and the Body is like a Bear, and the Tail as a Lion. And there be also Mice as great as Hounds, and yellow Mice as great as Ravens. And there be Geese, all red, 3 Times more great than

ours here, and they have the Head, the Neck and the Breast all black.

And many other diverse Beasts be in those Countries, and elsewhere there-about, and many diverse Birds also, of the which it were too long to tell you. And therefore, I pass them over at this Time.

CHAPTER XXIX

*Of the Goodness of the Folk of the Isle
of Bragman. Of King Alexander.
And wherefore the Emperor of Ind
is clept Prester John*

WOMAN OF BRAGMAN

ND beyond that Isle is another Isle, great and good and plenteous, where there be good Folk and true, and of good Living after their Belief and of good Faith. And albeit that they be not christened, nor have any perfect Law, yet, nevertheless, by natural Law they be full of all Virtue, and they eschew all Vices and all Malices and all Sins. For they be not proud, nor covetous, nor envious, nor wrathful, nor Gluttons, nor lecherous. Nor do they to any Man otherwise than they would that other Men did to them, and in this Point they fulfill the 10 Commandments of God. And they set no Weight on Possessions or on Riches. And they lie not, nor swear they, on any Occasion, but they say simply, Yea and Nay; for they say, " He that sweareth will deceive his Neighbour," and therefore, all that they do, they do it without Oath.

And Men call that Isle the Isle of Bragman, and some Men call it the Land of Faith.   And through that Land runneth a great River that is clept Thebe. And, in general, all the Men of those Isles and of all the Borders thereabout be more true than in any other Countries thereabout, and more righteous than others in all Things.   In that Isle is no Thief, nor Murderer, nor common Woman, nor poor Beggar, nor ever was Man slain in that Country.   And they be as chaste, and lead as good a Life, as though they were religious Men, and they fast all Days. And because they be so true and so righteous, and so full of all good Conditions, they were never grieved with Tempests, nor with Thunder, nor with Lightning, nor with Hail, nor with Pestilence, nor with War, nor with Hunger, nor with any other Tribulation, as we be, many times, amongst us, for our Sins.   Wherefore, it seemeth well, that God loveth them and is pleased with their Faith and their good Deeds.   They believe well in God, that made all Things, and Him they worship.   And they prize not earthly Riches ; and so they be all righteous.   And they live full orderly, and so soberly in Meat and Drink, that they live right long.   And the most Part of them die without Sickness, when Nature faileth them, for old Age.

And it befell in King Alexander's Time, that he

purposed him to conquer that Isle and to make them
to hold it of him. And when they of the Country
heard it, they sent Messengers to him with Letters,
that said thus; "What may be enough for that Man

THE MESSENGERS FROM BRAGMAN

to whom all the World is insufficient? Thou shalt
find nothing in us, that may cause thee to war
against us. For we have no Riches, nor covet we
any, and all the Goods of our Country be in
common. Our Meat, that we sustain withal our
Bodies, is our Riches. And, instead of Treasure of
Gold and Silver, we make our Treasure of Accord
and Peace, and the Love of every Man for the other.

And to apparel our Body with, we use a simple little Clout to wrap our Carrion in. Our Wives be not arrayed to make any Man Pleasure, but in suitable Array to eschew Folly. When Men pain themselves to array the Body, to make it seem fairer than God made it, they do great Sin. For Man should not devise nor ask greater Beauty, than God hath ordained Man to be at his Birth. The Earth ministereth to us 2 Things,—our Livelihood, that cometh of the Earth that we live by, and our Sepulture after our Death. We have been in perpetual Peace till now, that thou be come to disinherit us. And also we have a King, not to do Justice to every Man, for he shall find no Forfeit among us, but to keep Nobleness, and to shew that we be obeissant, we keep a King. For Justice hath not among us any Place, for we do no Man otherwise than we desire that Men do to us. So that Righteousness and Vengeance have nought to do among us. So that nothing may thou take from us, but our good Peace, that always hath endured among us."

And when King Alexander had read those Letters, he thought that he should do great Sin, to trouble them. And then he sent them Sureties, that they should keep their good Manners and their good Peace, as they had used before, of Custom. And so he let them alone.

Another Isle there is, that Men call Oxidrate, and another Isle, that Men call Gynosophe, where there is also good Folk, and full of good Faith. And they hold, for the most Part, the good Conditions and Customs and good Manners, as Men of the Country abovesaid ; but they go all naked.

Into that Isle entered King Alexander, to see the Manners. And when he saw their great Faith, and their Truth that was amongst them, he said he would not grieve them, and bade them ask of him what that they would have of him, Riches or anything else, and they should have it, with good Will. And they answered, that he was rich enough that had Meat and Drink to sustain the Body with, for the Riches of this World, that is transitory, be not of Worth ; but if it were in his Power to make them immortal, thereof would they pray him, and thank him. And Alexander answered them that it was not in his Power to do it, because he was mortal, as they were. And then they asked him why he was so proud and so fierce, and so busy to put all the World under his Subjection, "right as thou wert a God, and hast no Term of this Life, neither Day nor Hour, and willest to have all the World at thy Commandment, that shall leave thee without Fail, or thou leave it. And right as it hath been to other Men before thee, right so it shall be to other after thee. And from hence shalt thou bear nothing ; but as thou wert born naked, right so all naked shall thy Body be turned into Earth that thou wert made of. Wherefore thou shouldest think and impress it in thy Mind, that nothing is immortal, but only God, that made all Things." By the which Answer Alexander was greatly astonished and abashed, and all confused departed from them.

And albeit that these Folk have not the Articles of our Faith as we have, nevertheless, for their good natural Faith, and for their good Intent, I trow fully, that God loveth them, and that God taketh their Service in Favour, right as He did of Job, that was a Paynim, and held him for His true Servant. And therefore, albeit that there be many diverse Laws in the World, yet I trow, that God loveth always them that love Him, and serve Him meekly in Truth, and especially them that despise the vain Glory of this World, as this Folk do and as Job did also.

And therefore said our Lord by the Mouth of Hosea the Prophet, "*Ponam eis multiplices Leges Meas;*" ("*I have written to him the great Things of my Law;*") and also in another Place, "*Qui totum Orbem subdit suis Legibus,*" ("*Who subjected the whole World to His Laws.*") And also our Lord saith in the Gospel, "*Alias Oves habeo, que non sunt ex hoc Ovilis,*" ("*And other Sheep I have which are not of this Fold;*") that is to say, that he had other Servants than those that be under Christian Law. And to that accordeth the Vision that Saint Peter saw at Jaffa, how the Angel came from Heaven, and brought before him divers Beasts, as Serpents and creeping Beasts of the Earth, and of other also, great Plenty, and bade him take and eat. And Saint Peter answered; "I eat never," quoth he, "of unclean Beasts." And then said the Angel, "*Non dicas immunda, que Deus mundavit,*" ("*What God hath cleansed, that*

call thou not common.") And that was in Token that no Man should have in Despite any earthly Man for their diverse Laws, for we know not whom God loveth, nor whom God hateth. And for that Example, when Men say, "*De Profundis*," they say it in common and in general, with the Christians, "*Pro animabus omnium defunctorum, pro quibus sit orandum,*" ("*On behalf of the Souls of the Dead, for whom we ought to pray*").

And therefore say I of this Folk, that be so true and so faithful, that God loveth them. For He hath amongst them many of the Prophets, and always hath had. And in those Isles, they prophesied the Incarnation of our Lord Jesu Christ, how he should be born of a Maiden, 3000 Year or more ere our Lord was born of the Virgin Mary. And they believe well in the Incarnation, and that full perfectly, but they know not the Manner, how He suffered His Passion and Death for us.

And beyond these Isles there is another Isle that is clept Pytan. The Folk of that Country neither till, nor labour the Earth, for they eat no manner of Thing. And they be of good Colour and of fair Shape, after their Greatness. But the small be as Dwarfs, but not so little as be the Pigmies. These Men live by the Smell of wild Apples. And when they go any far Way, they bear the Apples with them; for if they had lost the Savour of the Apples, they should die anon. They be not full reasonable, but they be simple and bestial.

After that is another Isle, where the Folk be all

full of feathers and rough as a rough Beast, save only
the Face and the Palm of the Hand. These Folk
go as well under the Water of the Sea, as they do
above the Land all dry. And they eat both Flesh

THE FEATHERED MAN SWIMMING

and Fish all raw. In this Isle is a great River that
is well a 2 Mile and an half of Breadth that is clept
Beumare.

And from that River a 15 Days' Journey in
Length, going by the Deserts of the tother Side of
the River, whoso might go it,—for I was not there
but it was told us by them of the Country,—that
within those Deserts were the Trees of the Sun and
of the Moon, that spake to King Alexander, and
warned him of his Death. And Men say that the
Folk that keep those Trees, and eat of the Fruit
and of the Balm that groweth there, live well 400

2 A

Year or 500 Year, by Virtue of the Fruit and of the Balm. For Men say that Balm groweth there in great Plenty and nowhere else, save only at Babylon, as I have told you before. We would have gone toward the Trees full gladly if we had might. But I trow that 100,000 Men of Arms might not pass the Deserts safely, for the great Multitude of wild Beasts and of great Dragons and of great Serpents that there be, that slay and devour all that come anent them. In that Country be many white Elephants without Number, and Unicorns and Lions of many Manners, and many of such Beasts that I have told of before, and of hideous Beasts without Number.

Many other Isles there be in the Land of Prester John, and many great Marvels, that were too long all to tell, both of his Riches and of his Nobleness and of the great Plenty also of precious Stones that he hath. I trow that ye know well enough, and have heard say, wherefore this Emperor is clept Prester John. But, nevertheless, for them that know not, I shall say to you the Cause.

It was sometime an Emperor there, that was a worthy and a full noble Prince, that had Christian Knights in his Company; as he hath that is now there. So it befell, that he had great List to see the Service in the Church among Christian Men. And then endured Christendom beyond the Sea, through all Turkey, Syria, Tartary, Jerusalem, Palestine, Arabia, Aleppo and all the Land of Egypt. And so it befell that this Emperor came with a Christian

Knight with him into a Church in Egypt. And it was a Saturday in Whitsun Week. And the Bishop was conferring Orders. And he beheld, and listened to the Service full attentively. And he asked the Christian Knight what Men of Degree they should be that the Prelate had before him. And the Knight answered and said that they should be Priests. And the Emperor said that he would no longer be clept King nor Emperor, but Priest, and that he would have the Name of the first Priest that went out of the Church, and his Name was John. And so ever-more since, he is clept Prester John.

In his Land be many Christian Men of good Faith and of good Law, and especially them of the same Country, and have commonly their Priests, that sing the Mass, and make the Sacrament of the Altar, of Bread, right as the Greeks do ; but they say not so many Things at the Mass as Men do here. For they say not but only that, that the Apostles said, as our Lord taught them, right as Saint Peter and Saint Thomas and the other Apostles sung the Mass, saying the *Pater Noster* and the Words of the Sacrament. But we have many more Additions that divers Popes have made, that they know not of.

CHAPTER XXX

*Of the Hills of Gold that Pismires keep. And of the
4 Rivers that come from Terrestrial Paradise*

THE KING OF TAPROBANE

OWARD the East Part
of Prester John's Land is
an Isle good and great,
that Men call Taprobane,
that is full noble and full
fruitful. And the King
thereof is full rich, and is
under the Obeissance of
Prester John. And always
there they make their King by Election. In that
Isle be 2 Summers and 2 Winters, and Men harvest
the Corn twice a Year. And in all the Seasons of
the Year be the Gardens in Blossom. There dwell
good Folk and reasonable, and many Christian Men
amongst them, that be so rich that they wit not
what to do with their Goods. Of old Time, when
Men passed from the Land of Prester John unto

that Isle, Men made Disposition to pass by Ships,
23 Days, or more ; but now Men pass by Ship in
7 Days.   And Men may see the Bottom of the Sea
in many Places, for it is not full deep.

Beside that Isle, toward the East, be 2 other Isles.
And Men call the one Orille, and the other Argyte,
of the which all the Land is a Mine of Gold and
Silver.   And those Isles be right where that the Red
Sea departeth from the Sea Ocean.   And in those
Isles Men see there no Stars so clearly as in other
Places.   For there appear no Stars, but only one
clear Star that Men call Canapos.   And there is the
Moon not seen in all the Lunation, save only in the
second Quarter.

In the Isle also of this Taprobane be great Hills
of Gold, that Pismires keep full diligently.   And
they refine the purified Gold, and cast away the
un-purified.   And these Pismires be as great as
Hounds.   So that no Man dare come to those Hills,
for the Pismires would assail them and devour them
anon.   So that no Man may get of that Gold, but
by great Sleight.   And when it is great Heat, the
Pismires rest them in the Earth, from Prime of the
Day unto Noon.   And then the Folk of the Country
take Camels, Dromedaries, and Horses and other
Beasts, and go thither, and charge them in all Haste
that they may ; and after that, they flee away in all
Haste that the Beasts may go, ere the Pismires
come out of the Earth.   And in other times, when
it is not so hot, and that the Pismires rest them not
in the Earth, then they get Gold by this Subtlety.

They take Mares that have young Colts or Foals, and lay upon the Mares empty Vessels made there for; and they be all open above, and hanging low to the Earth. And then they send forth those Mares to pasture about those Hills, and with-hold the Foals with them at Home. And when the Pismires see those Vessels, they leap in anon : and they have this Nature that they let nothing be empty among them, but anon they fill it, be it what manner of Thing that it be ; and so they fill those Vessels with Gold. And when that Folk suppose that the Vessels be full, they put forth anon the young Foals, and make them to neigh after their Dams. And then anon the Mares return towards their Foals with their Charges of Gold. And then Men uncharge them, and get Gold enough by this subtlety. For the Pismires will suffer Beasts to go and pasture amongst them, but no Man in no wise.

And beyond the Land and the Isles and the Deserts of Prester John's Lordship, in going straight toward the East, Men find nothing but Mountains and Rocks, full great. And there is the dark Region, where no Man may see, neither by Day nor by Night, as they of the Country say. And that Desert and that Place of Darkness endure from this Side unto Terrestrial Paradise, where that Adam, our first Father, and Eve were put, that dwelled there but little while : and that is towards the East at the Beginning of the Earth. But that is not that East that we call our East, on this Side, where the Sun riseth to us. For when the Sun is East in those

Parts towards Terrestrial Paradise, it is then Midnight in our Parts of this Side, for the Roundness of the Earth, of the which I have told you before. For our Lord God made the Earth all round in the mid Place of the Firmament.   And there be Mountains and Hills and Valleys that be only from Noah's Flood, that wasted the soft Ground and the tender, that fell down into Valleys, and the hard Earth and the Rocks abode as Mountains, when the soft Earth and tender waxed soft through Water, and fell and became Valleys.

Of Paradise cannot I speak properly.   For I was not there.   It is far beyond.   And that grieveth me. And also I was not worthy.   But as I have heard say of wise Men beyond, I shall tell you with good Will.

Terrestrial Paradise, as wise Men say, is the highest Place of Earth, that is in all the World. And it is so high that it toucheth nigh to the Circle of the Moon, there where the Moon maketh her Turn ; for she is so high that there might not come to her the Flood of Noah, that covered all the Earth of the World all about and above and beneath, save only Paradise alone.   And this Paradise is enclosed all about with a Wall, and Men wit not whereof it is ; for the Walls be covered all over with Moss, as it seemeth.   And it seemeth not that the Wall is Stone of Nature.   And that Wall stretcheth from the South to the North, and it hath but one Entry that is closed with Fire, burning ; so that no Man that is mortal dare enter.

And in the most high Place of Paradise, evenly in the middle Place, is a Well that casteth out the 4 Rivers that run by divers Lands.   Of the which, the first is clept Pison, or Ganges, that are one and the same ; and it runneth throughout Ind or Emlak, in the which River be many precious Stones, and much of Lignum Aloes and much Gravel of Gold.   And that other River is clept Nile, or Gison, that goeth by Ethiopia and after by Egypt.   And that other is clept Tigris, that runneth by Assyria and by Armenia the Great.   And that other is clept Euphrates, that runneth also by Media and Armenia and by Persia.   And Men there beyond say, that all the sweet Waters of the World, above and beneath, take their Beginning from the Well of Paradise, and out of that Well all Waters come and go.

The first River is clept Pison, that is to say in their Language, Assembly ; for many other Rivers meet there, and go into that River.   And some Men call it Ganges, from a King that was in Ind, that was hight Gangeres, and as it ran throughout his Land.   And that Water is in some Places clear, and in some Places troubled, in some Places hot, and in some Places cool.

The second River is clept Nile, or Gison ; for it is always troubled ; and Gison, in the Language of Ethiopia, is to say, Troubled, and in the Language of Egypt also.

The third River, that is clept Tigris, is as much as

"AND SOME WERE

    PERISHED AND LOST

        WITHIN THE WAVES"

to say as, Fast-running; for he runneth more fast
than any of the tother; and also there is a Beast,
that is clept Tiger, that is fast-running.

The fourth River is clept Euphrates, that is to
say, Well-bearing; for there grow many Goods upon
that River, as Corns, Fruits and other Goods plenty
enough.

And ye shall understand that no Man that is
mortal may approach to that Paradise. For by Land
no Man may go for wild Beasts that be in the
Deserts, and for the high Mountains and great huge
Rocks that no Man may pass by, for the dark
Places that be there, and that many. And by the
Rivers may no Man go. For the Water runneth so
rudely and so sharply, because that it cometh down
so outrageously from the high Places above, that it
runneth in Waves so great, that no Ship may row
or sail against it. And the Water roareth so, and
maketh so huge Noise and so great Tempest, that
no Man may hear another in the Ship, though he
cried with all the Strength that he could in the
highest Voice that he might. Many great Lords
have assayed with great Will, many Times, to pass
by those Rivers towards Paradise, with full great
Companies. But they might not speed in their
Voyage. And many died for Weariness of rowing
against those strong Waves. And many of them
became blind, and many deaf, for the Noise of the
Water. And some were perished and lost within
the Waves. So that no mortal Man may approach

to that Place, without special Grace of God, so that
of that Place I can say you no more ; and therefore,
I shall hold me still, and return to that, that I have
seen.

WOMAN OF TAPROBANE

THE KING OF CASSON

CHAPTER XXXI

Of the Customs of Kings and others that dwell in the
Isles coasting to Prester John's Land. And
of the Worship that a Son doth to his
Father when he is dead

FROM these Isles that I have spoken of before, in
the Land of Prester John, that be under Earth as to
us that be of this Side, and from other Isles that be
more further beyond, whoso will, may pursue his
Journey to come again right to the Parts that he
came from, and so environ all the Earth. But what
for the Isles, what for the Sea, and what for strong

THE LOBASSY AND THE IDOL

Fruit and all other Riches. And the Folk of that Country have no Houses, but they dwell and lie all under Tents made of black Fern, in all the Country. And the principal City and the most royal is all walled with black Stone and white. And all the Streets also be paved of the same Stones. In that City is no Man so hardy as to shed Blood of any Man, nor of any Beast, for the Reverence of an Idol that is worshipped there. And in that Isle dwelleth the Pope of their Law, that they call Lobassy. This Lobassy giveth all the Benefices, and all other Dignities and all other Things that belong to the Idol. And all those that hold anything of their Churches, religious Men and others, obey him, as Men do here of the Pope of Rome.

In that Isle they have a Custom by all the Country, that when the Father is dead of any Man, and the Son list to do great Worship to his Father, he sendeth to all his Friends and to all his Kin, and for religious Men and Priests, and for Minstrels also, great Plenty. And then Men bear the dead Body unto a great Hill with great Joy and Solemnity. And when they have brought it thither, the Chief Prelate smiteth off the Head, and layeth it upon a great Platter of Gold and of Silver, if so be that he be a rich Man. And then he taketh the Head to the Son. And then the Son and his other Kin sing and say many Orisons. And then the Priests and the religious Men smite all the Body of the dead Man in Pieces. And then they say certain Orisons. And the Fowls of Ravin of all the

Country about know the Custom of long time before, and come flying above in the Air; as Eagles, Kites, Ravens and other Fowls of Ravin, that eat Flesh. And then the Priests cast the Gobbets of the Flesh; and then the Fowls, each of them, take that they may, and go a little thence and eat it; and so they do whilst any Piece lasteth of the dead Body.

And after that, as Priests amongst us sing for the Dead, "*Subvenite Sancti Dei, etc.*" "*Come to his Assistance, ye Saints of God, etc.*," right so the Priests sing in high Voice in their Language; "Behold how worthy a Man and how good a Man this was, that the Angels of God come to seek him and bring him into Paradise." And then seemeth it to the Son, that he is highly worshipped, when that many Birds and Fowls and Ravens come and eat his Father; and he that hath most Number of Fowls is most worshipped.

Then the Son bringeth Home with him all his Kin, and his Friends, and all the others to his House, and maketh them a great Feast. And then all his Friends make their Vaunt and their Dalliance, how the Fowls come thither, here 5, here 6, here 10, and there 20, and so forth; and they rejoice them hugely to speak thereof. And when they be at Meat, the Son makes bring forth the Head of his Father, and thereof he giveth of the Flesh to his most special Friends, instead of a Dainty, or a Sweet-meat. And of the Brain Pan, he has made a Cup, and there from drinketh he and his other Friends also, with great Devotion, in Remembrance of the holy Man, that the Angels of God have eaten. And that Cup the Son shall keep to drink from, all his Life-time, in Remembrance of his Father.

From that Land, in returning by a 10 Days' Journey throughout the Land of the great Chan, is another good Isle and a great Kingdom, where the King is full rich and mighty.

And amongst the rich Men of his Country is a passing rich Man, that is neither Prince, nor Duke, nor Earl, but he hath more that hold of him Lands and other Lordships, for he is more rich. For he hath, every Year, of annual Rent 300,000 Horses charged with Corn of diverse Grains and of Rice. And so he leadeth a full noble Life and a delicate, after the Custom of the Country. For he hath, every Day, 50 fair Damsels, all Maidens, that serve him evermore at his Meat, and to lie with him at Night, and to do with them what is to his Pleasure. And when he is at Table, they bring him his Meat at every Time, 5 and 5 together; and in bringing their Service they sing a Song. And after that, they cut his Meat, and put it in his Mouth; for he toucheth nothing, nor handles nought, but holdeth evermore his Hands before him upon the Table. For he hath Nails so long, that he may take nothing, nor handle anything. For the Nobleness of that Country is to have long Nails, and to make them grow always to be as long as Men may. And there be many in that Country, that have their Nails so long, that they environ all the Hand. And that is a great Nobleness. And the Nobleness of the

Women is to have small Feet and little. And
therefore anon when they be born, they make bind
their Feet so straitly, that they may not grow half
as Nature would. And always these Damsels, that
I spake of before, sing all the Time that this rich
Man eateth. And when that he eateth no more of
his first Course, then other 5 and 5 of fair Damsels
bring him his second Course, always singing as they
did before. And so they do continually to the End
of his Meat. And in this Manner he leadeth his
Life. And so did they before him, that were his
Ancestors. And so shall they that come after him,
without doing of any Deeds of Arms, but live evermore thus in Ease, as a Swine that is fed in a Sty
to be made fat. He hath a full fair Palace and
full rich, that he dwelleth in, of the which the
Walls be, in Circuit, 2 Mile. And he hath within
many fair Gardens, and many fair Halls and
Chambers; and the Pavement of his Halls and
Chambers be of Gold and Silver. And in the mid
Place of one of his Gardens is a little Mountain,
where there is a little Meadow. And in that
Meadow is a little Hill with Towers and Pinnacles,
all of Gold. And on that little Hill will he sit
often-time, to take the Air and disport him.

From that Country Men come to the Land of the
great Chan also, that I have spoken of before.

And ye shall understand, that of all these Countries, and of all these Isles, and of all the divers Folk,
that I have spoken of before, and of divers Laws, and
of Beliefs that they have, is there yet none of these

all but have some Reason within them and Under-
standing, unless it be a few, and that have certain
Articles of our Faith and some good Points of our
Belief, and that believe in God, that formed all
Things and made the World, and that call Him
God of Nature ; after what the Prophet saith, "*Et
metuent Eum omnes Fines Terrae*," ("*And all the
Ends of the Earth fear Him*,") and also in another
Place, "*Omnes Gentes servient Ei*," that is to say,
"*All Folk shall serve Him.*"

But they cannot speak perfectly, for there is no
Man to teach them, but only what they can devise
by their natural Wit.   For they have no Knowledge
of the Son, nor of the Holy Ghost.   But they can
all speak of the Bible, and especially of Genesis, of
the Prophets' Laws and of the Books of Moses.
And they say well, that the Creatures that they
worship be no Gods ; but they worship them for
the Virtue that is in them, that may not be but only
by the Grace of God.   And of Simulacres and Idols,
they say, that there be no Folk, but that they have
Simulacres.   And that they say, just as we Christian
Men have Images, as of our Lady and of other
Saints that we worship ; not the Images of Wood or
of Stone, but the Saints, in whose Names they be
made after.   For right as their Books of the Scriptures teach the Clerks how and in what Manner they
shall believe, right so the Images and the Paintings
teach the lay Folk to worship the Saints and to
have them in their Mind, in whose Names that the
Images be made after.   They say also, that the

Angels of God speak to them in those Idols, **and** that they do many great Miracles. And they say Truth, that there is an Angel within them. For there be 2 Manner of Angels, a good and an evil, as the Greeks say, Kakos and Kalos. This Kakos is the Wicked Angel, and Kalos is the good Angel. But the tother, that is within the Idols, is not the good Angel, but the wicked Angel, to deceive them and maintain them in their Error.

There be many other divers Countries and many other Marvels beyond, that I have not seen. Wherefore, of them I cannot speak properly to tell you the Manner of them. And also in the Countries where I have been, be many Diversities of many wonderful Things, more than I make Mention of; for it were too long a Thing to advise you of the Manner. And therefore, as that I have advised you of certain Countries, that I have spoken of before, I beseech your worthy and excellent Nobleness, that it suffice to you at this Time. For if that I advised you of all that is beyond the Sea, another Man, perchance, that would pain him and travail his Body to go into those Borders, to search those Countries, might be blamed by my Words in rehearsing many strange Things; for he might not say anything new, in the which the Hearers might have either Solace, or Sport, or Lust, or Liking in the Hearing. For Men say always, that new Things and new Tidings be pleasant to hear. Wherefore I will hold me still, without any more rehearsing of Diversities or of Marvels that be beyond, to that Intent and End, that whoso will go into these Countries, he shall find enough to speak of, that I have not touched on in any wise.

And ye shall understand, if it like you, that at mine Home-coming, I came to Rome, and shewed my Life to our Holy Father the Pope, and was assoiled of all that lay on my Conscience, on many a diverse grievous Point ; as Men must needs that be in Company, dwelling amongst so many diverse Folk of diverse Sects and Beliefs, as I have been.

And amongst all, I shewed him this Treatise, that I had made after Information of Men that knew of Things that I had not seen myself, and also of Marvels and Customs that I had seen myself, as far as God would give me Grace ; and besought his Holy Father-hood, that my Book might be examined and corrected by Advice of his wise and discreet Council. And our Holy Father, of his special Grace, remitted my Book to be examined and proved by the Advice of his said Counsel.   By the which my Book was proved for true, insomuch, that they shewed me a Book, that my Book was examined by, that comprehended full much more, by an 100th Part, after the which the *Mappa Mundi* was made.   And so my Book, (albeit that many Men list not to give Credence to anything, but to that, that they have seen with their Eye, be the Author or the Person never so true,) is affirmed and proved by our Holy Father, in Manner and Form as I have said.

And I, John Mandevile, Knight, abovesaid, although I be unworthy, that departed from our

Countries and passed the Sea, the Year of Grace 1322, that have passed many Lands and many Isles and Countries, and searched many full. strange Places, and have been in many a full good honourable Company, and at many a fair Deed of Arms, albeit that I did none myself, for mine incapable Insufficiency, now am come Home, maugre myself, to rest. For Gouts and Rheumatics, that distress me—those define the End of my Labour ; against my Will, God knoweth !

And thus, taking Solace in my wretched Rest, recording the Time passed, I have fulfilled these Things, and put them written in this Book, as it would come into my Mind, the Year of Grace 1356, in the 34th Year that I departed from our Countries.

Wherefore, I pray to all the Readers and Hearers of this Book, if it please them, that they would pray to God for me ; and I shall pray for them. And all those that say for me a *Pater Noster*, with an *Ave Maria*, that God forgive me my Sins, I make them Partners, and grant them Part of all the good Pilgrimages and of all the good Deeds that I have done, if any be to His Pleasure ; and not only of those, but of all that ever I shall do unto my Life's End. And I beseech Almighty God, from Whom all Goodness and Grace cometh, that He vouchsafe of His excellent Mercy and abundant Grace, to fulfil their Souls with Inspiration of the Holy Ghost, in making Defence against all their ghostly Enemies here on Earth, to their Salvation both of

Body and Soul ; to the Worship and Thanking of Him, that is Three in One, without Beginning and without Ending ; that is without Quality, good, and without Quantity, great ; that in all Places is Present, and all Things Containing ; the Which that no Goodness may amend, nor any Evil impair ; that in perfect Trinity, liveth and reigneth, God, for all Worlds, and for all Times !

Amen ! Amen ! Amen !

INDEX

A

B

G

S

14TH CENTURY JESTER

Printed by BALLANTYNE HANSON & Co.
London & Edinburgh